천주

PUBLISHER
MIKE RICHARDSON

EDITOR
TIM ERVIN

BOOK DESIGN
SCOTT COOK

ART DIRECTOR
LIA RIBACCHI

English-language version produced by DARK HORSE COMICS.

Chunchu: Genocide Fiend #1

Dark Horse Manhwa
A division of Dark Horse Comics, Inc.
10956 SE Main Street
Milwaukie, OR 97222

darkhorse.com

First edition: August 2007

ISBN-10: 1-59307-753-X
ISBN-13: 978-1-59307-753-2

10 9 8 7 6 5 4 3 2 1

Printed in the United States of America

To find a comics shop in your area, call the Comic Shop Locator Service
toll-free at 1-888-266-4226.

1

WRITTEN BY
KIM SUNG-JAE

ILLUSTRATED BY
KIM BYUNG-JIN

TRANSLATED BY
JAY SO

LETTERED BY
KATHRYN RENTA

DARK
HORSE
MANHWA

"WE ANNOUNCE THIS TO THE WORLD.

AGAINST ALL ODDS, WE SURVIVED THE WAR WITH THE YOONG CLAN...

BUT STILL,

NO ONE IS CONTENT. BECAUSE,

HE...

IS STILL ALIVE..."

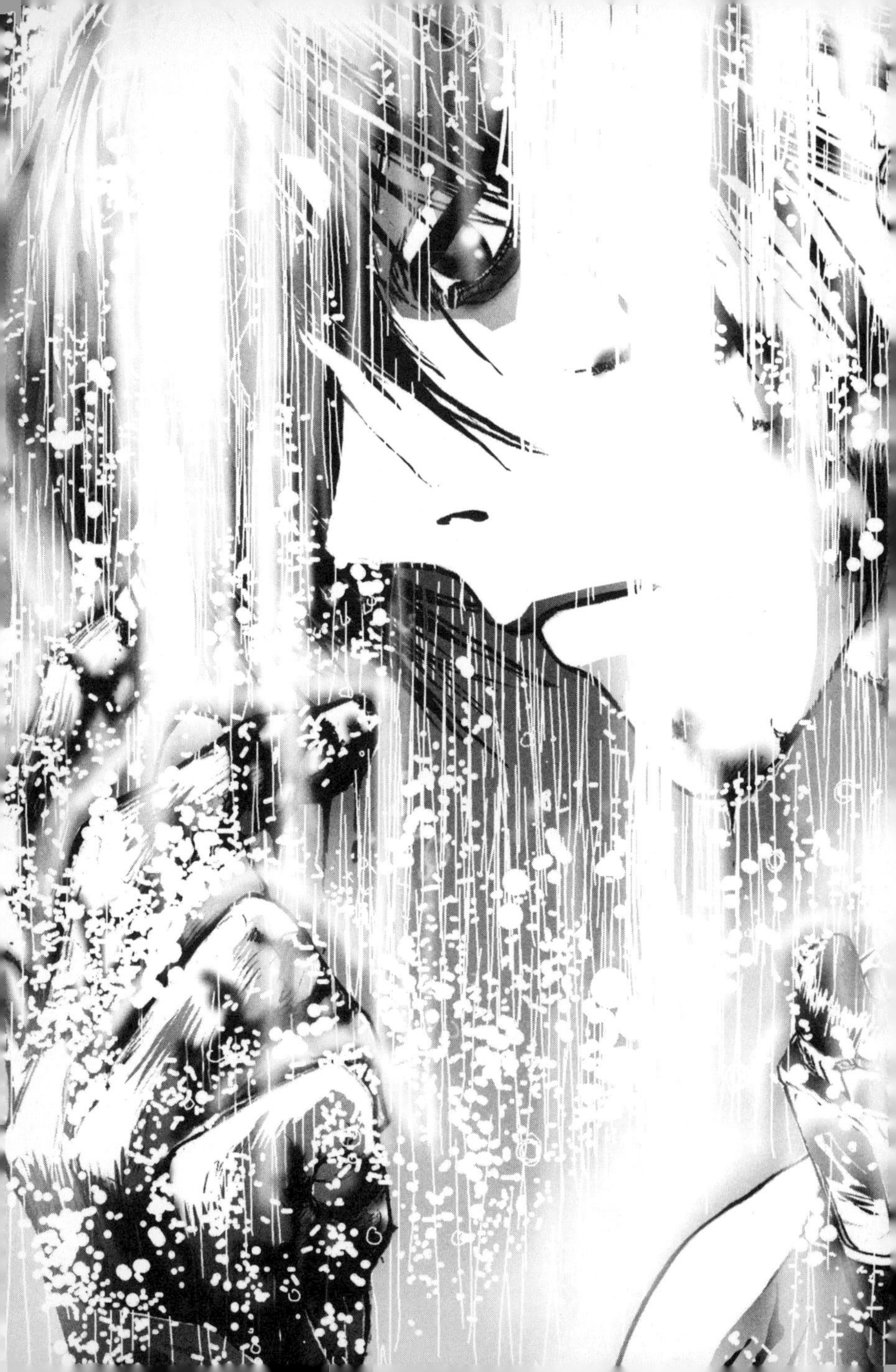

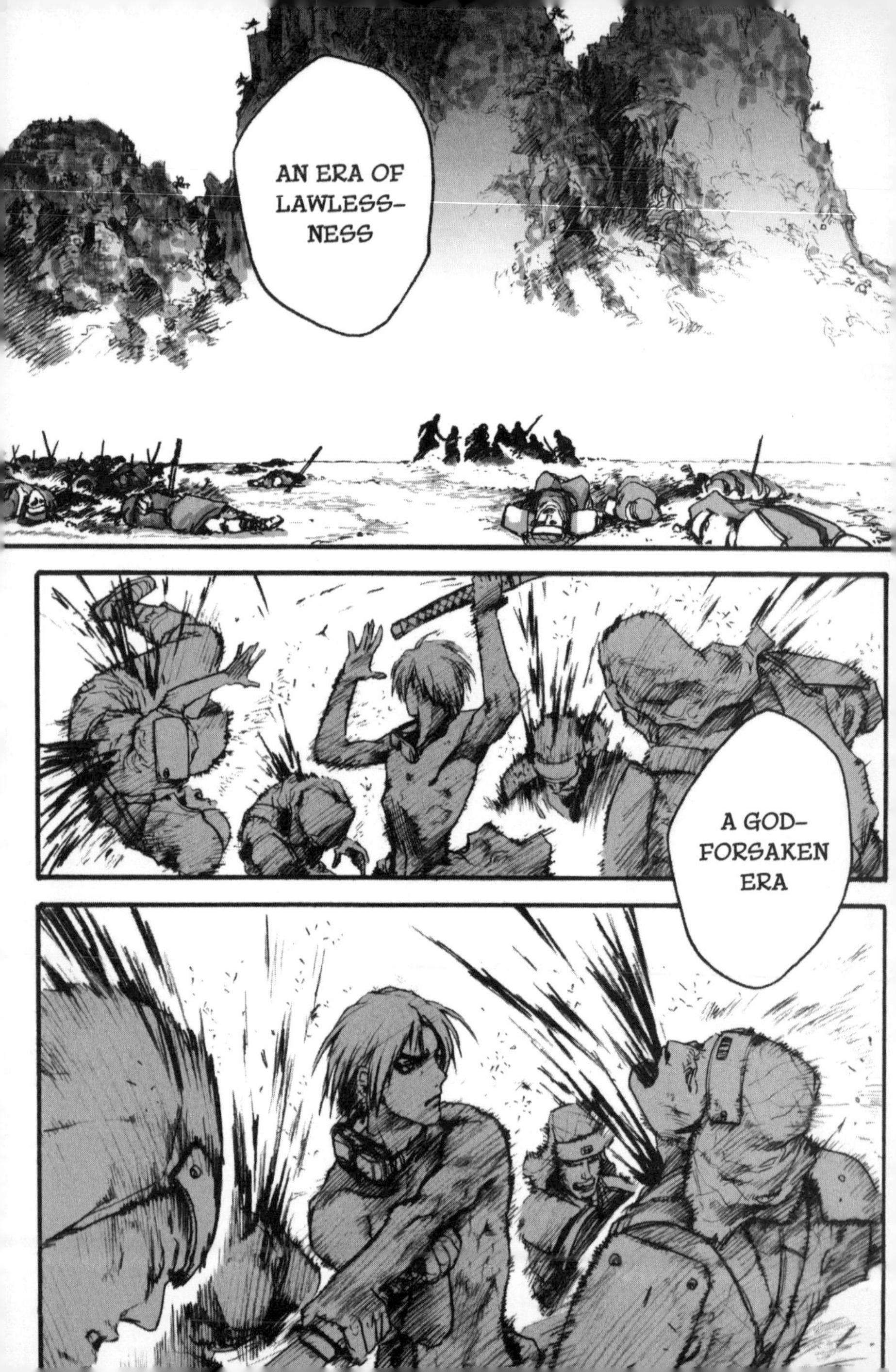
AN ERA OF LAWLESS-NESS
A GOD-FORSAKEN ERA

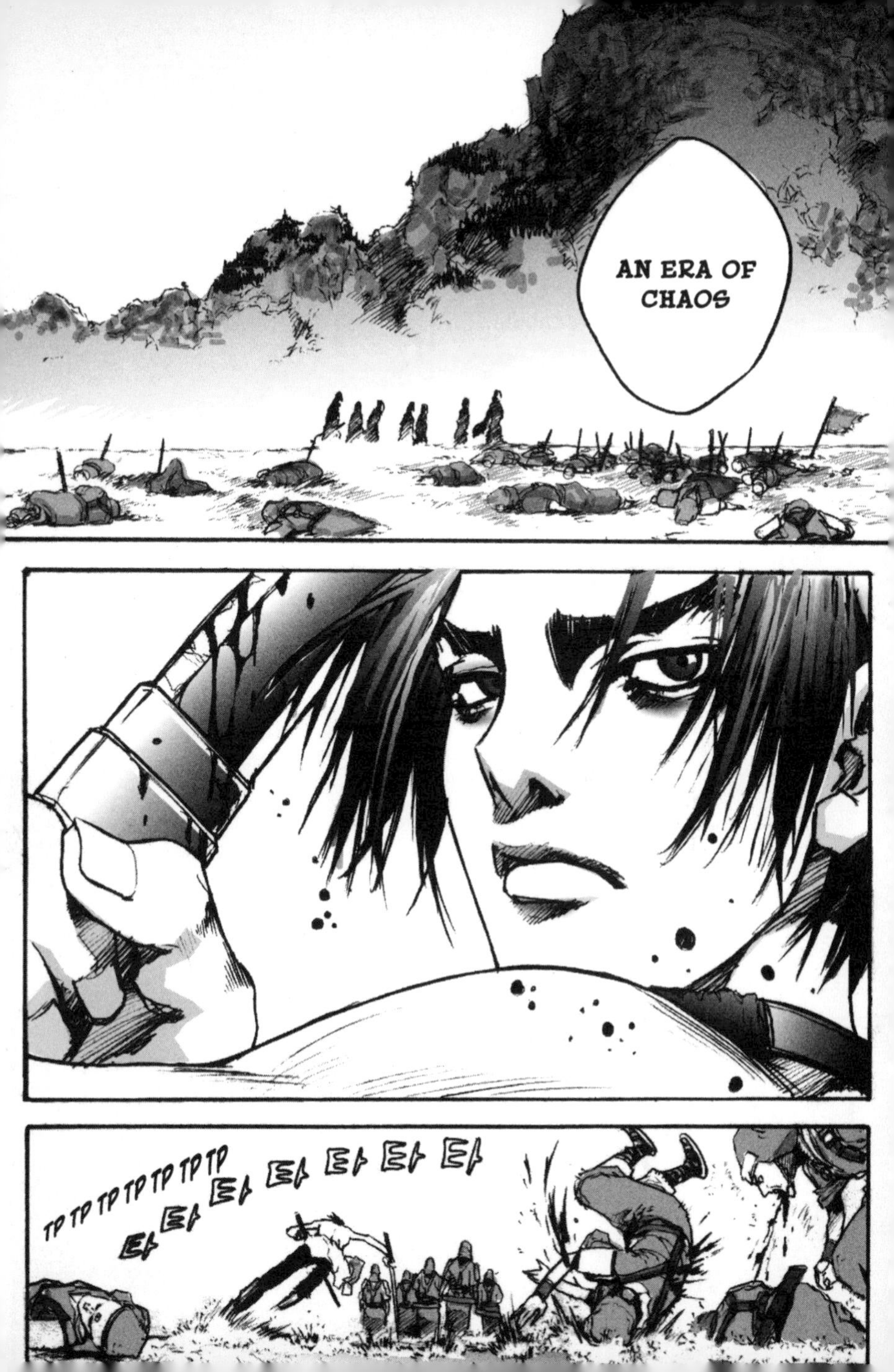
AN ERA OF CHAOS
TP TP TP TP TP TP TP

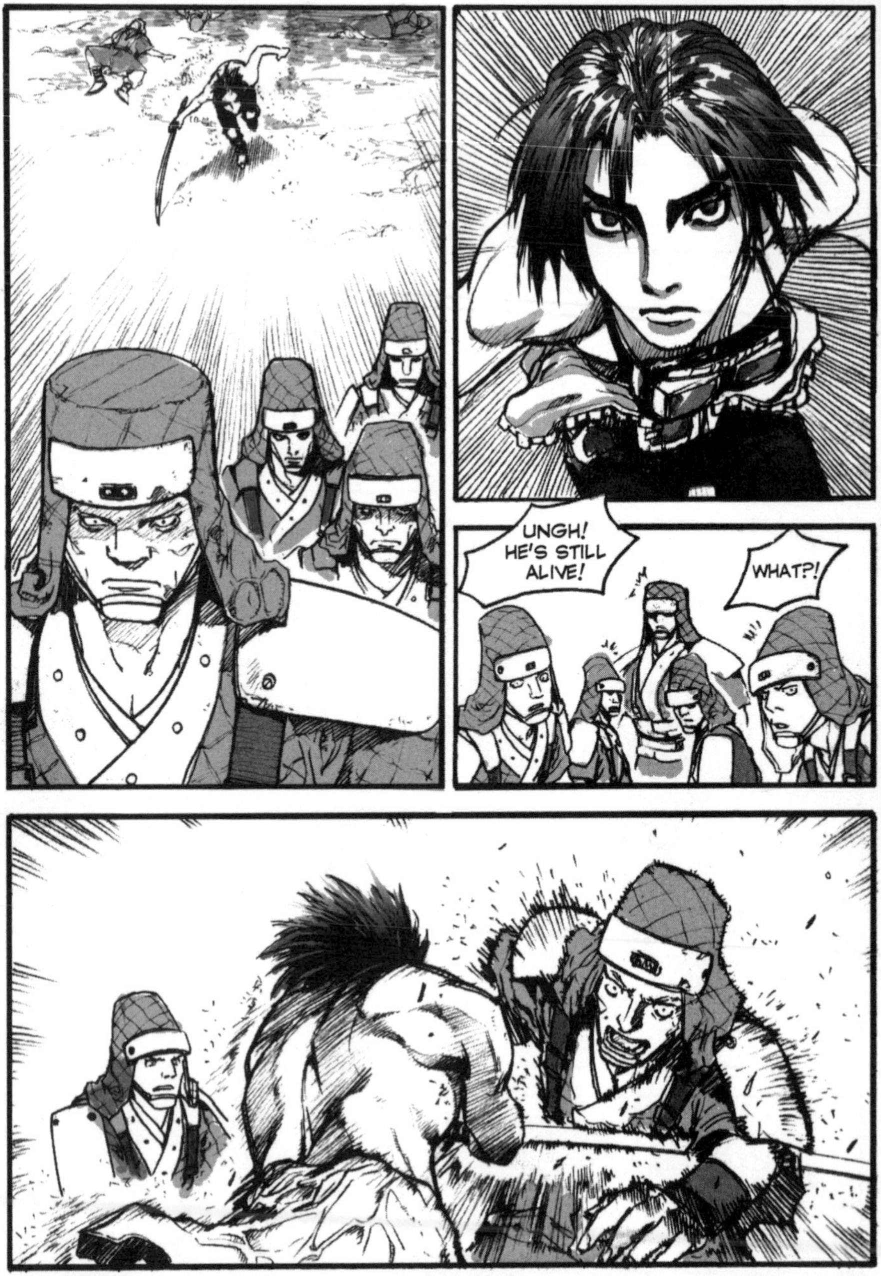
UNGH! HE'S STILL ALIVE!
WHAT?!

파 SNA AAK 아!

KYAAA!

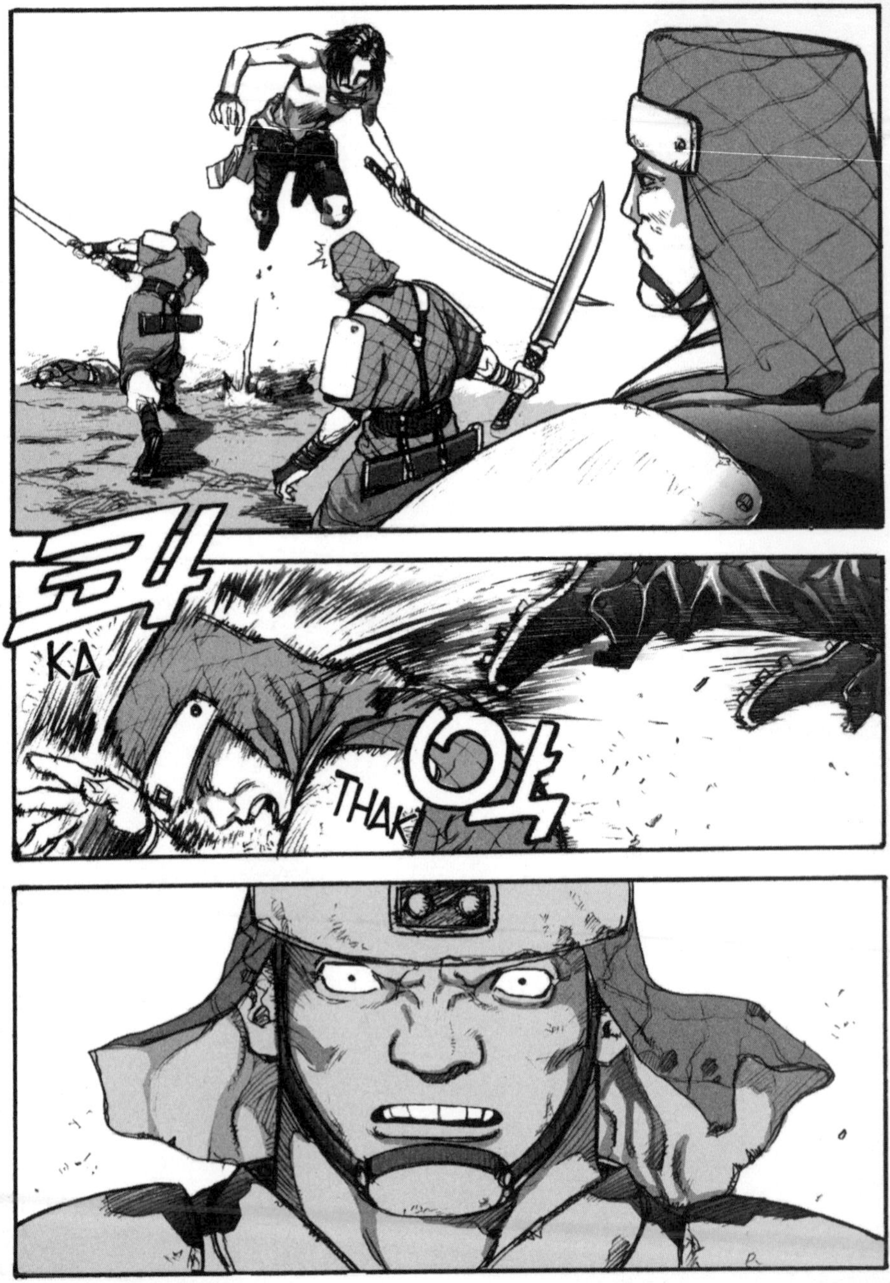
KA
THAK

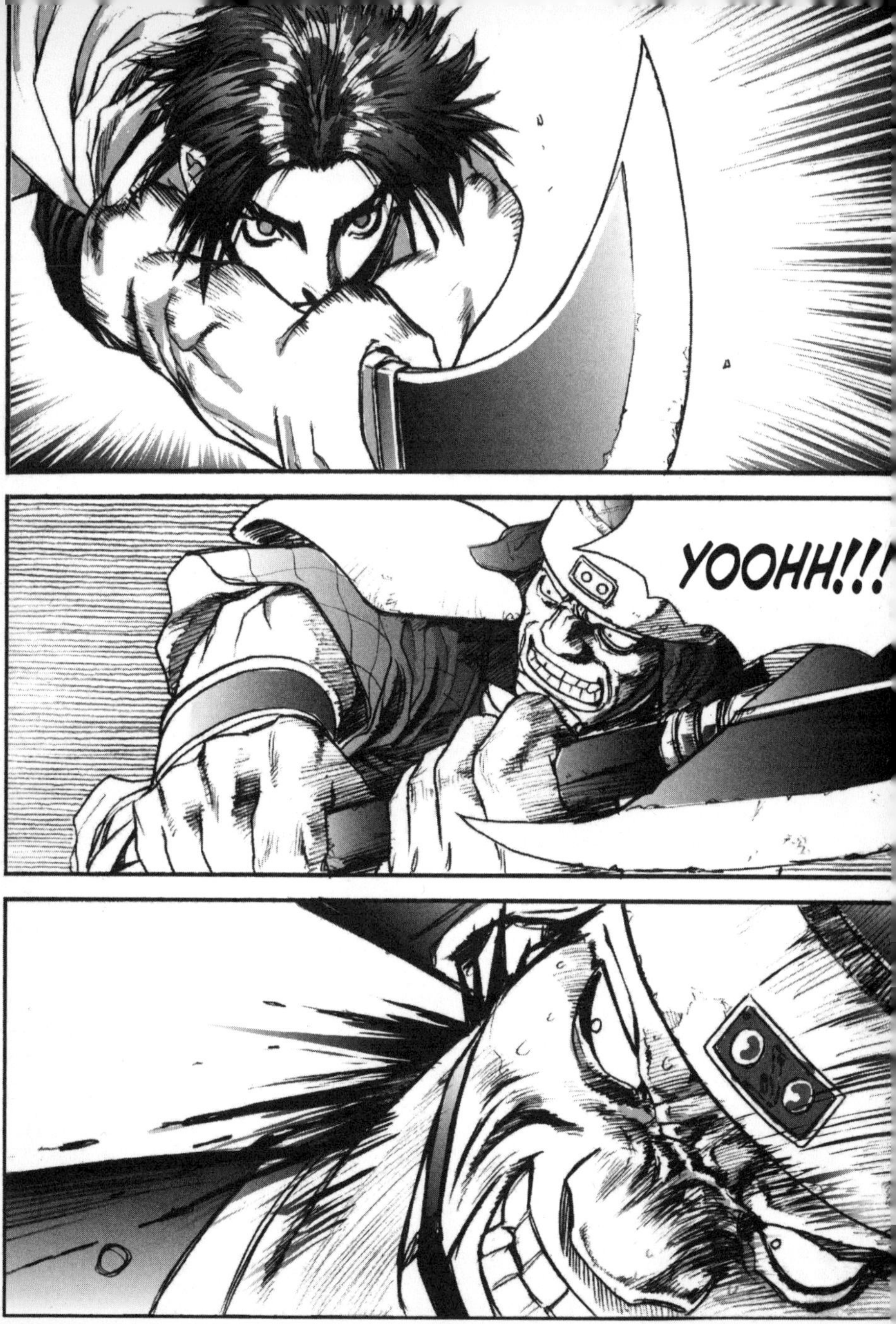
YOOHH!!!

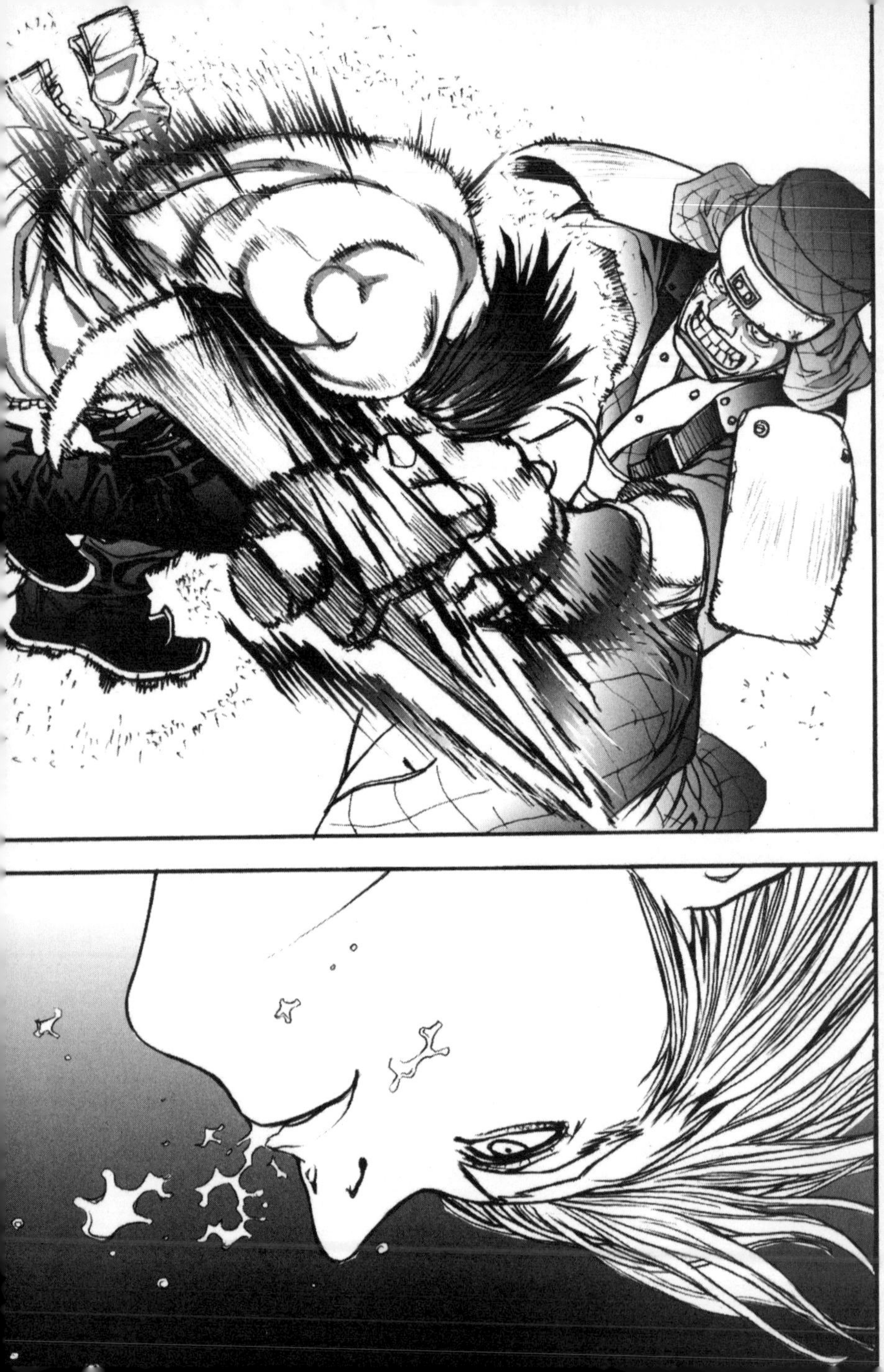

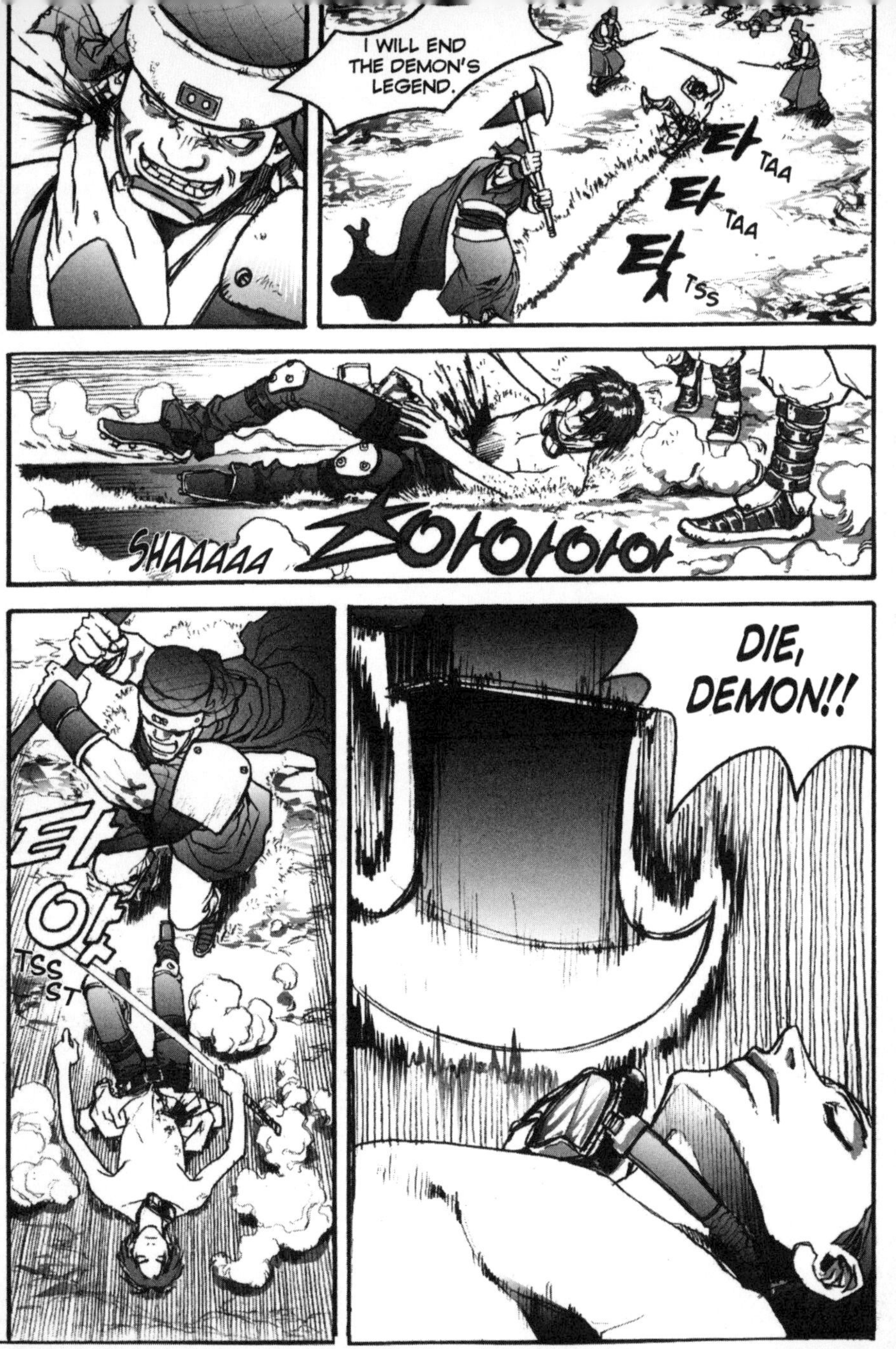
I WILL END THE DEMON'S LEGEND.
타 TAA
타 TAA
탓 TSS
SHAAAAA
좌아아아아아
타앗 TSS ST
DIE, DEMON!!

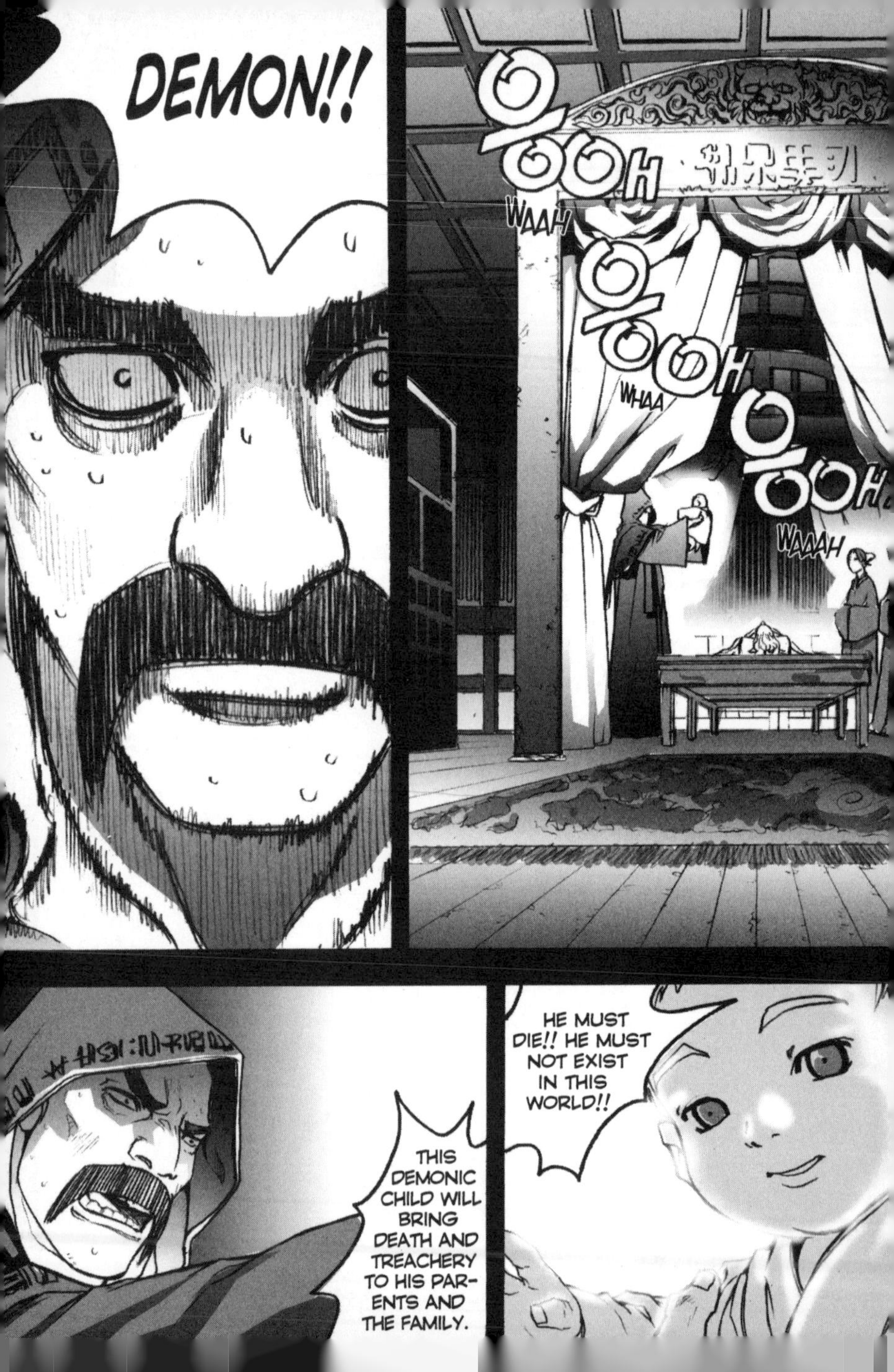
DEMON!!
OOOH
WAAH
OOOOOH
WHAA
OOOOH
WAAAH
THIS DEMONIC CHILD WILL BRING DEATH AND TREACHERY TO HIS PARENTS AND THE FAMILY.
HE MUST DIE!! HE MUST NOT EXIST IN THIS WORLD!!

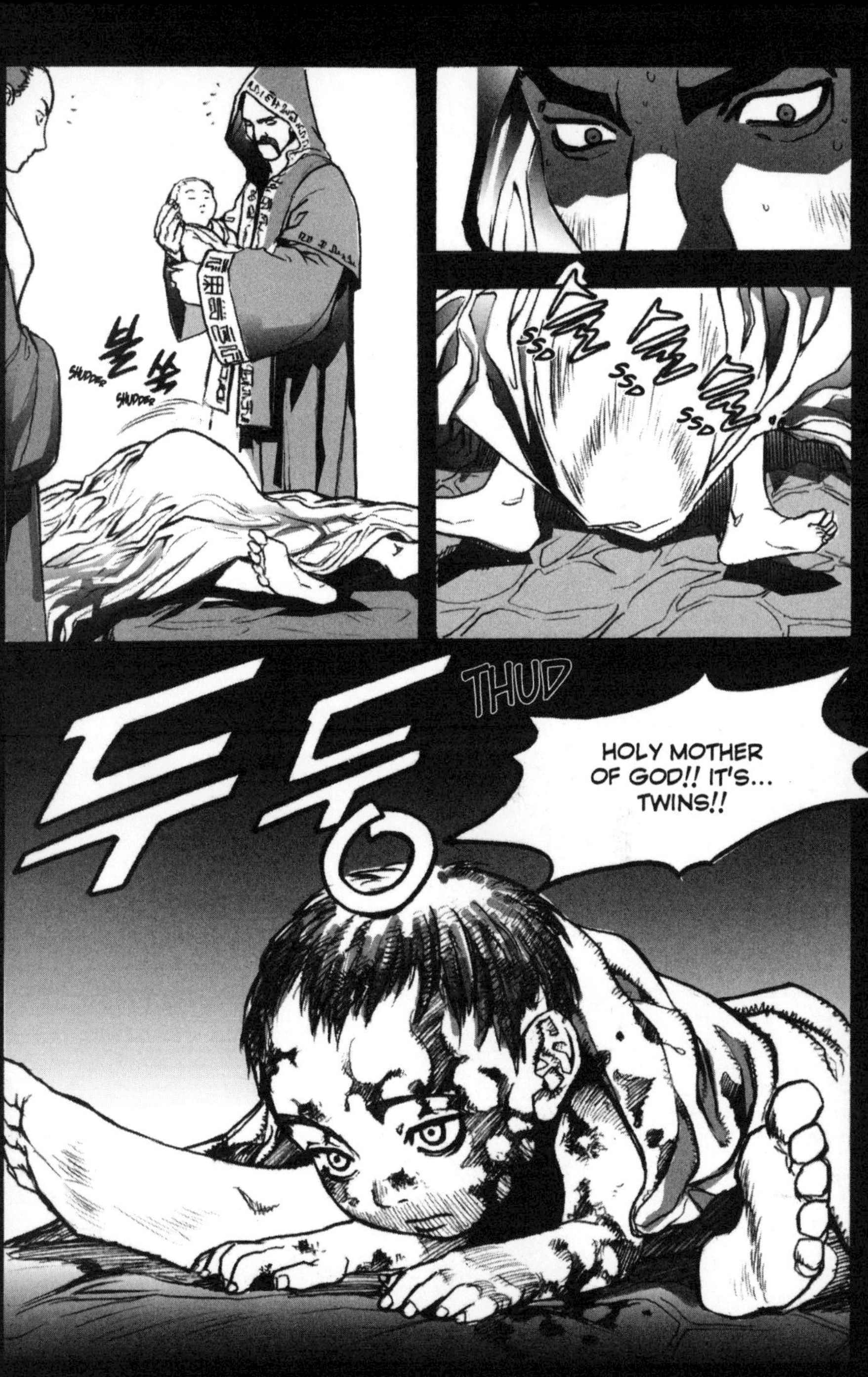
불 쑥
SHUDDER
SHUDDER
SSD
SSD
SSD
두둥
THUD
HOLY MOTHER OF GOD!! IT'S... TWINS!!

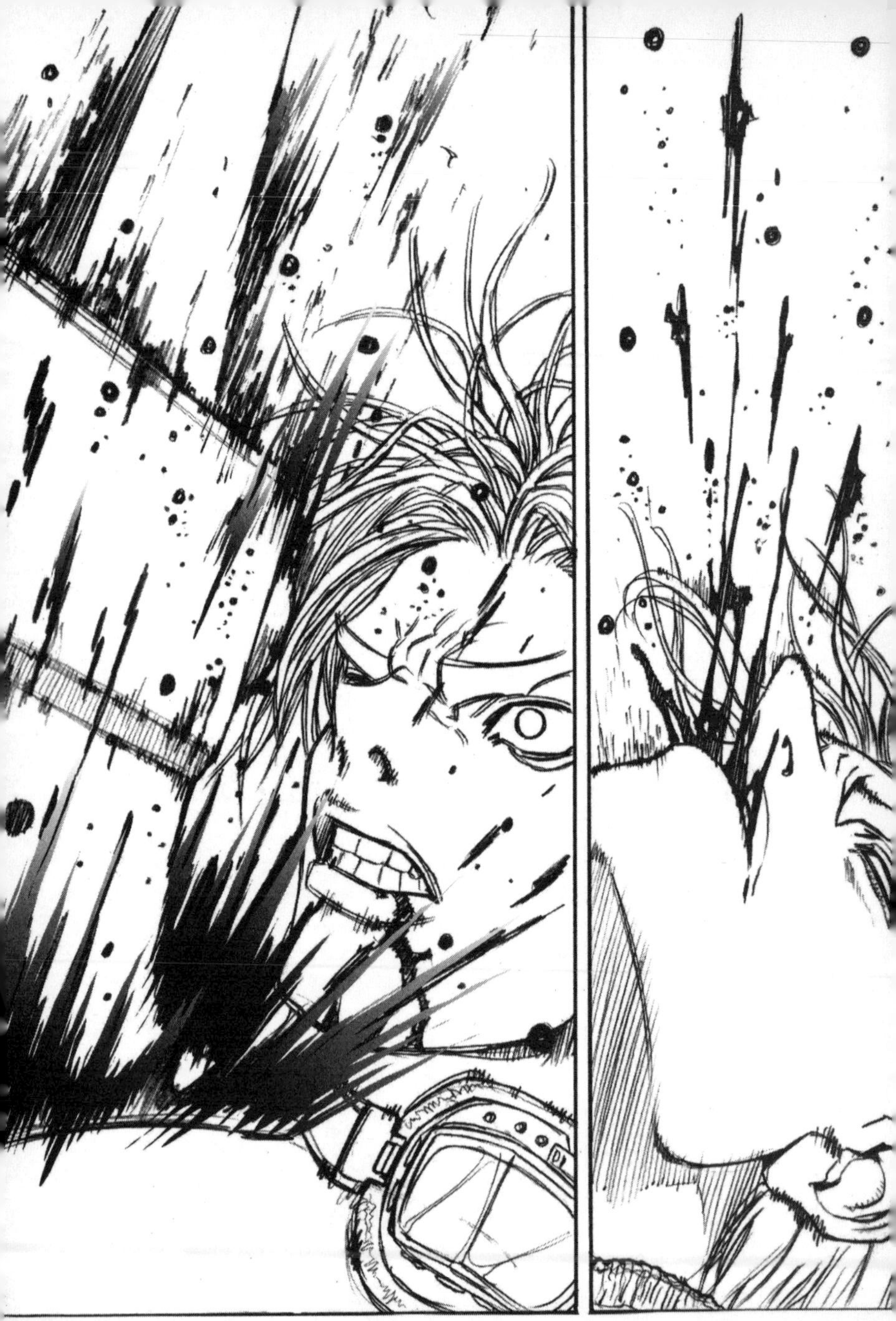

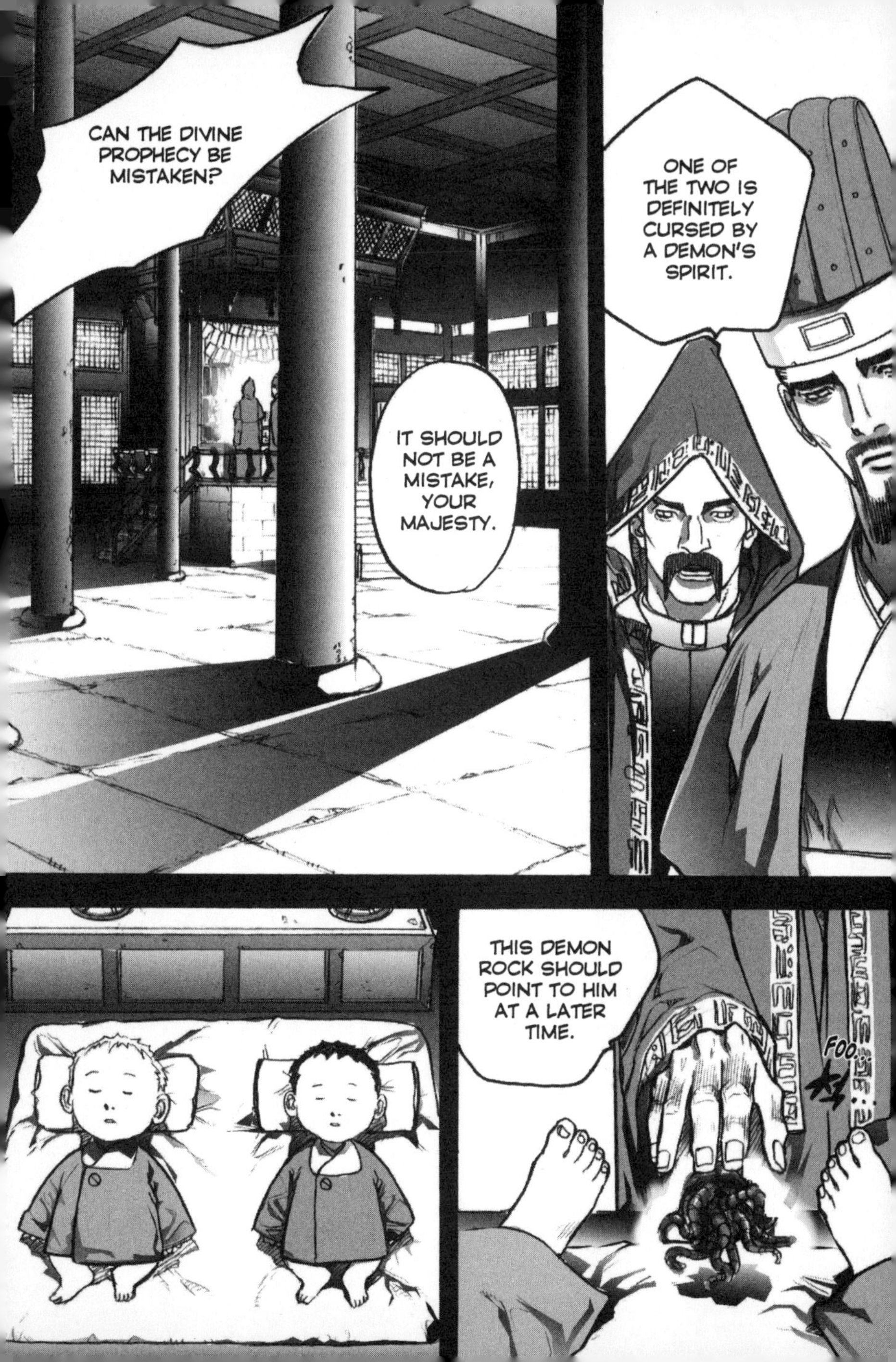
CAN THE DIVINE PROPHECY BE MISTAKEN?
ONE OF THE TWO IS DEFINITELY CURSED BY A DEMON'S SPIRIT.
IT SHOULD NOT BE A MISTAKE, YOUR MAJESTY.
THIS DEMON ROCK SHOULD POINT TO HIM AT A LATER TIME.
FOO...

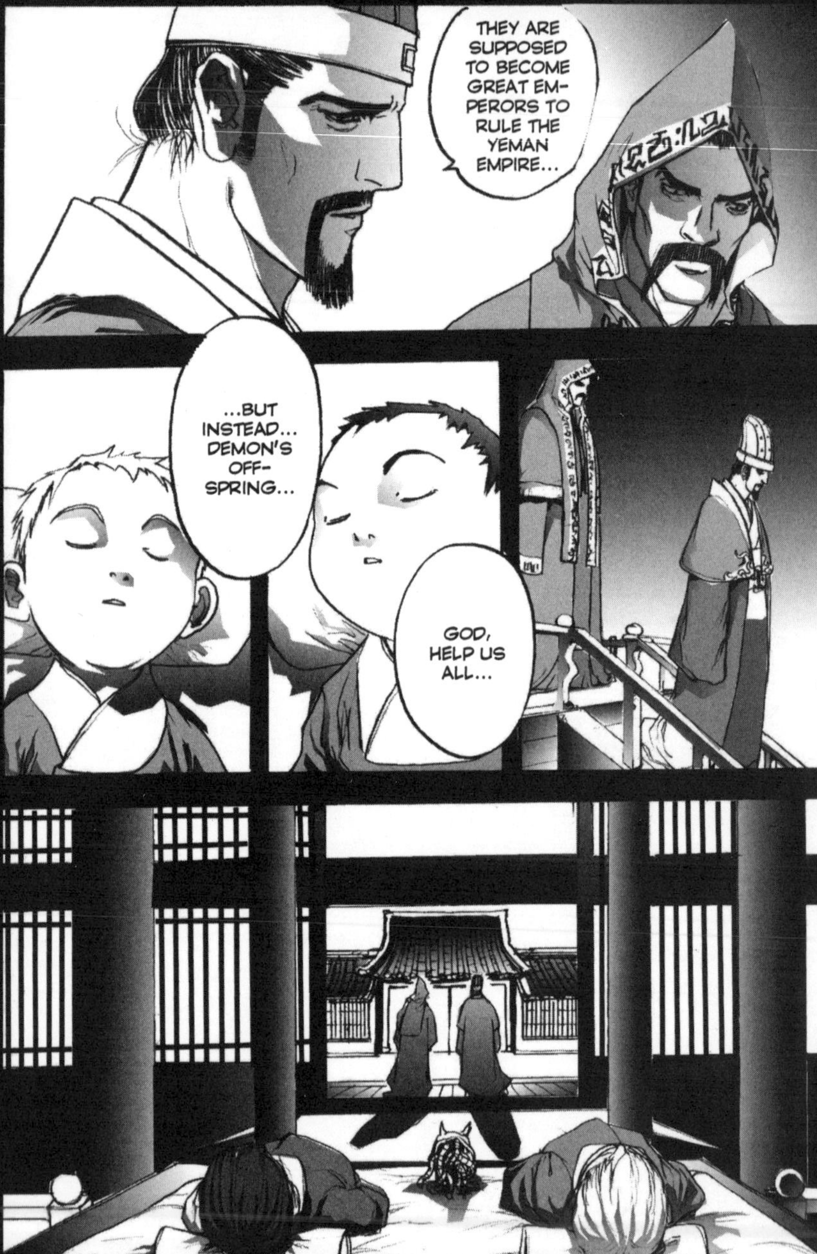
THEY ARE SUPPOSED TO BECOME GREAT EM-PERORS TO RULE THE YEMAN EMPIRE...
...BUT INSTEAD... DEMON'S OFF-SPRING...
GOD, HELP US ALL...

GSH

IT'S RED. DEMON'S BLOOD IS RED...

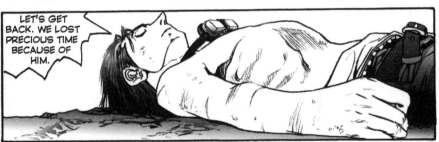

LET'S GET BACK. WE LOST PRECIOUS TIME BECAUSE OF HIM.

WHY DID FATE BRING ME TO THIS WORLD...

KNOWING I'M GOING TO BE CURSED ...

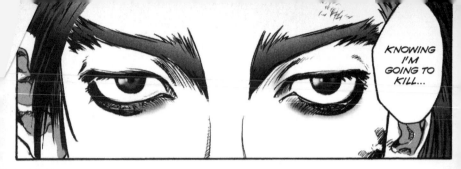

KNOWING I'M GOING TO KILL...

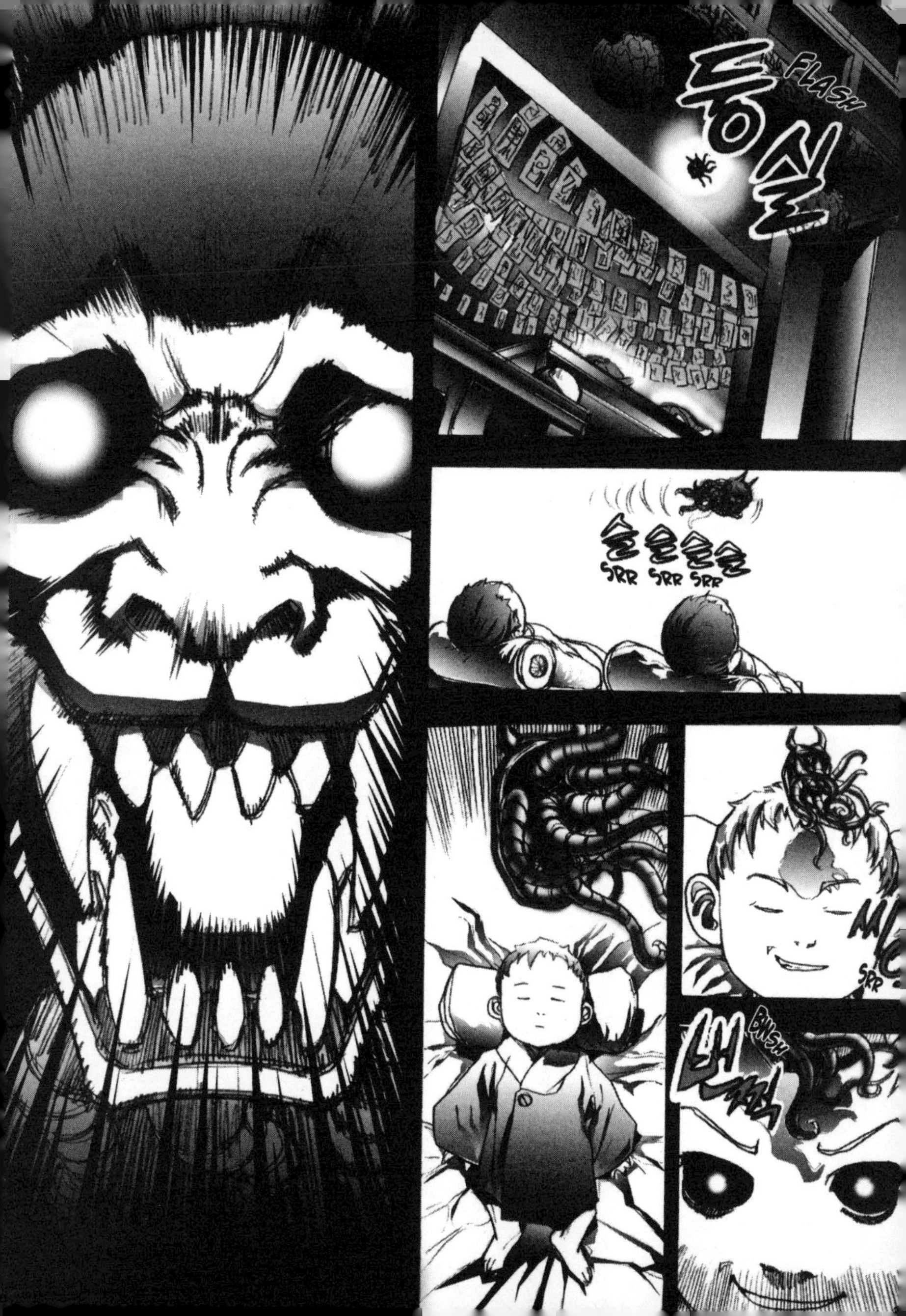
FLASH
슬슬슬슬
SRR SRR SRR
SRR
BWSH

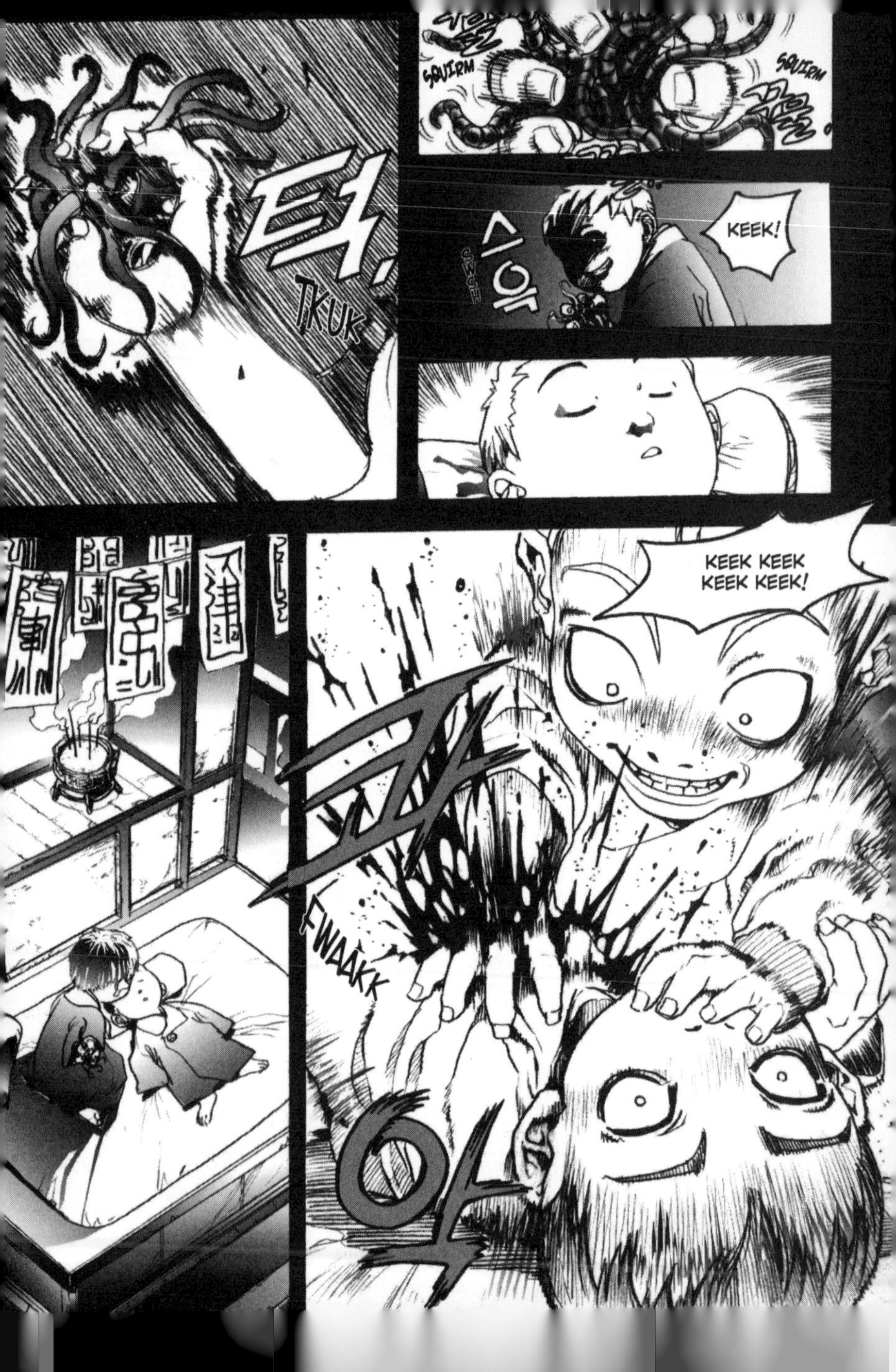
턱
TKUK
SQUIRM
SQUIRM
KEEK!
SWSH
KEEK KEEK
KEEK KEEK!
FWAAKK

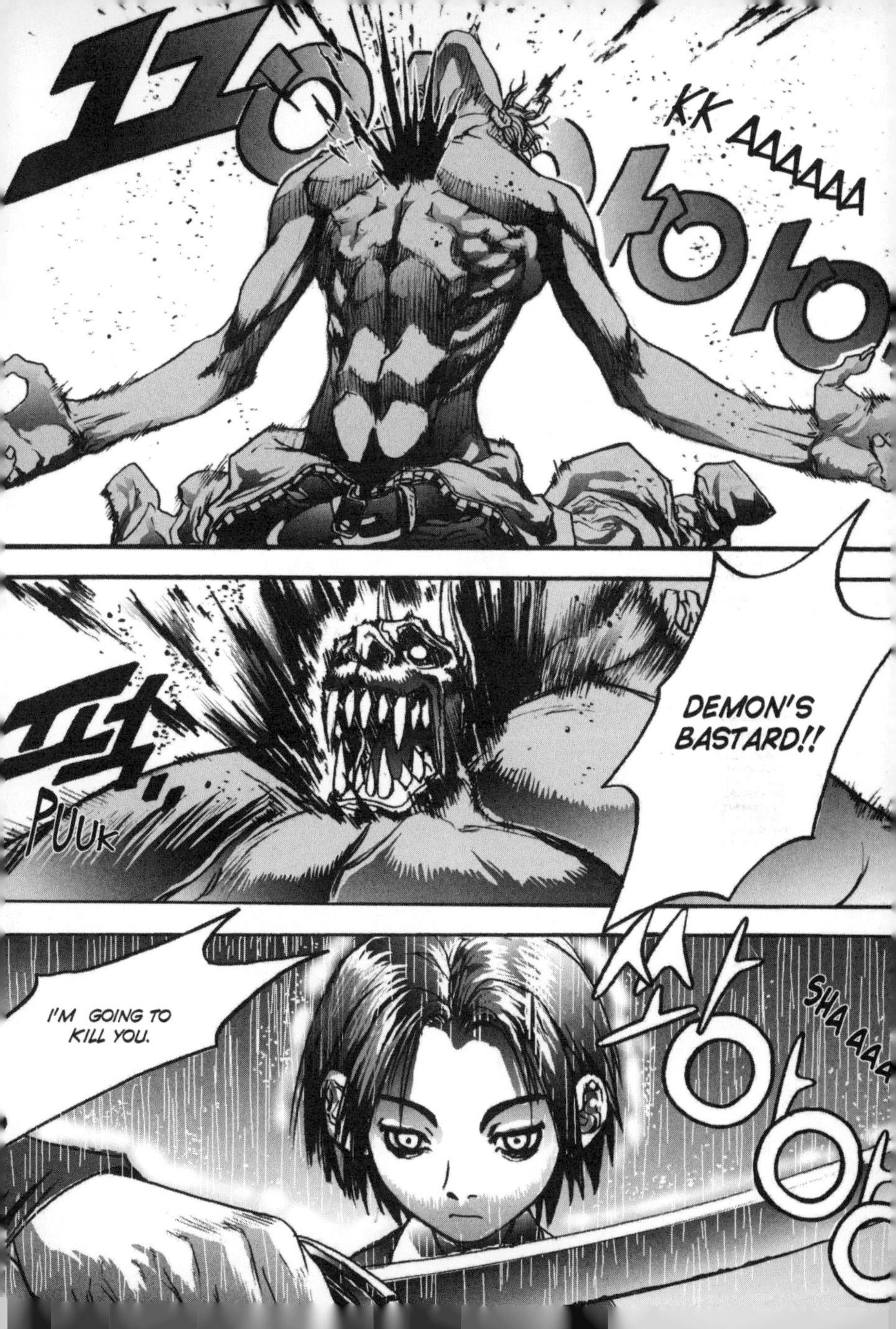
KK AAAAAAA
PUUK
DEMON'S BASTARD!!
I'M GOING TO KILL YOU.
SHA AAA

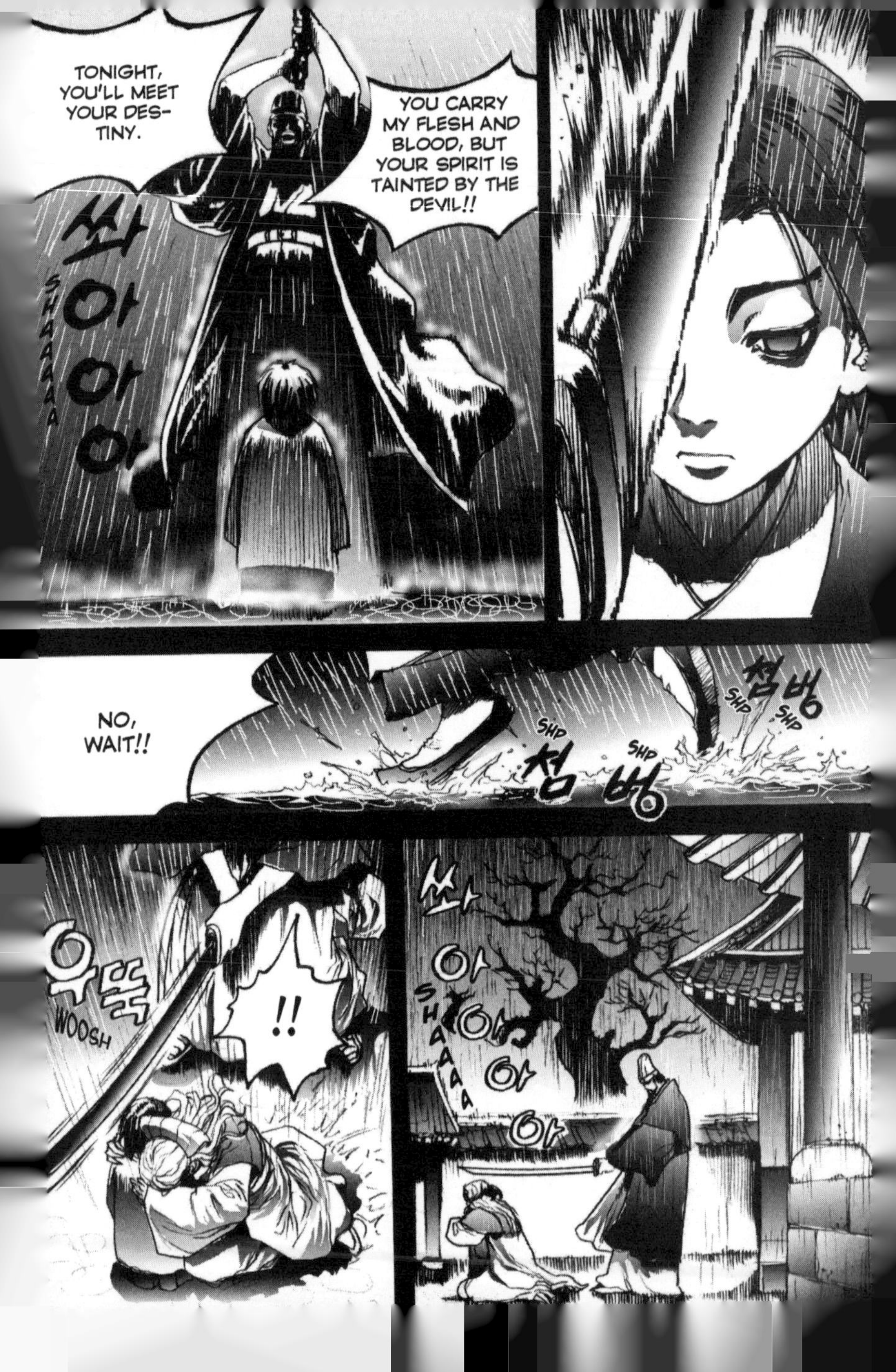
TONIGHT, YOU'LL MEET YOUR DES-TINY.
YOU CARRY MY FLESH AND BLOOD, BUT YOUR SPIRIT IS TAINTED BY THE DEVIL!!
쏴아아아
SHAAAAAA
NO, WAIT!!
첨벙
SHP
SHP
첨벙
SHP
SHP
우뚝
WOOSH
!!
쏴아아아아
SHAAAAA

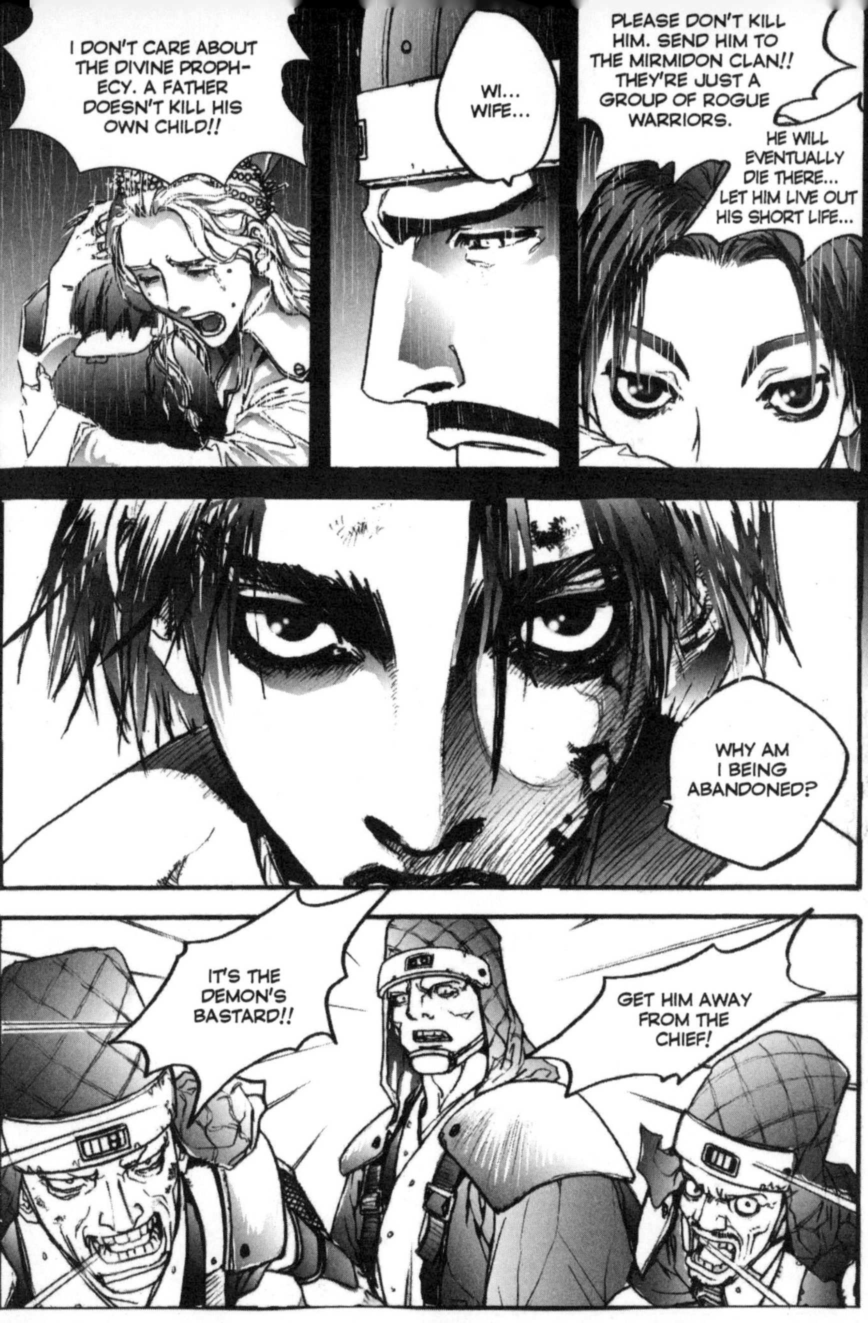
I DON'T CARE ABOUT THE DIVINE PROPHECY. A FATHER DOESN'T KILL HIS OWN CHILD!!
WI... WIFE...
PLEASE DON'T KILL HIM. SEND HIM TO THE MIRMIDON CLAN!! THEY'RE JUST A GROUP OF ROGUE WARRIORS.
HE WILL EVENTUALLY DIE THERE... LET HIM LIVE OUT HIS SHORT LIFE...
WHY AM I BEING ABANDONED?
IT'S THE DEMON'S BASTARD!!
GET HIM AWAY FROM THE CHIEF!

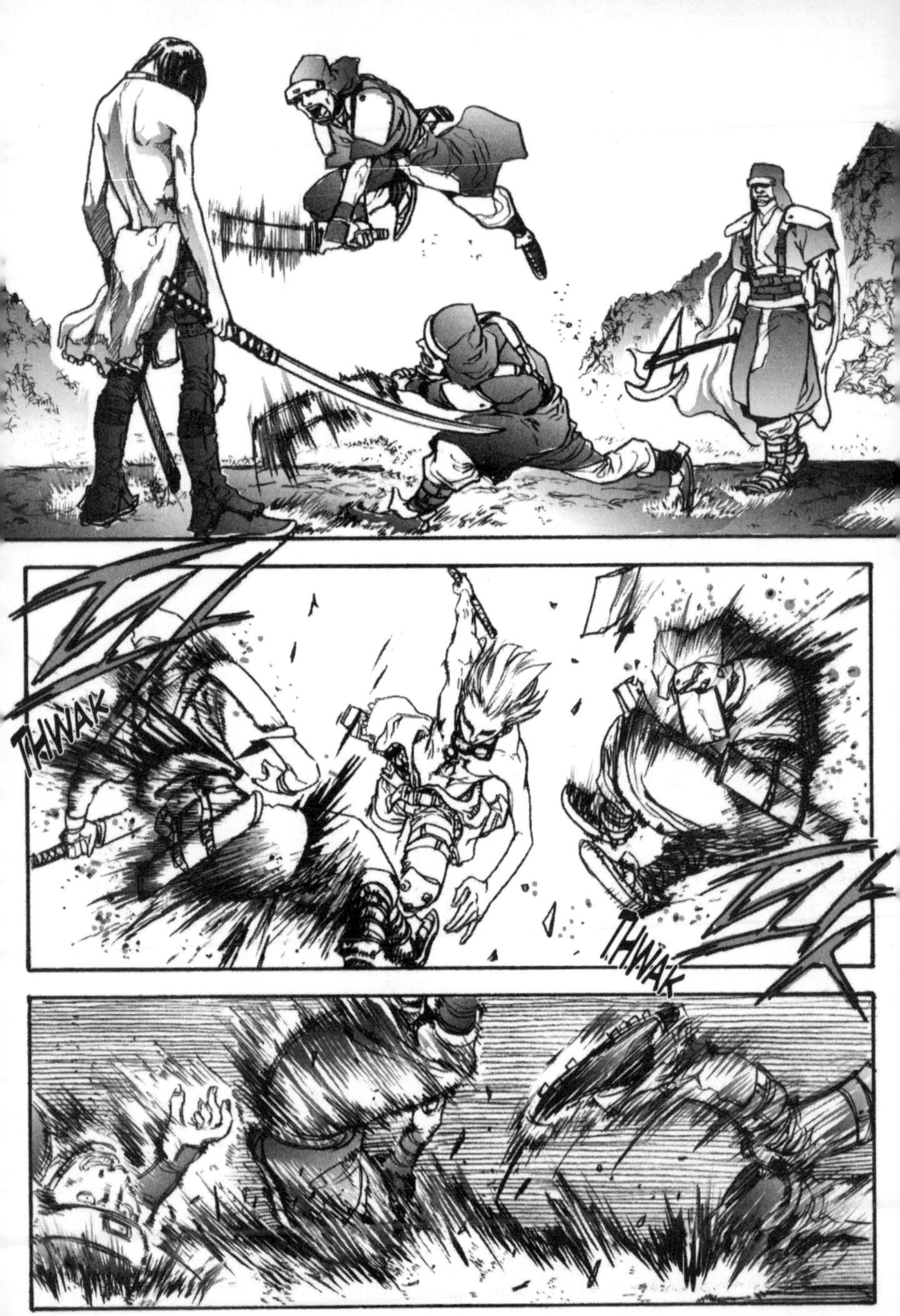
THWAK
THWAK

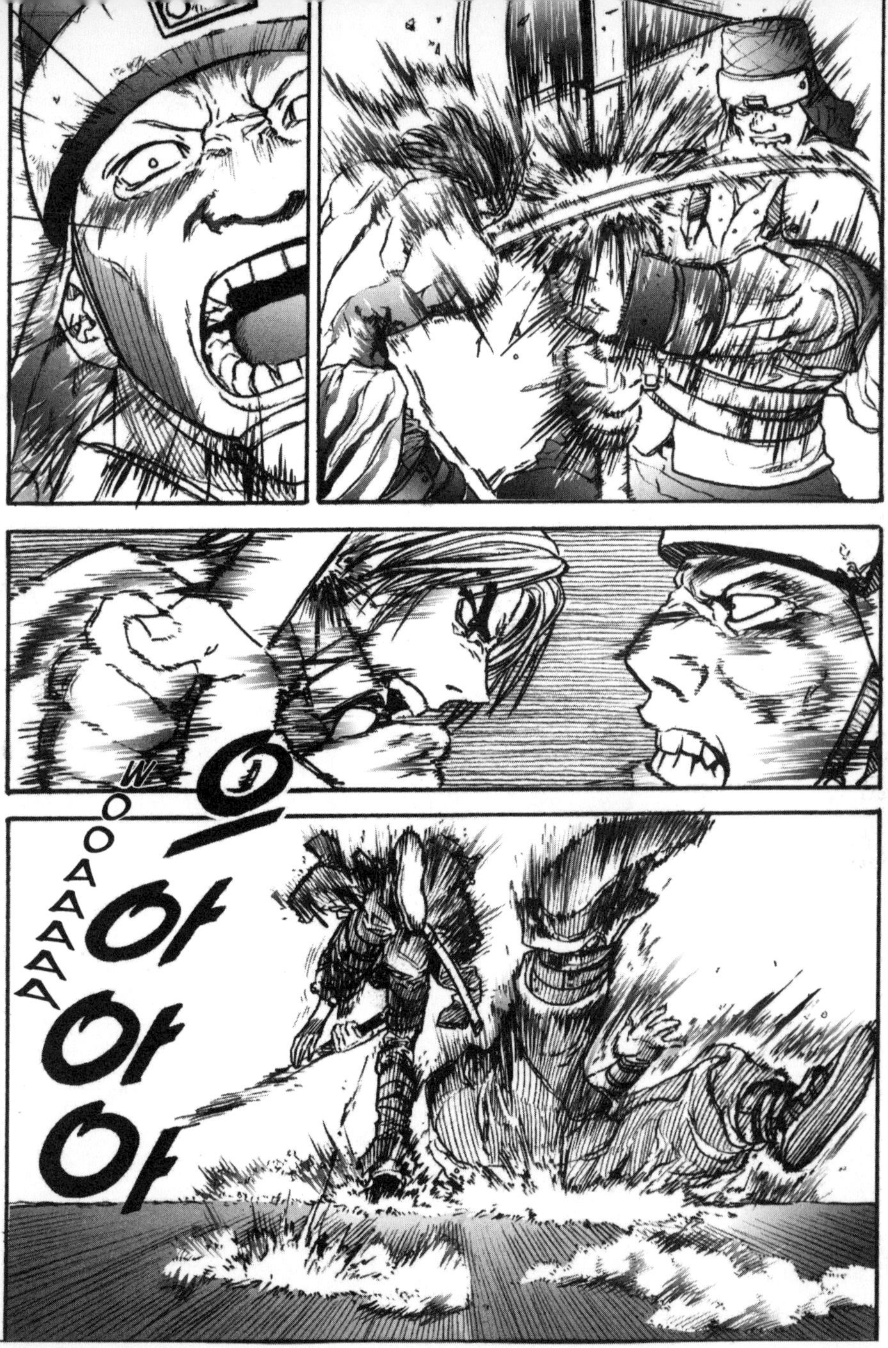
WOOAAAAA

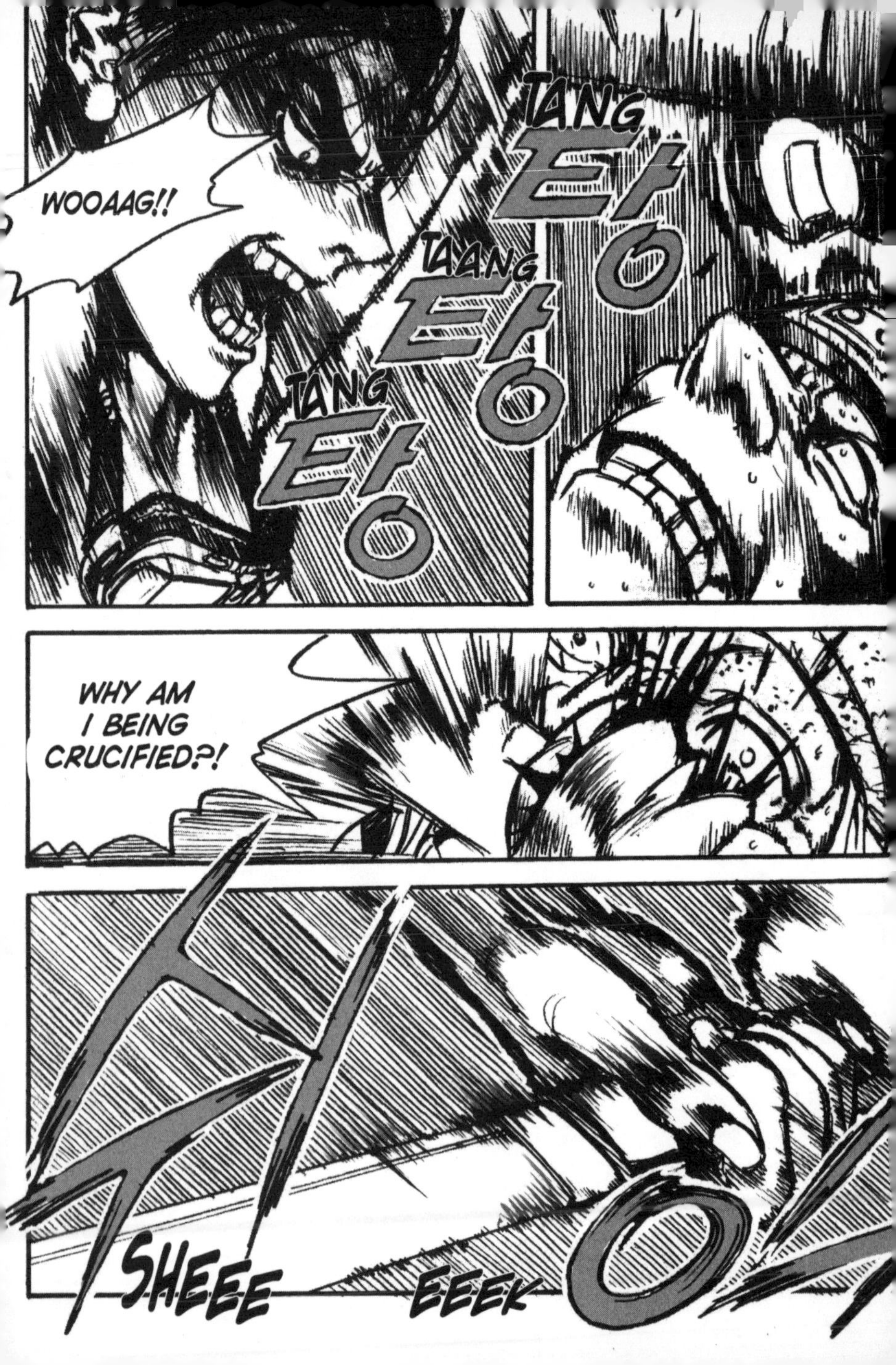
TANG
TAANG
TANG
WOOAAG!!
WHY AM I BEING CRUCIFIED?!
SHEEE
EEEK

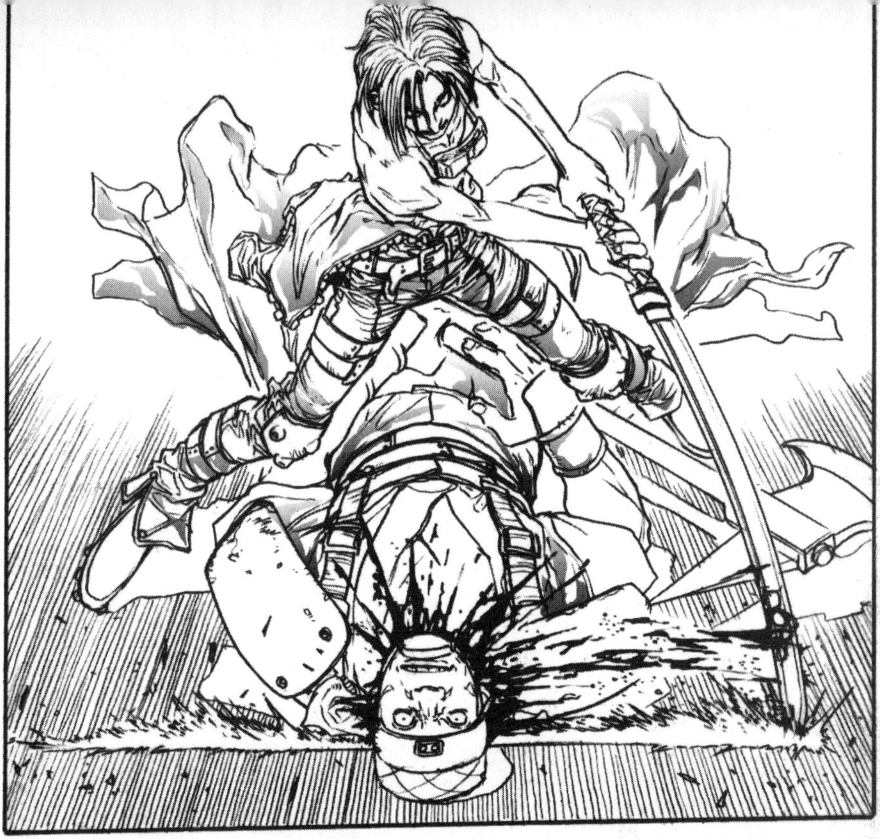

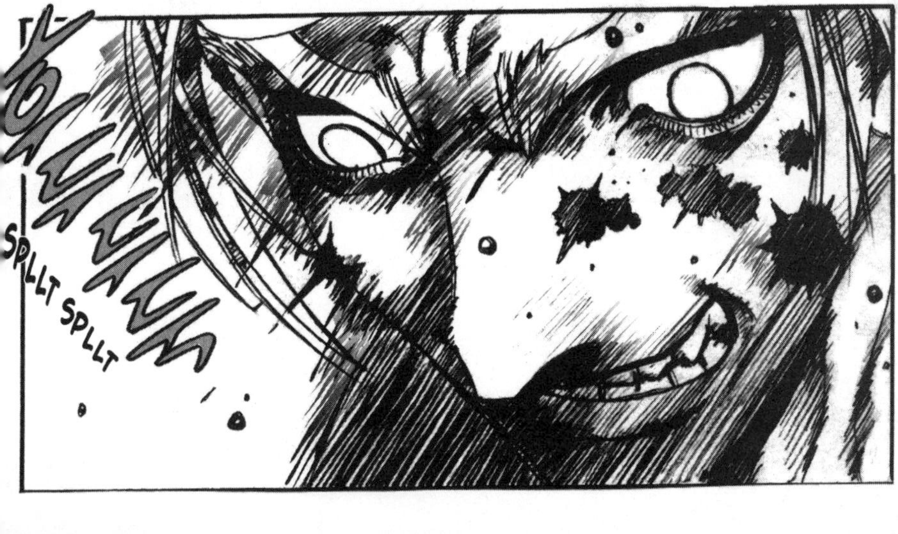
SPLLT SPLLT

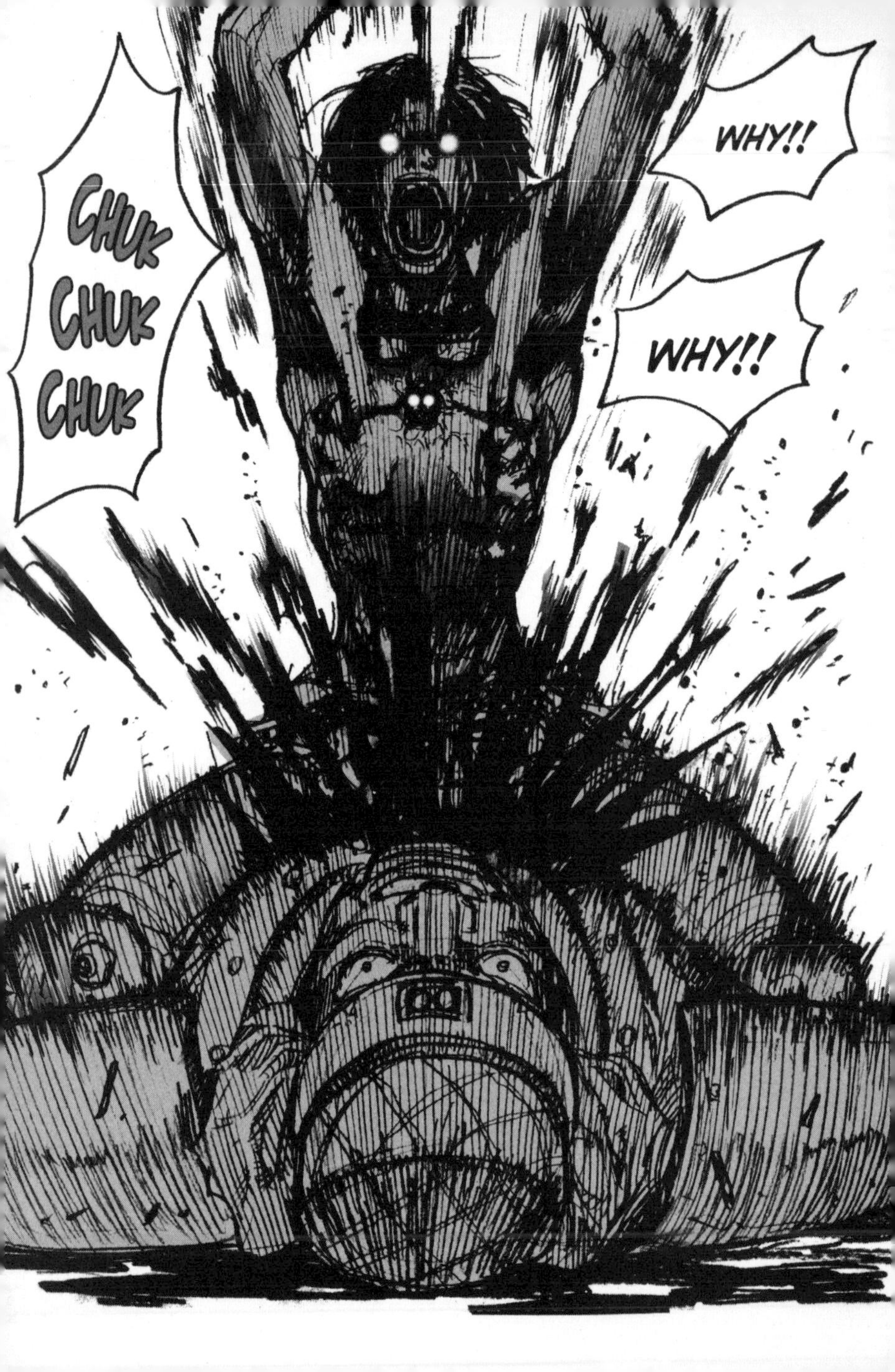
WHY!!
WHY!!
CHUK
CHUK
CHUK

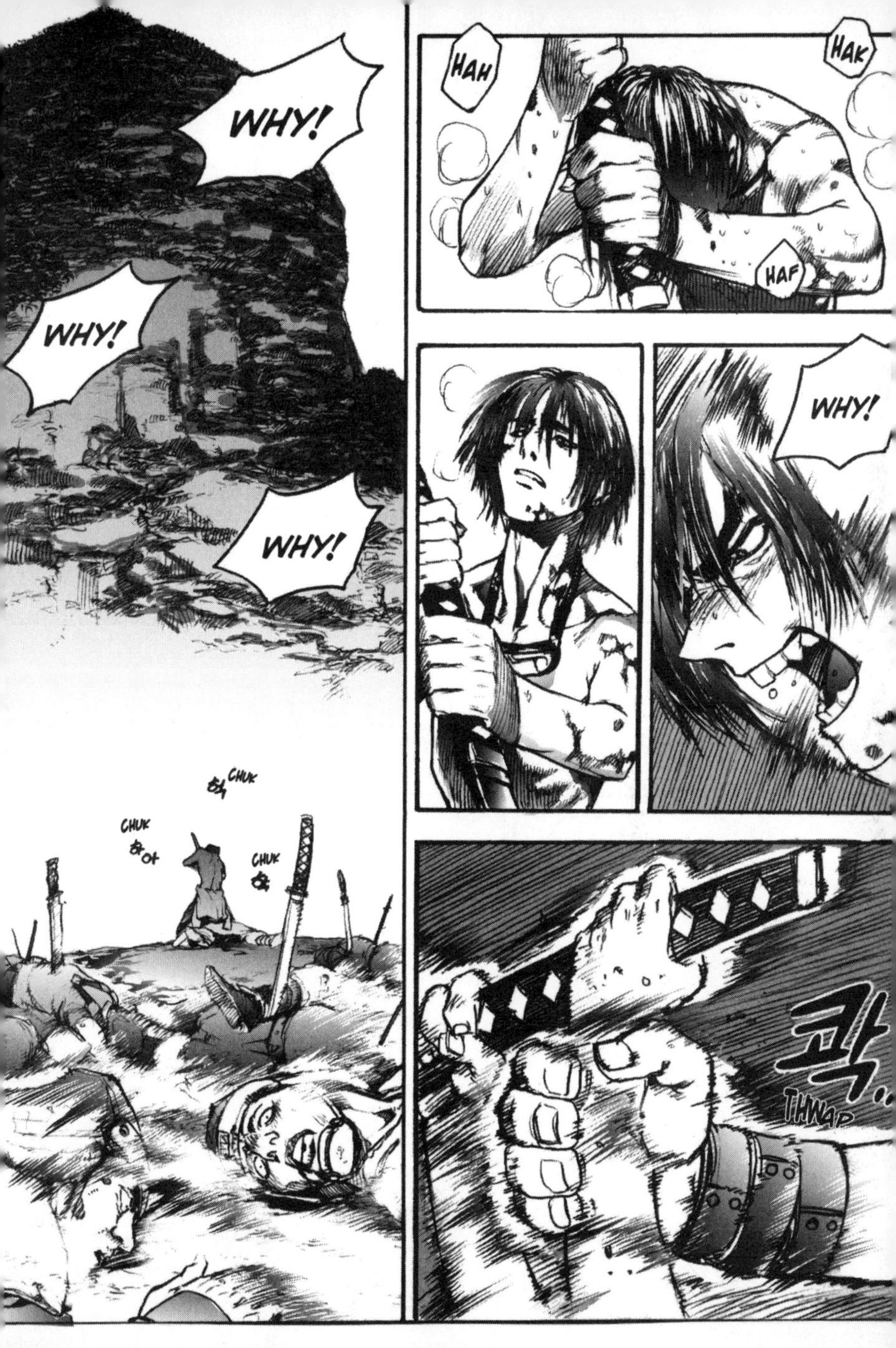
WHY!
WHY!
WHY!
CHUK
CHUK
CHUK
HAH
HAK
HAF
WHY!
콱..
THWAP

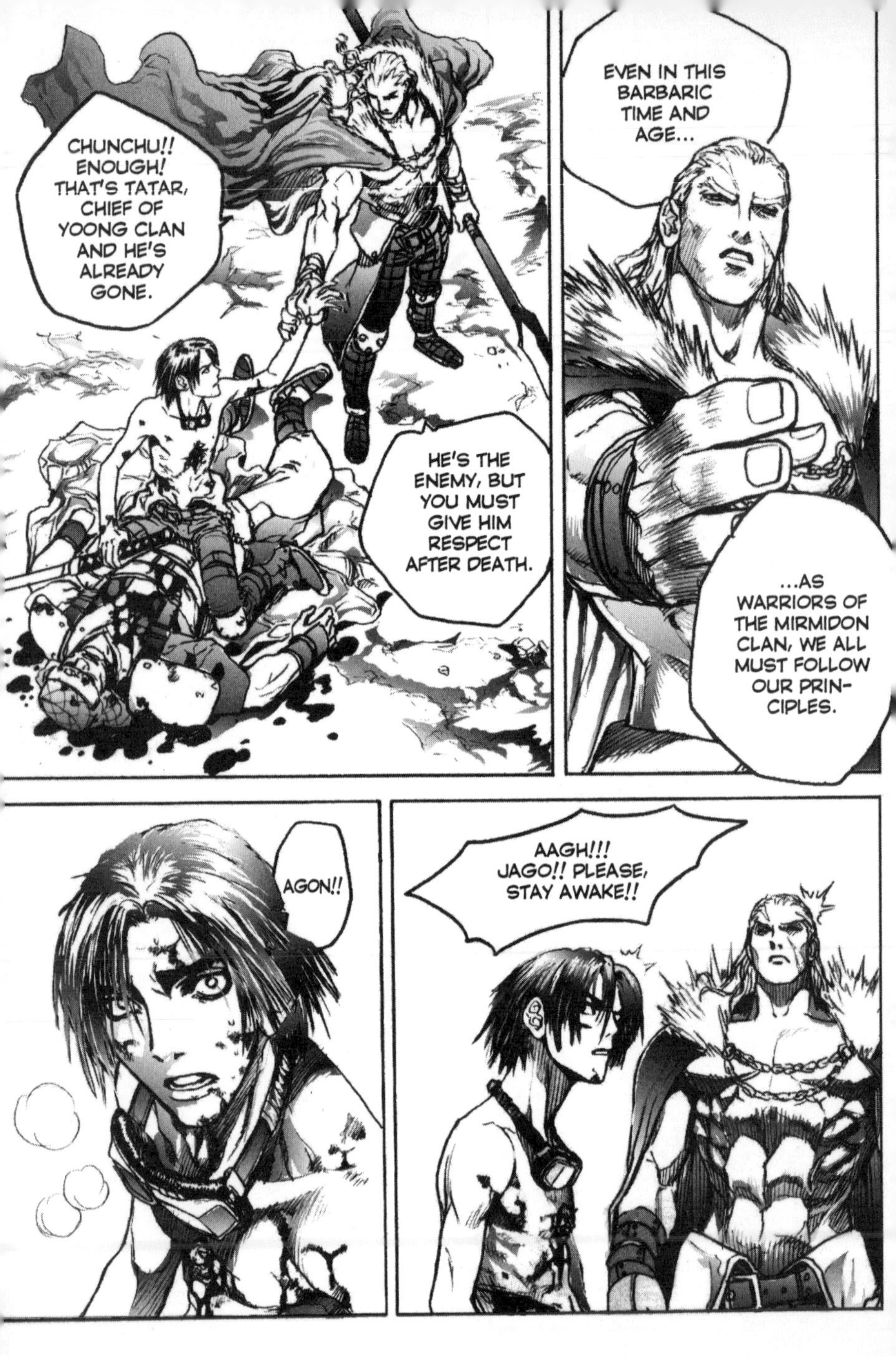
CHUNCHU!! ENOUGH! THAT'S TATAR, CHIEF OF YOONG CLAN AND HE'S ALREADY GONE.
HE'S THE ENEMY, BUT YOU MUST GIVE HIM RESPECT AFTER DEATH.
EVEN IN THIS BARBARIC TIME AND AGE...
...AS WARRIORS OF THE MIRMIDON CLAN, WE ALL MUST FOLLOW OUR PRIN-CIPLES.
AGON!!
AAGH!!! JAGO!! PLEASE, STAY AWAKE!!

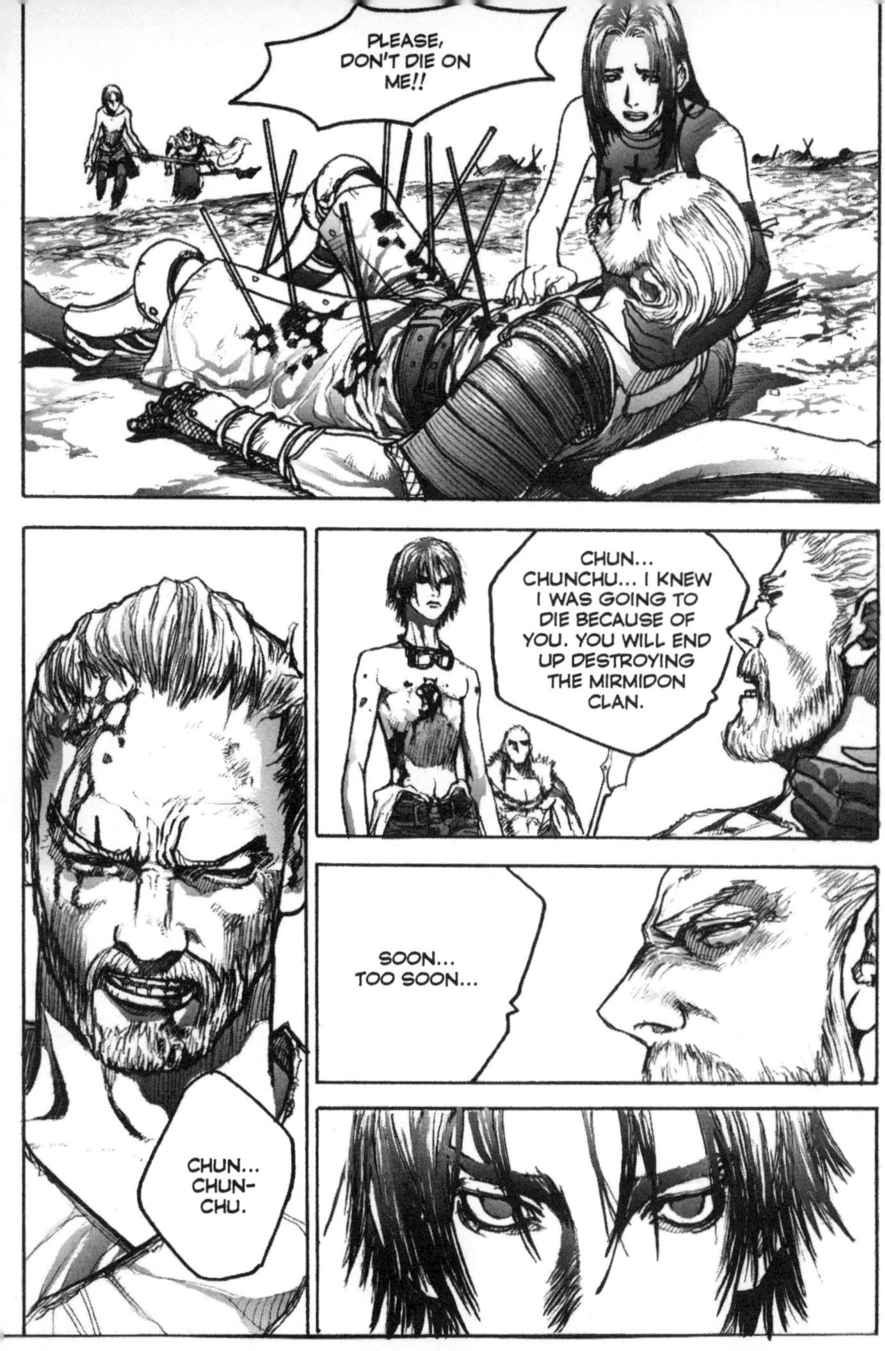
PLEASE, DON'T DIE ON ME!!
CHUN... CHUNCHU... I KNEW I WAS GOING TO DIE BECAUSE OF YOU. YOU WILL END UP DESTROYING THE MIRMIDON CLAN.
SOON... TOO SOON...
CHUN... CHUN-CHU.

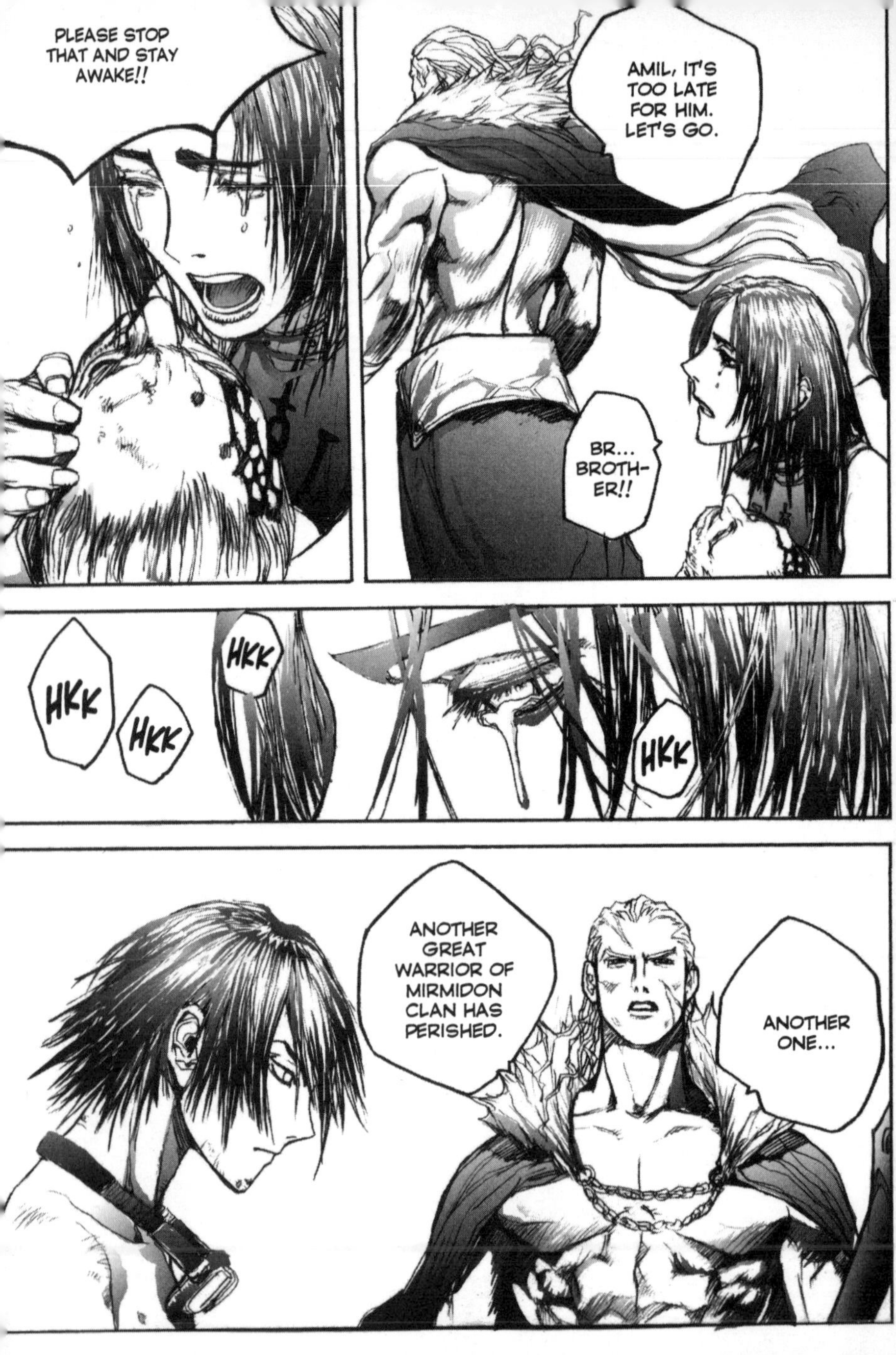
PLEASE STOP THAT AND STAY AWAKE!!
AMIL, IT'S TOO LATE FOR HIM. LET'S GO.
BR... BROTHER!!
HKK
HKK
HKK
HKK
ANOTHER GREAT WARRIOR OF MIRMIDON CLAN HAS PERISHED.
ANOTHER ONE...

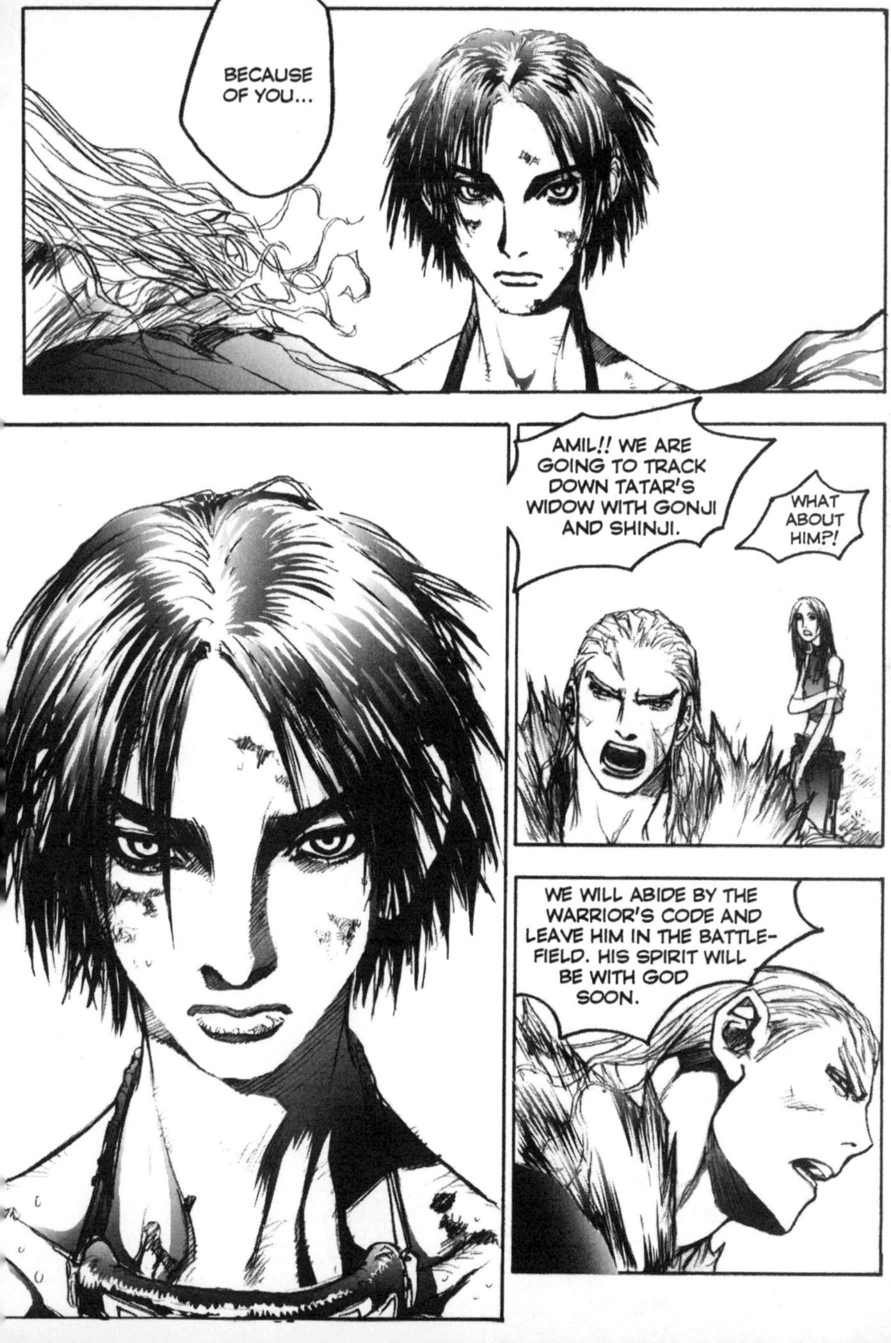
BECAUSE OF YOU...
AMIL!! WE ARE GOING TO TRACK DOWN TATAR'S WIDOW WITH GONJI AND SHINJI.
WHAT ABOUT HIM?!
WE WILL ABIDE BY THE WARRIOR'S CODE AND LEAVE HIM IN THE BATTLE-FIELD. HIS SPIRIT WILL BE WITH GOD SOON.

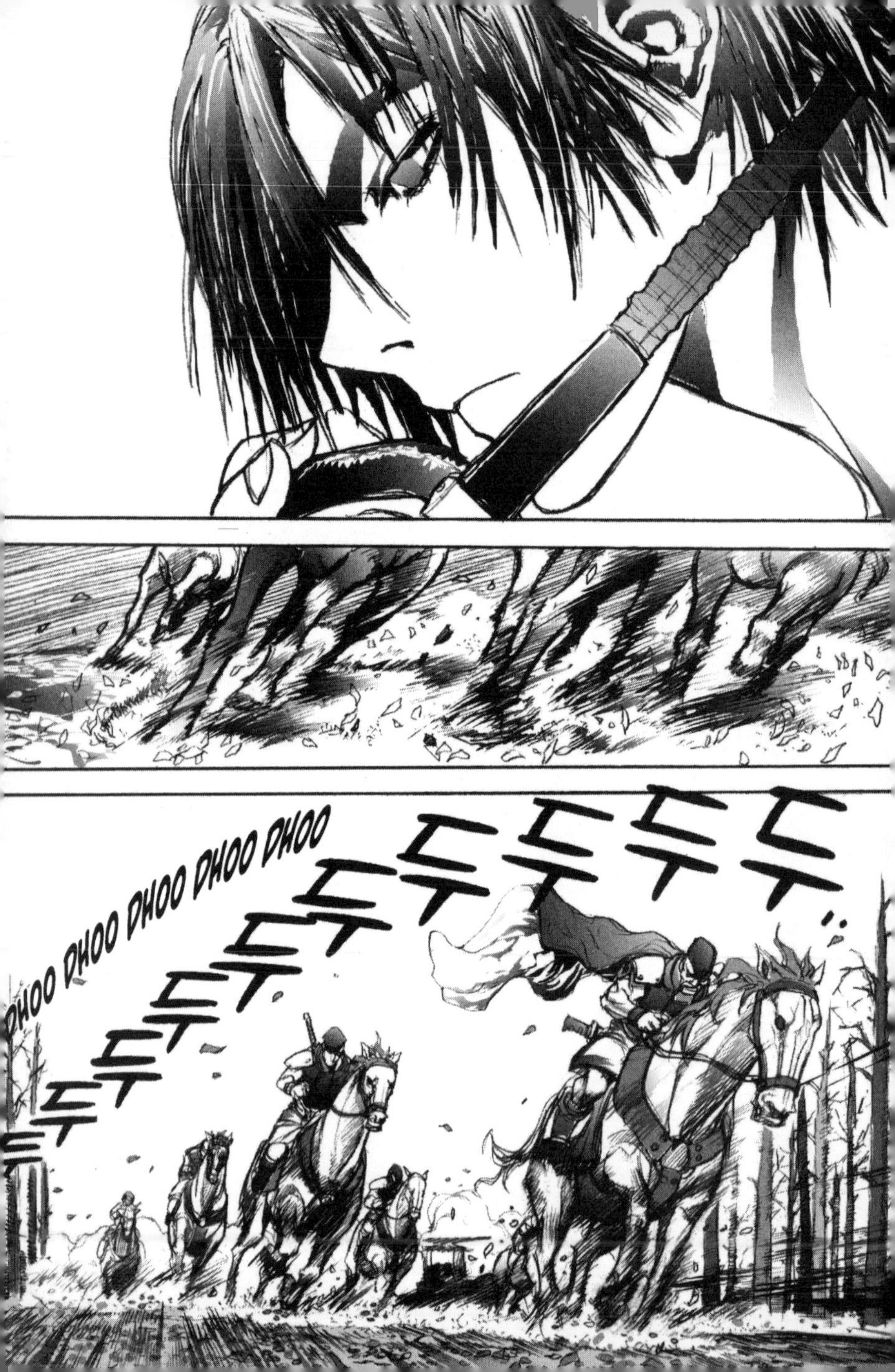
DHOO DHOO DHOO DHOO DHOO

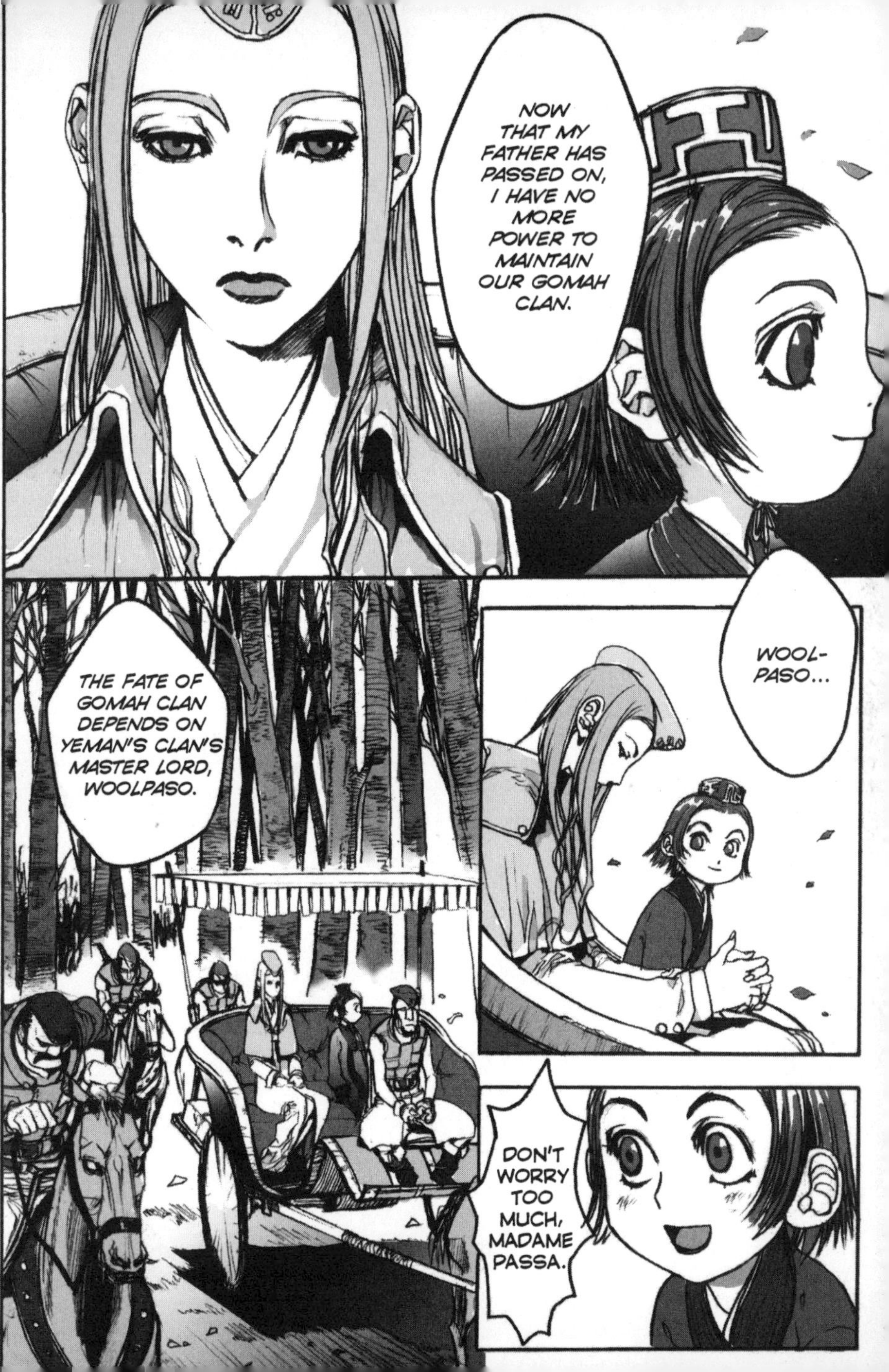
NOW THAT MY FATHER HAS PASSED ON, I HAVE NO MORE POWER TO MAINTAIN OUR GOMAH CLAN.
THE FATE OF GOMAH CLAN DEPENDS ON YEMAN'S CLAN'S MASTER LORD, WOOLPASO.
WOOL-PASO...
DON'T WORRY TOO MUCH, MADAME PASSA.

GRIN
씨익

I HEARD A RUMOR THAT LORD WOOLPASO IS SO HANDSOME AND SUCH A GENTLEMAN.

YOU GOT A REAL GOOD THING COMING, MADAME PASSA.

GOOD AND *BIG* THING!!

HOW CAN SHE BE SO VULGAR...

ANG-ANG! YOU NEED TO CHOOSE YOUR WORDS WISELY. THEY CAN BE TAKEN OUT OF CONTEXT SO EASILY.

SORRY, MA'AM.

HMM.

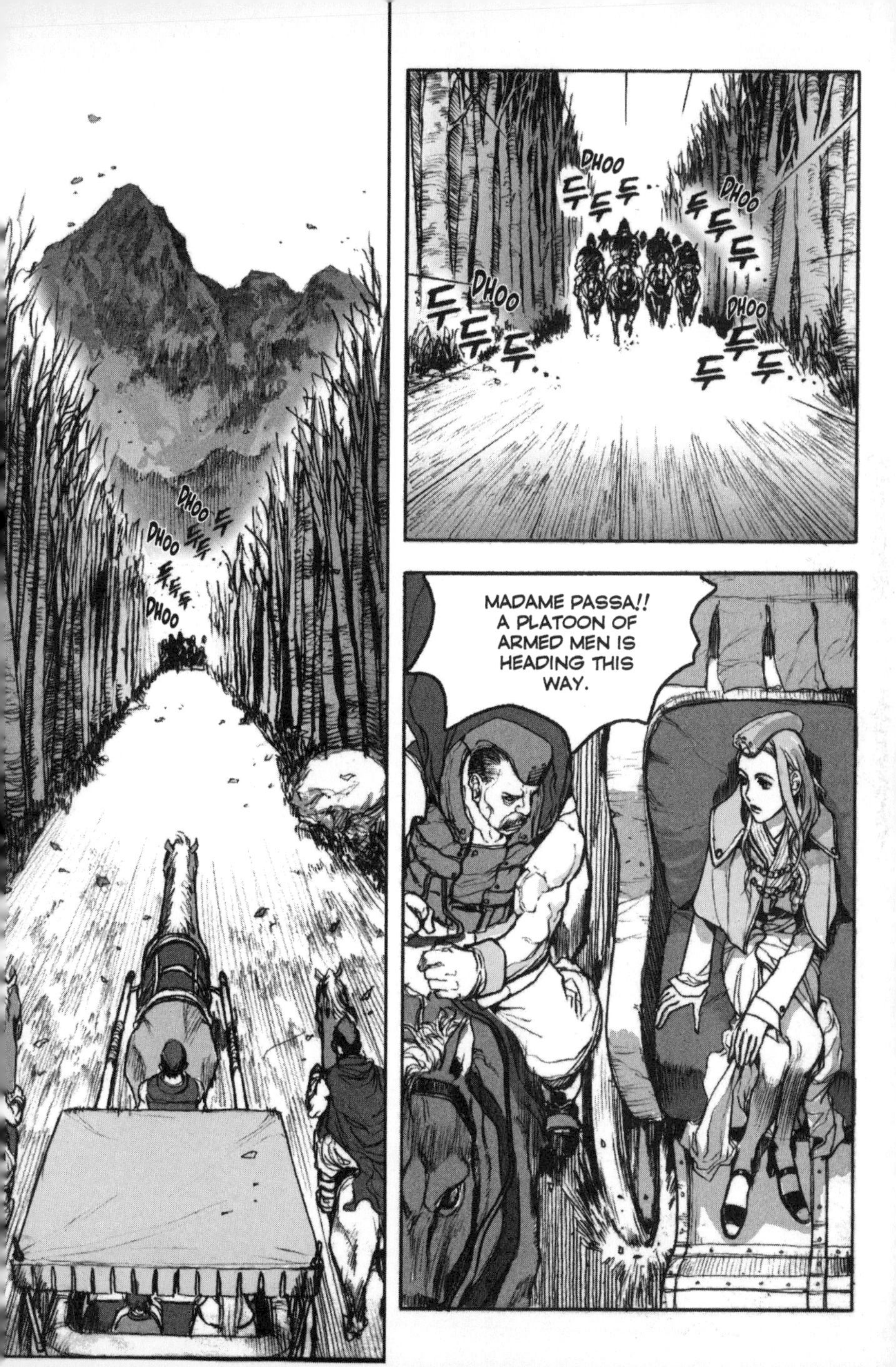

DHOO 두
DHOO 두두
두두두
DHOO
DHOO 두두두...
DHOO 두두두두
DHOO 두두두...
DHOO 두두두...
MADAME PASSA!! A PLATOON OF ARMED MEN IS HEADING THIS WAY.

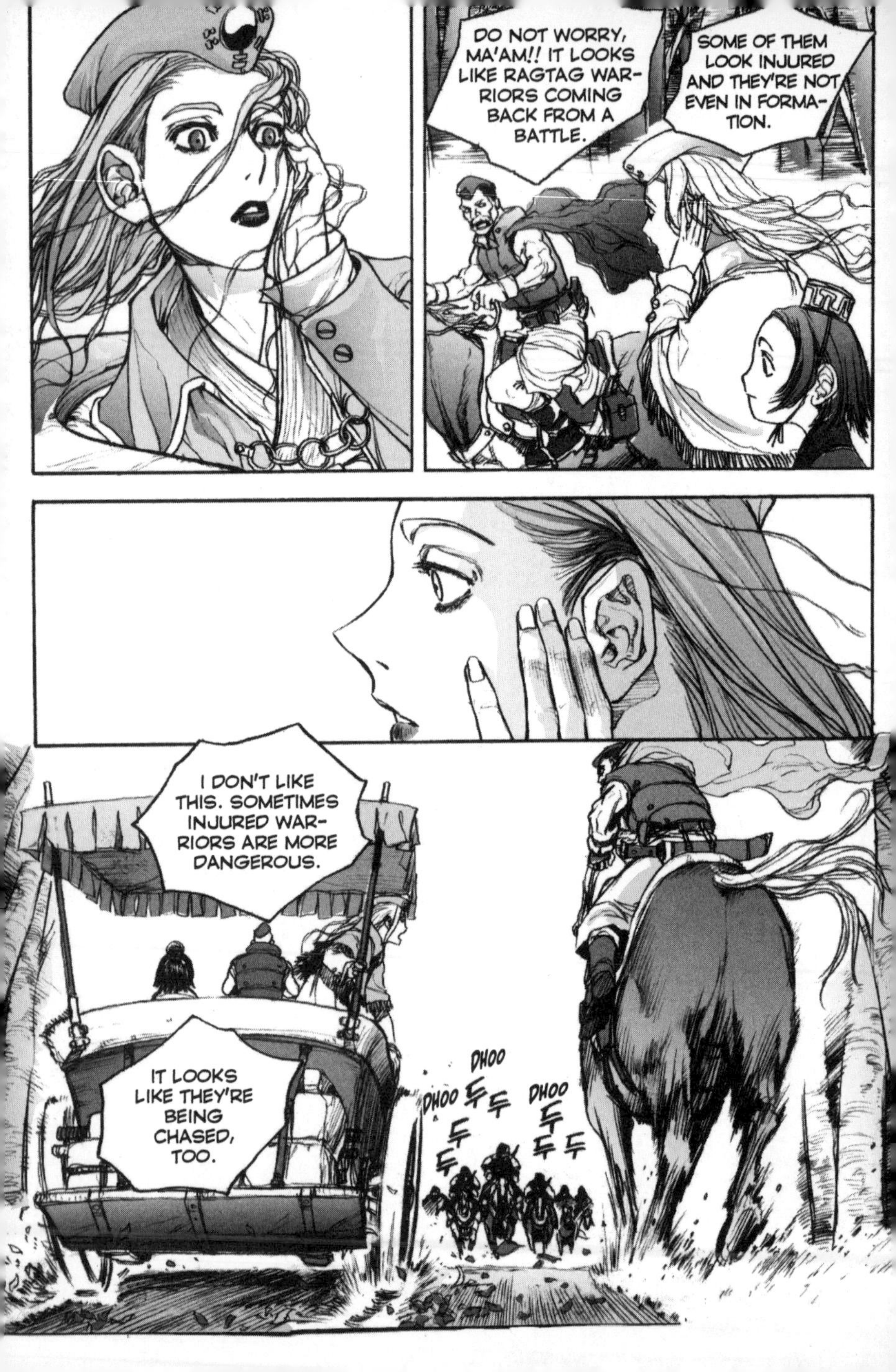
DO NOT WORRY, MA'AM!! IT LOOKS LIKE RAGTAG WARRIORS COMING BACK FROM A BATTLE.
SOME OF THEM LOOK INJURED AND THEY'RE NOT EVEN IN FORMATION.
I DON'T LIKE THIS. SOMETIMES INJURED WARRIORS ARE MORE DANGEROUS.
IT LOOKS LIKE THEY'RE BEING CHASED, TOO.
DHOO
두
DHOO
두
두
DHOO
두
두
두
두
두

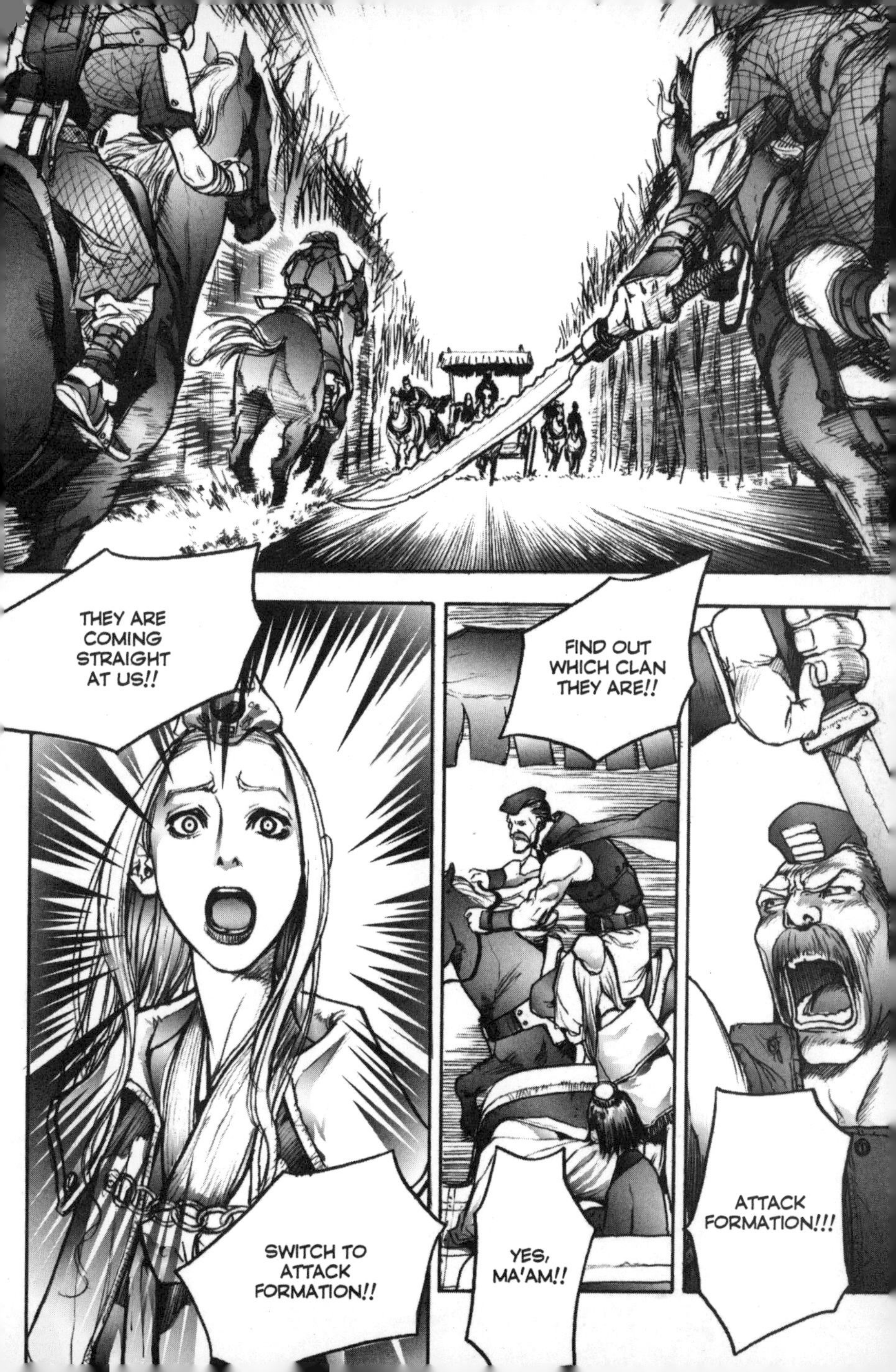
THEY ARE COMING STRAIGHT AT US!!
FIND OUT WHICH CLAN THEY ARE!!
SWITCH TO ATTACK FORMATION!!
YES, MA'AM!!
ATTACK FORMATION!!!

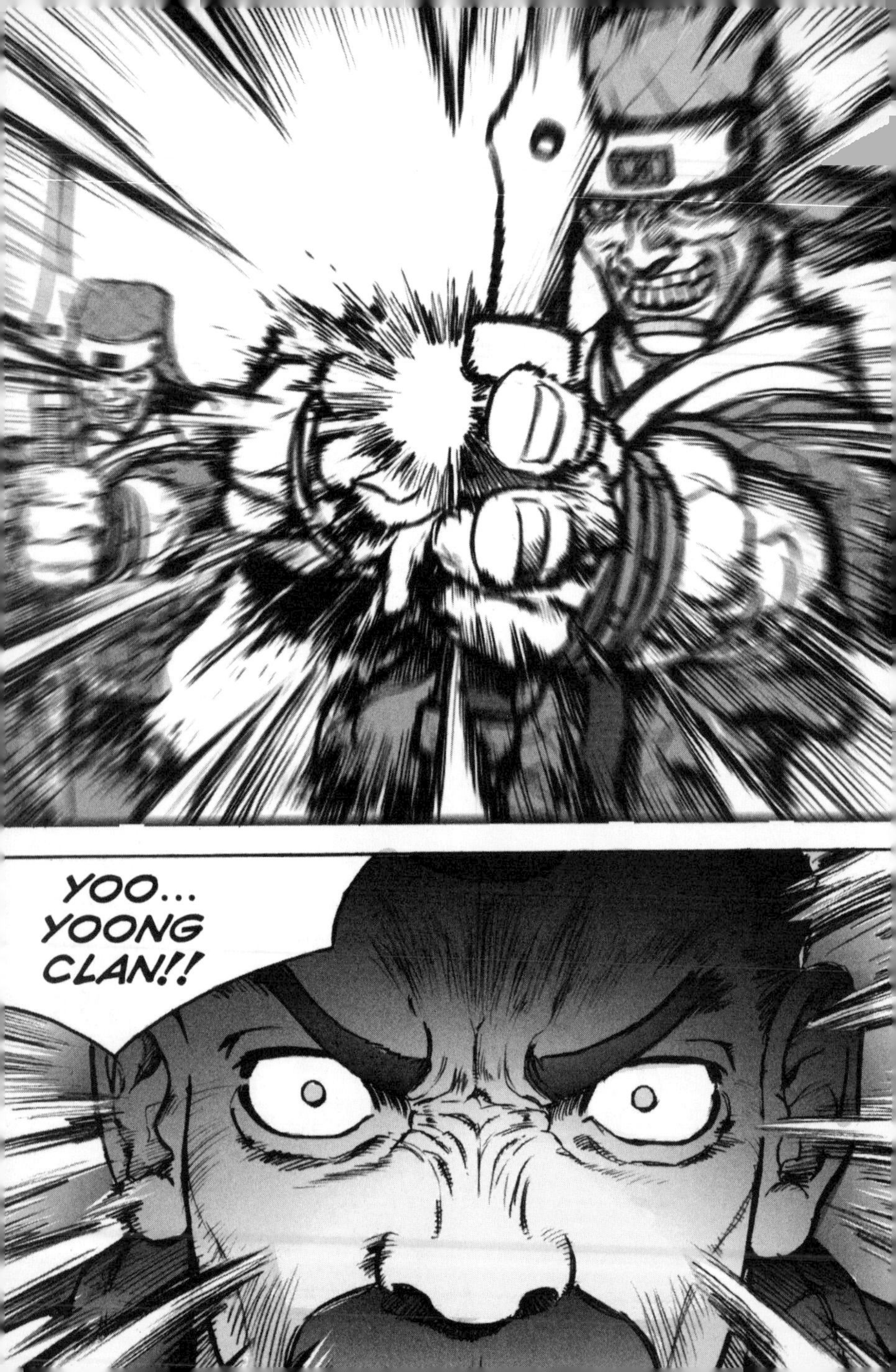
YOO...
YOONG
CLAN!!

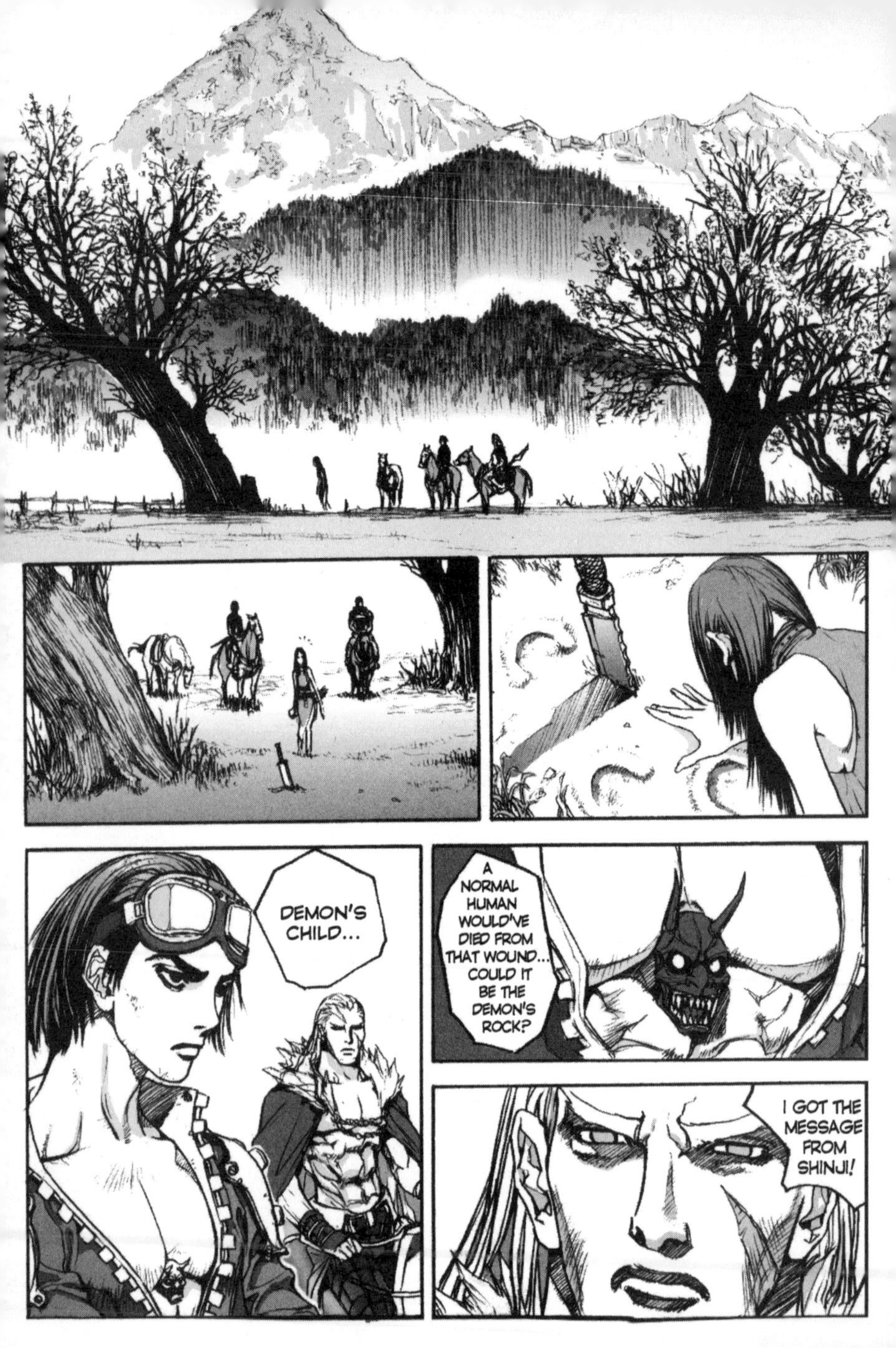
DEMON'S CHILD...
A NORMAL HUMAN WOULD'VE DIED FROM THAT WOUND... COULD IT BE THE DEMON'S ROCK?
I GOT THE MESSAGE FROM SHINJI!

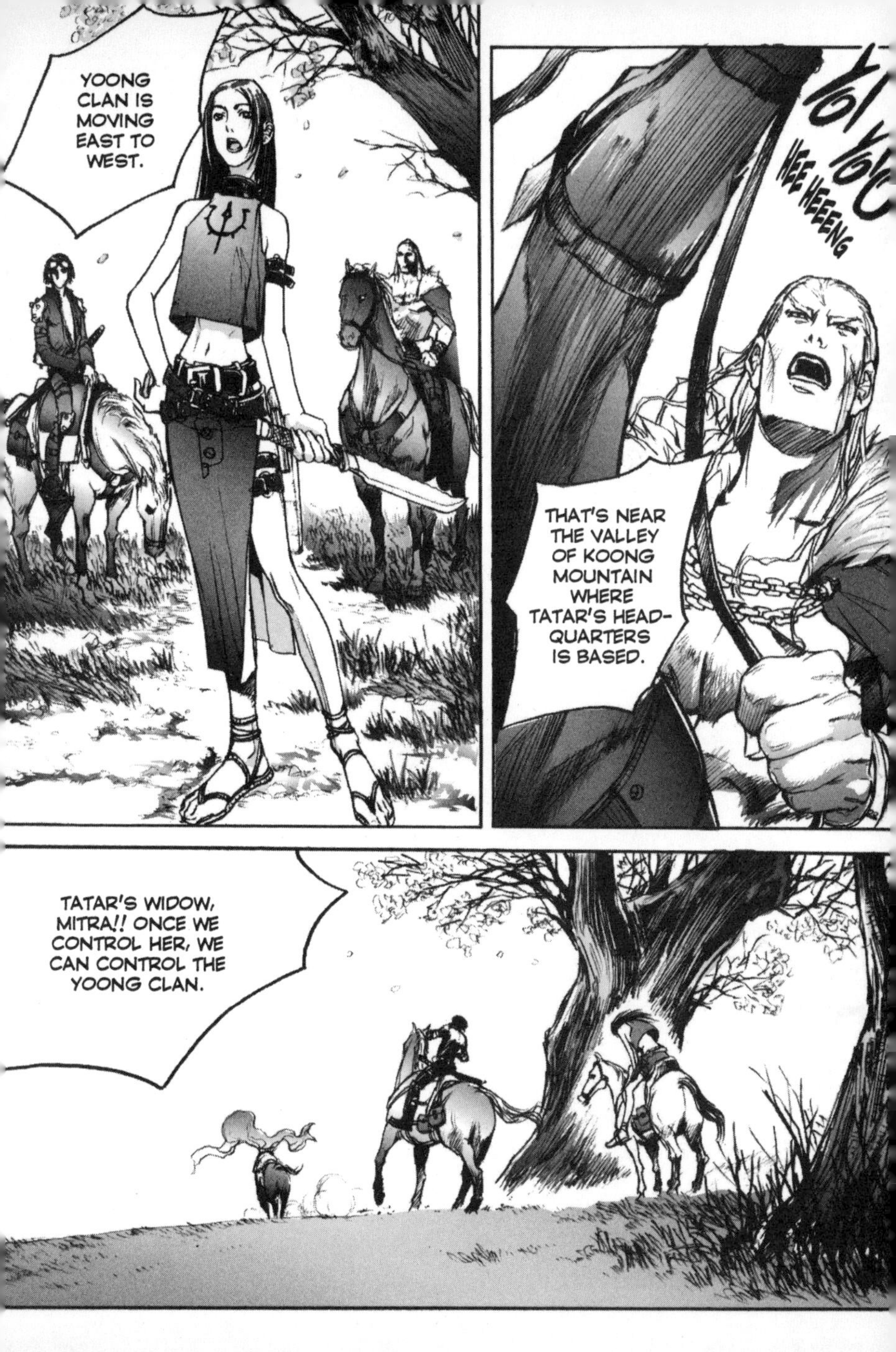
YOONG CLAN IS MOVING EAST TO WEST.
YOI YOIC
HEE HEEENG
THAT'S NEAR THE VALLEY OF KOONG MOUNTAIN WHERE TATAR'S HEAD-QUARTERS IS BASED.
TATAR'S WIDOW, MITRA!! ONCE WE CONTROL HER, WE CAN CONTROL THE YOONG CLAN.

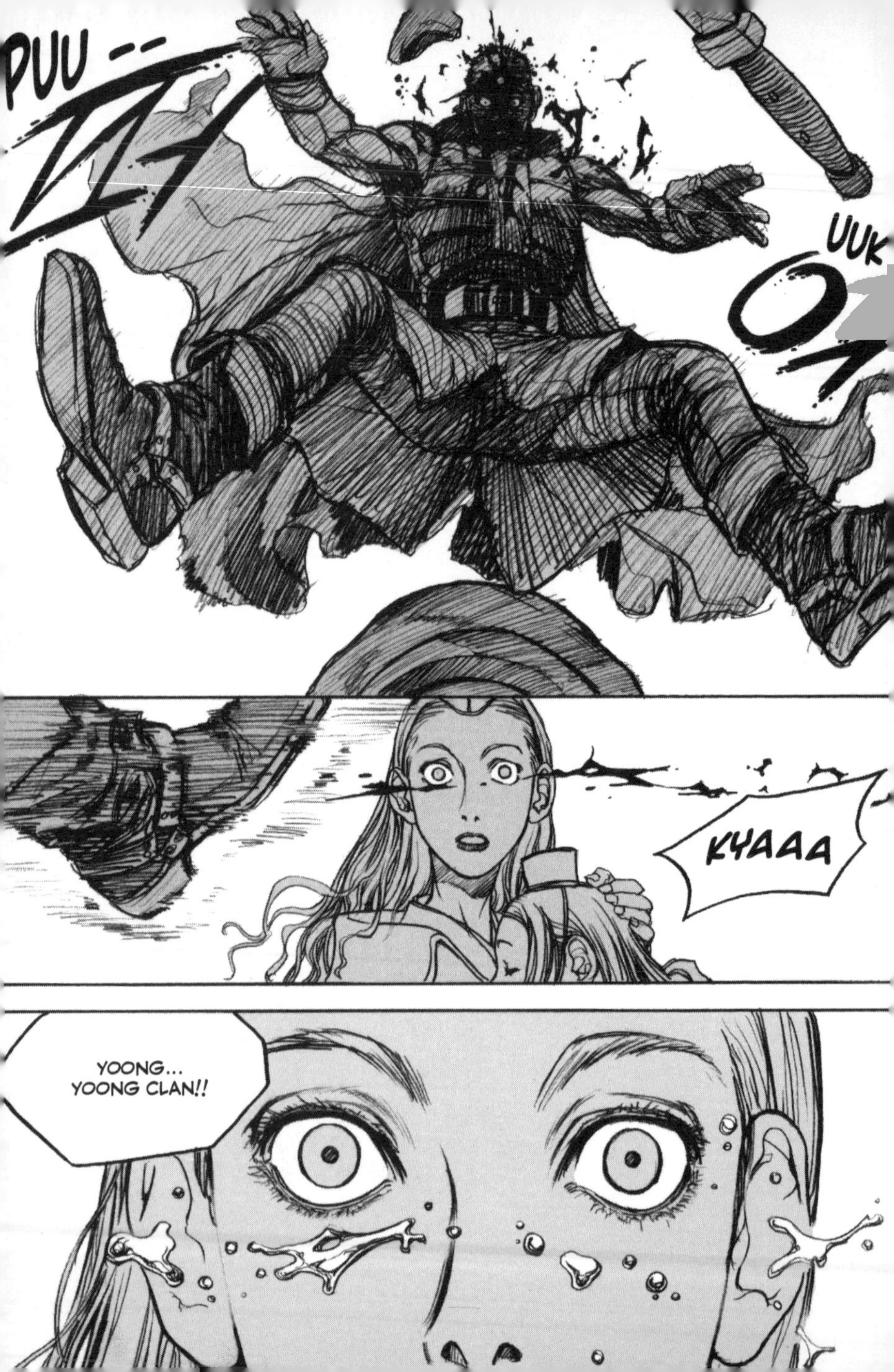
PUU --
UUK
KYAAA
YOONG...
YOONG CLAN!!

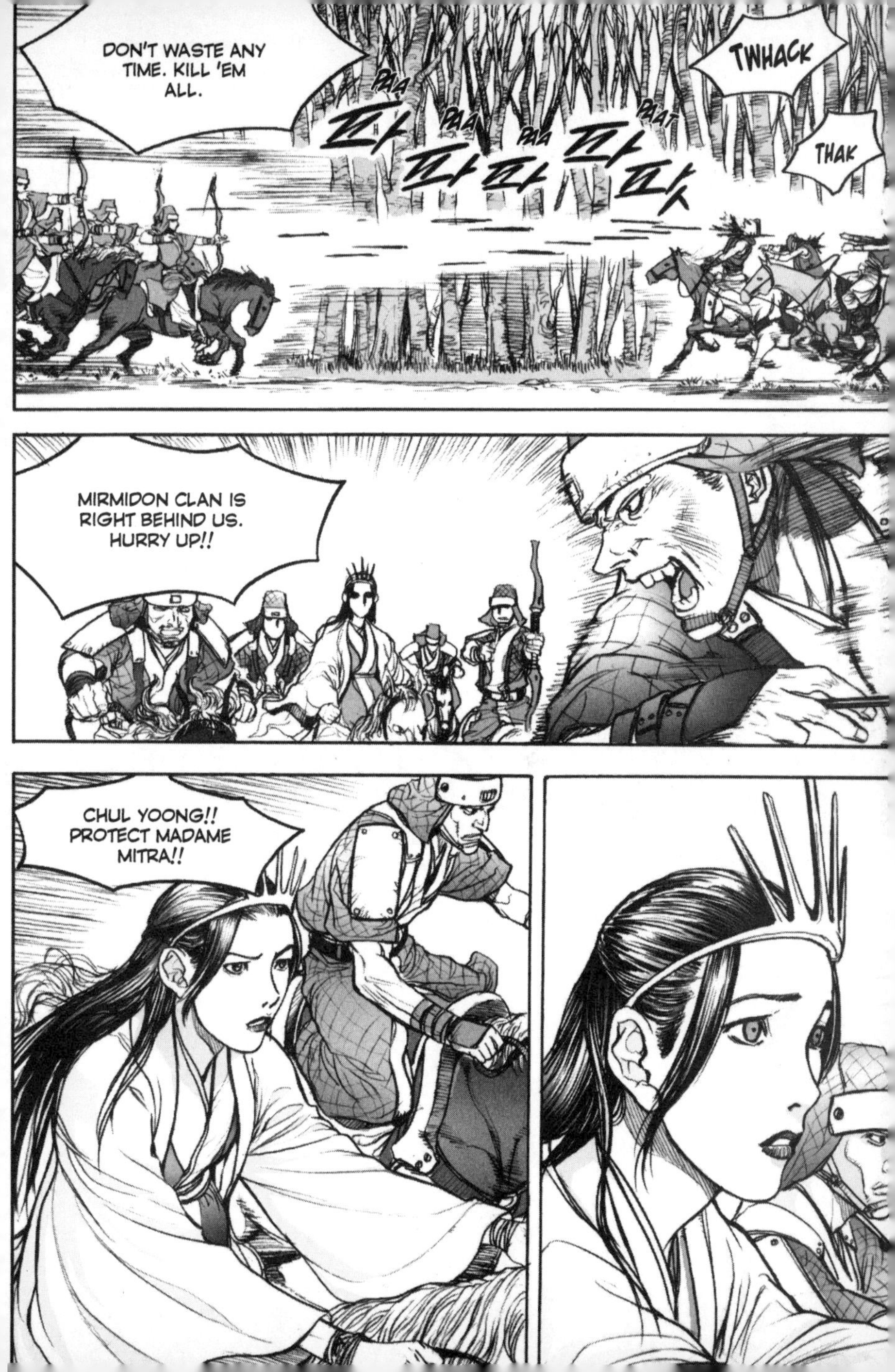
DON'T WASTE ANY TIME. KILL 'EM ALL.
PAA
PAA
PAA
PAAT
TWHACK
THAK
MIRMIDON CLAN IS RIGHT BEHIND US. HURRY UP!!
CHUL YOONG!! PROTECT MADAME MITRA!!

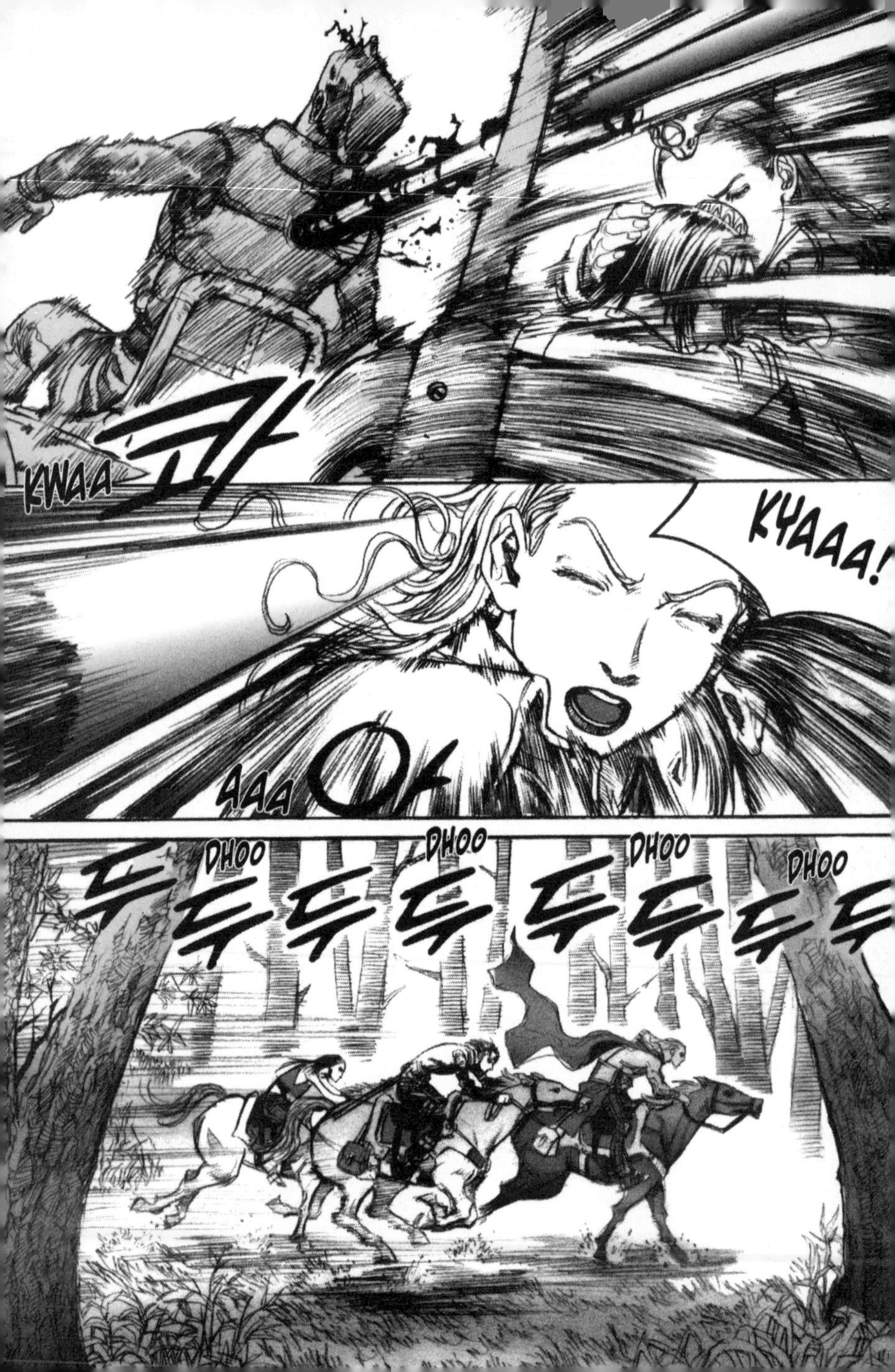
KWAA
KYAAA!
AAA
DHOO
DHOO
DHOO
DHOO

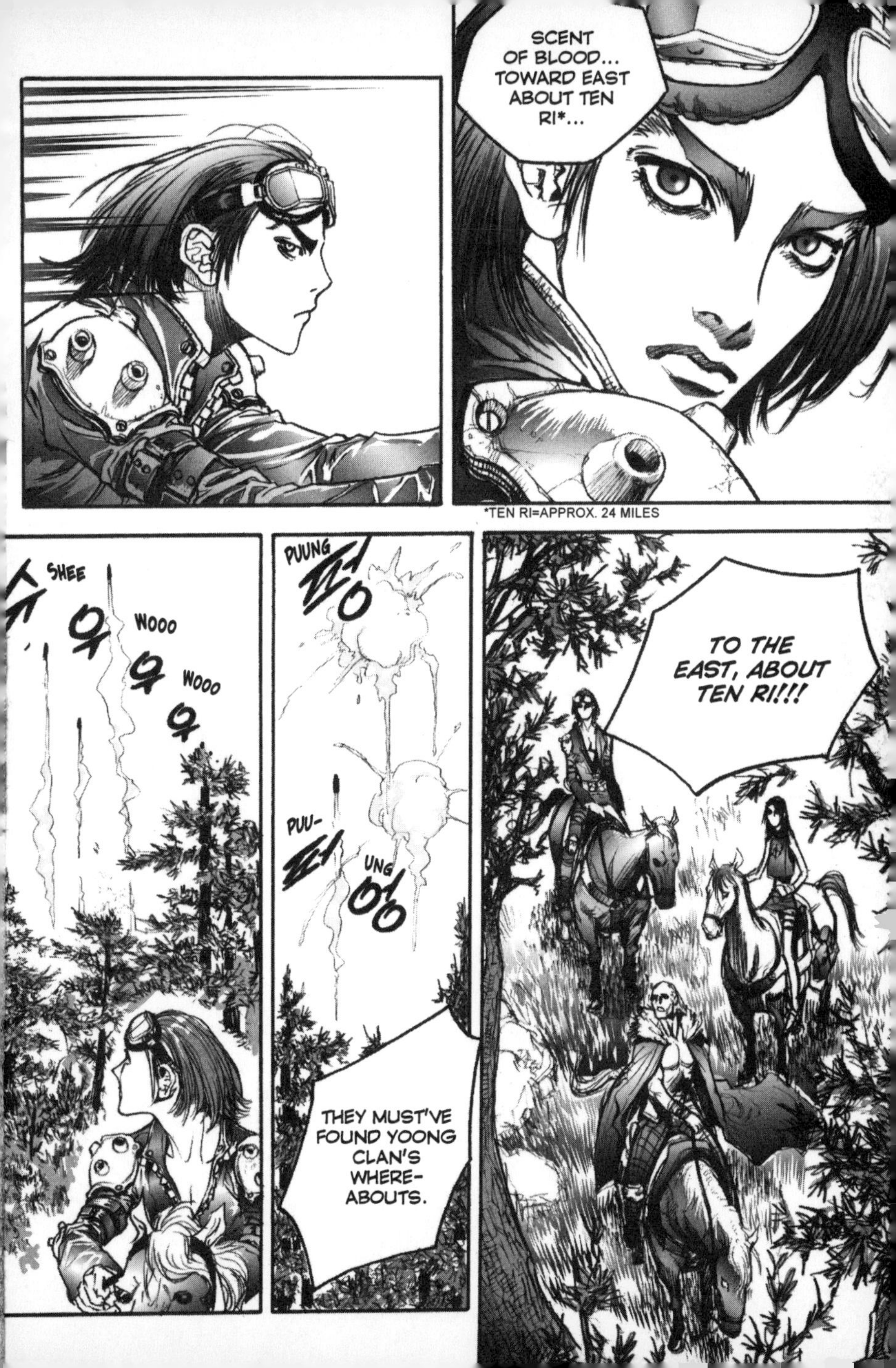
SCENT OF BLOOD... TOWARD EAST ABOUT TEN RI*...
SHEE
WOOO
WOOO
PUUNG
PUU-
UNG
THEY MUST'VE FOUND YOONG CLAN'S WHERE-ABOUTS.
TO THE EAST, ABOUT TEN RI!!!

*TEN RI=APPROX. 24 MILES

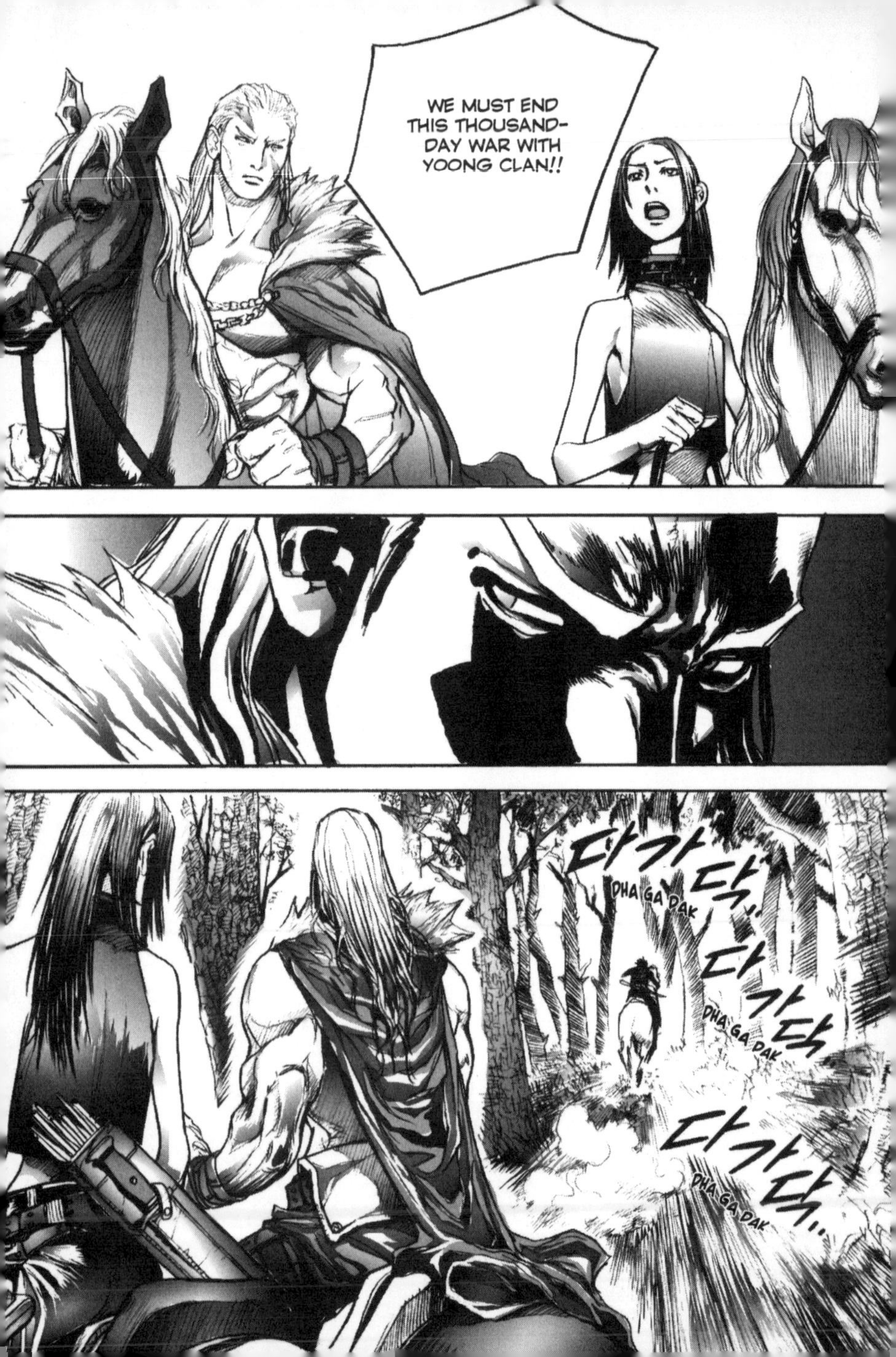
WE MUST END THIS THOUSAND-DAY WAR WITH YOONG CLAN!!
다가닥..
DHA GA DAK
다가닥
DHA GA DAK
다가닥..
DHA GA DAK

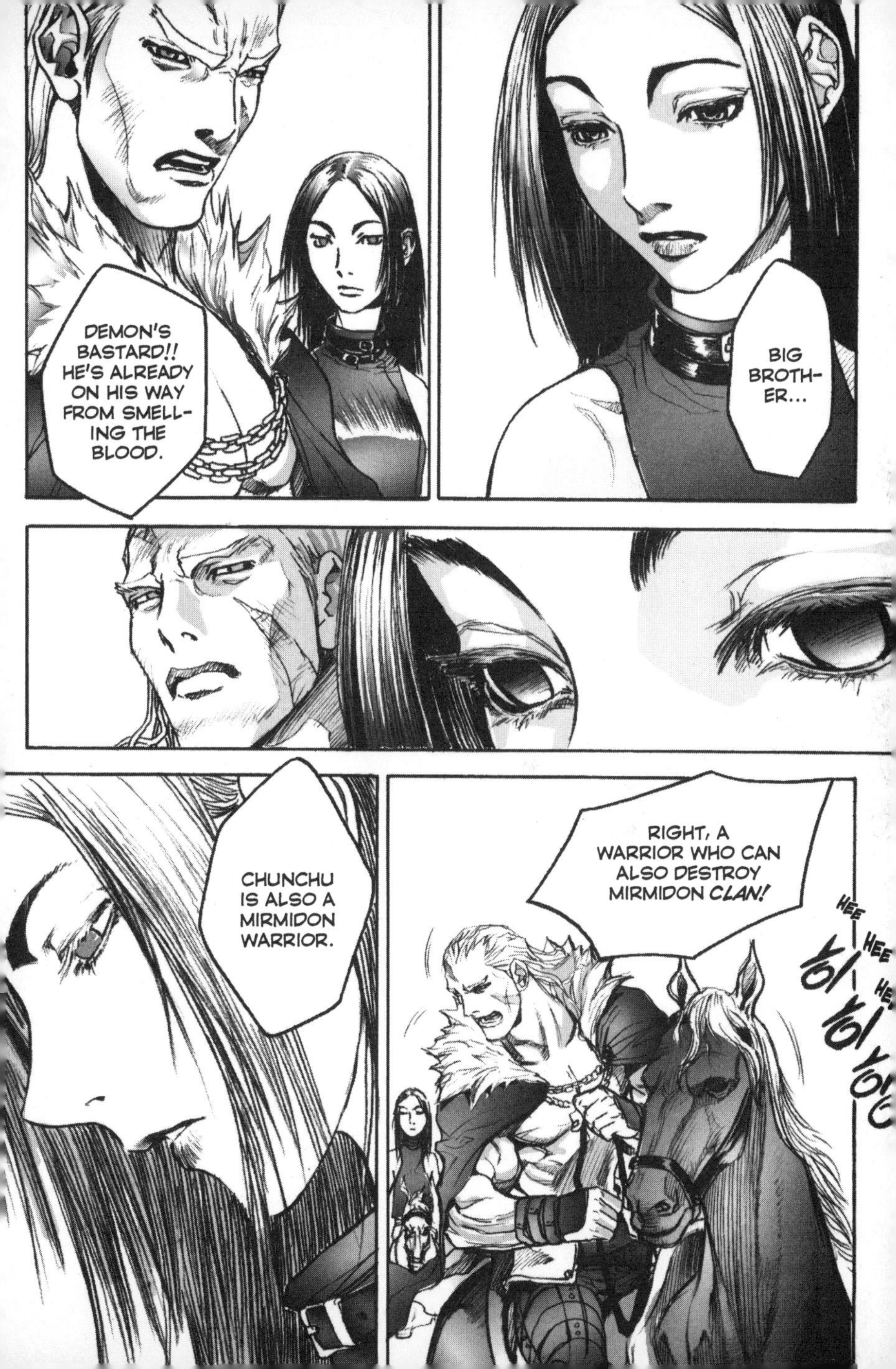
BIG BROTHER-ER...
DEMON'S BASTARD!! HE'S ALREADY ON HIS WAY FROM SMELLING THE BLOOD.
CHUNCHU IS ALSO A MIRMIDON WARRIOR.
RIGHT, A WARRIOR WHO CAN ALSO DESTROY MIRMIDON CLAN!
HEE HEE HEE
YO! YO! YO! YO!

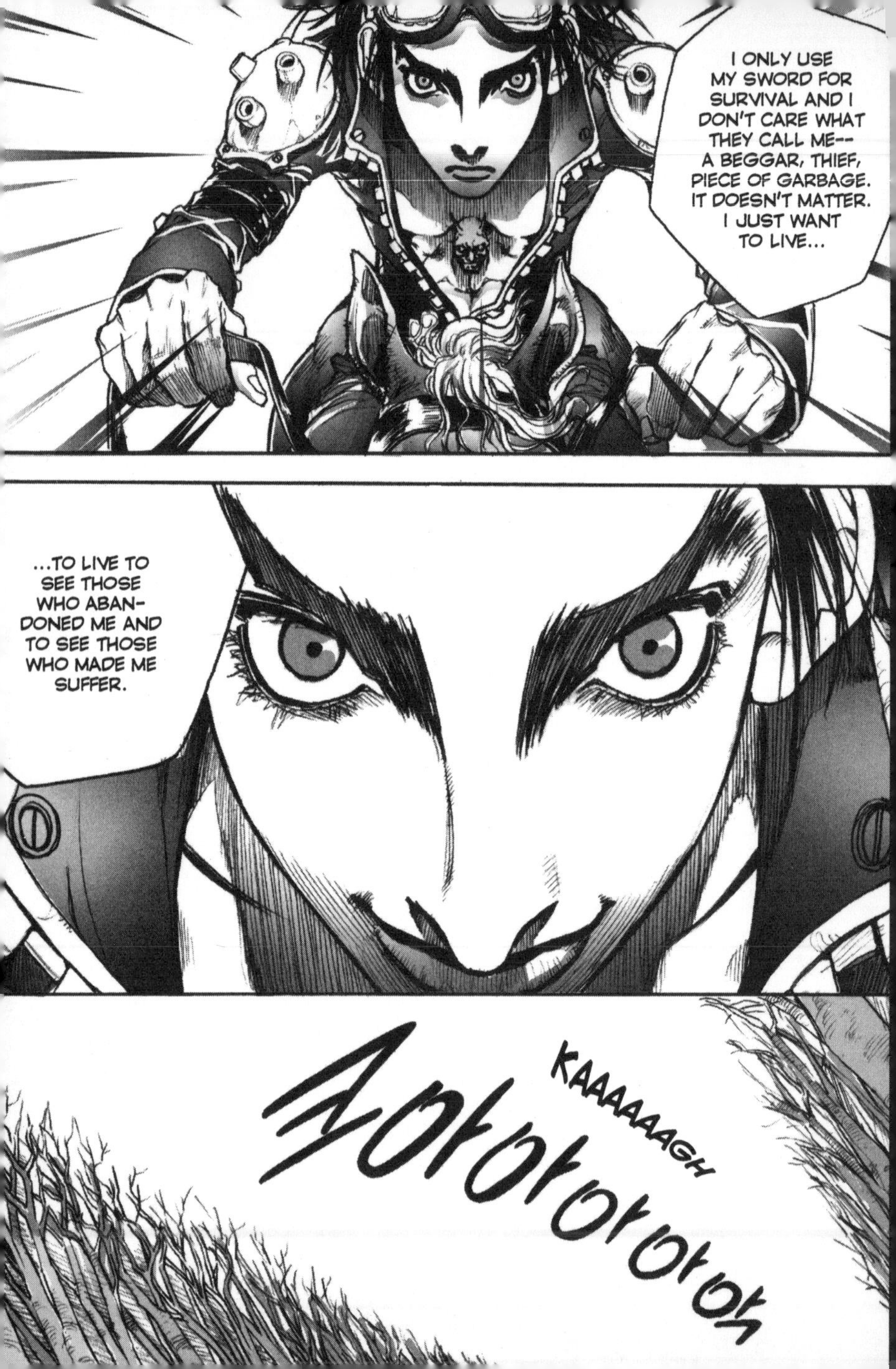
I ONLY USE MY SWORD FOR SURVIVAL AND I DON'T CARE WHAT THEY CALL ME-- A BEGGAR, THIEF, PIECE OF GARBAGE. IT DOESN'T MATTER. I JUST WANT TO LIVE...
...TO LIVE TO SEE THOSE WHO ABAN-DONED ME AND TO SEE THOSE WHO MADE ME SUFFER.
KAAAAAAAGH

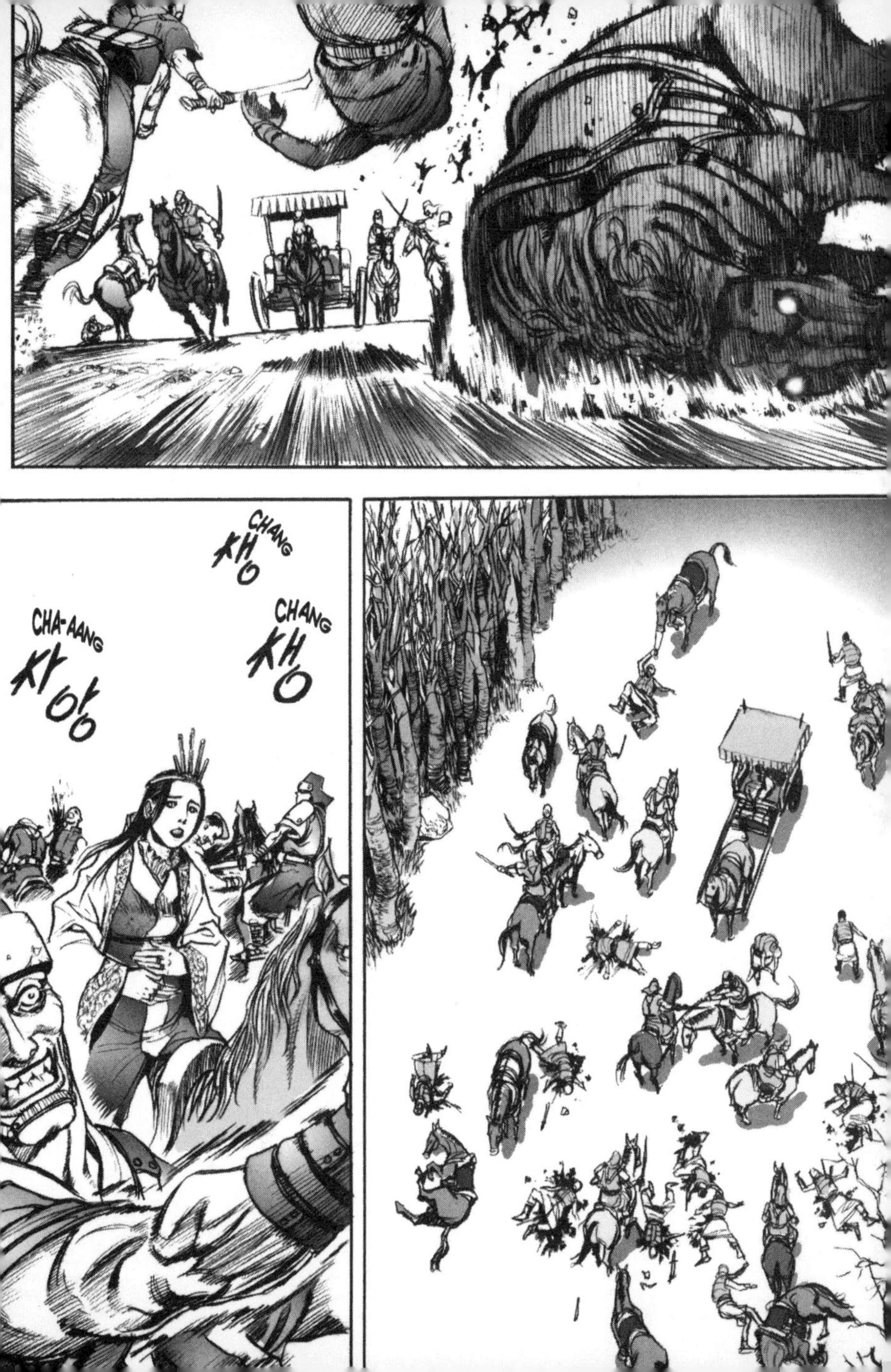
CHANG
챙
CHANG
챙
CHA-AANG
차앙

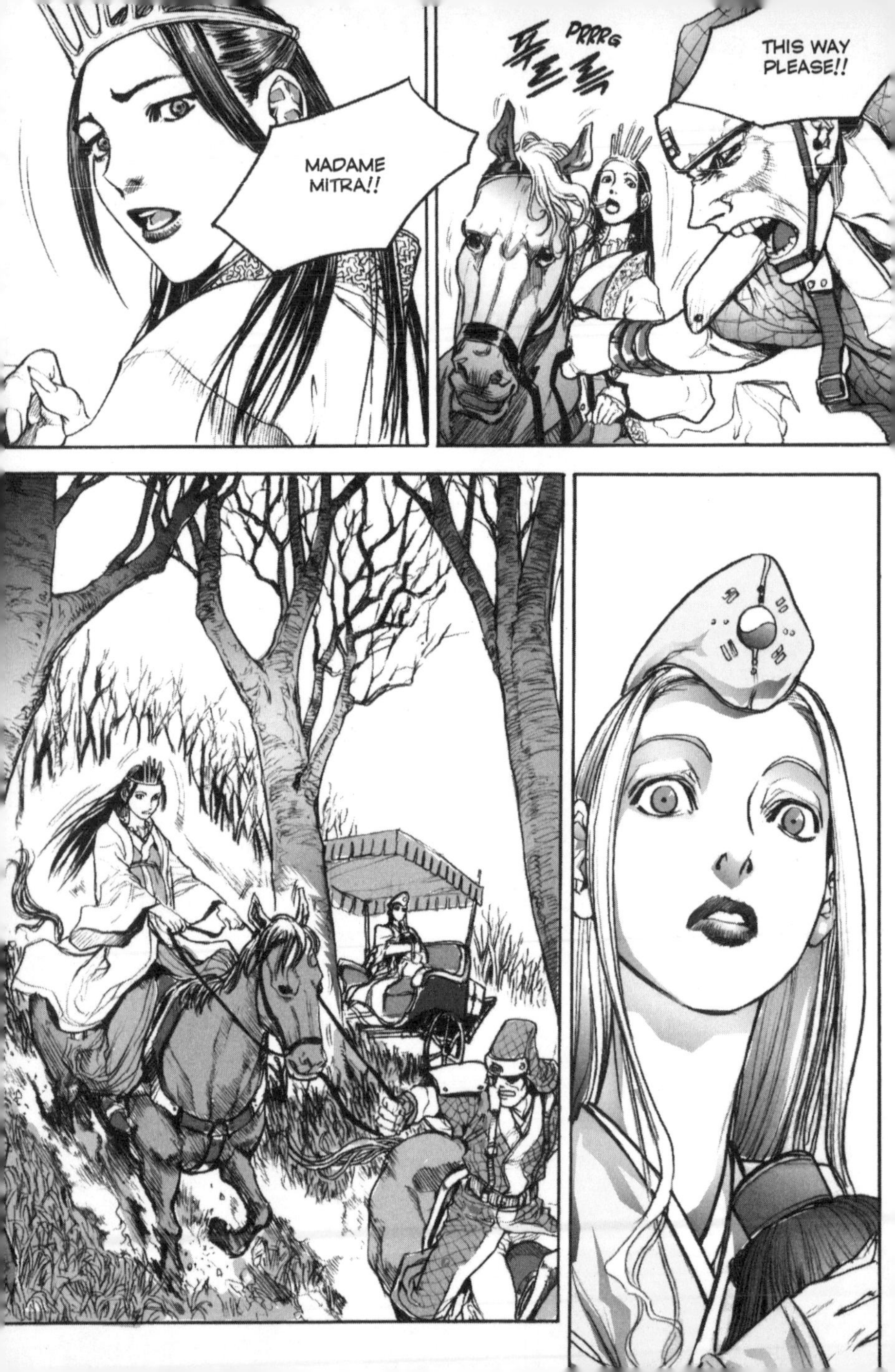
MADAME MITRA!!
PRRRG
THIS WAY PLEASE!!

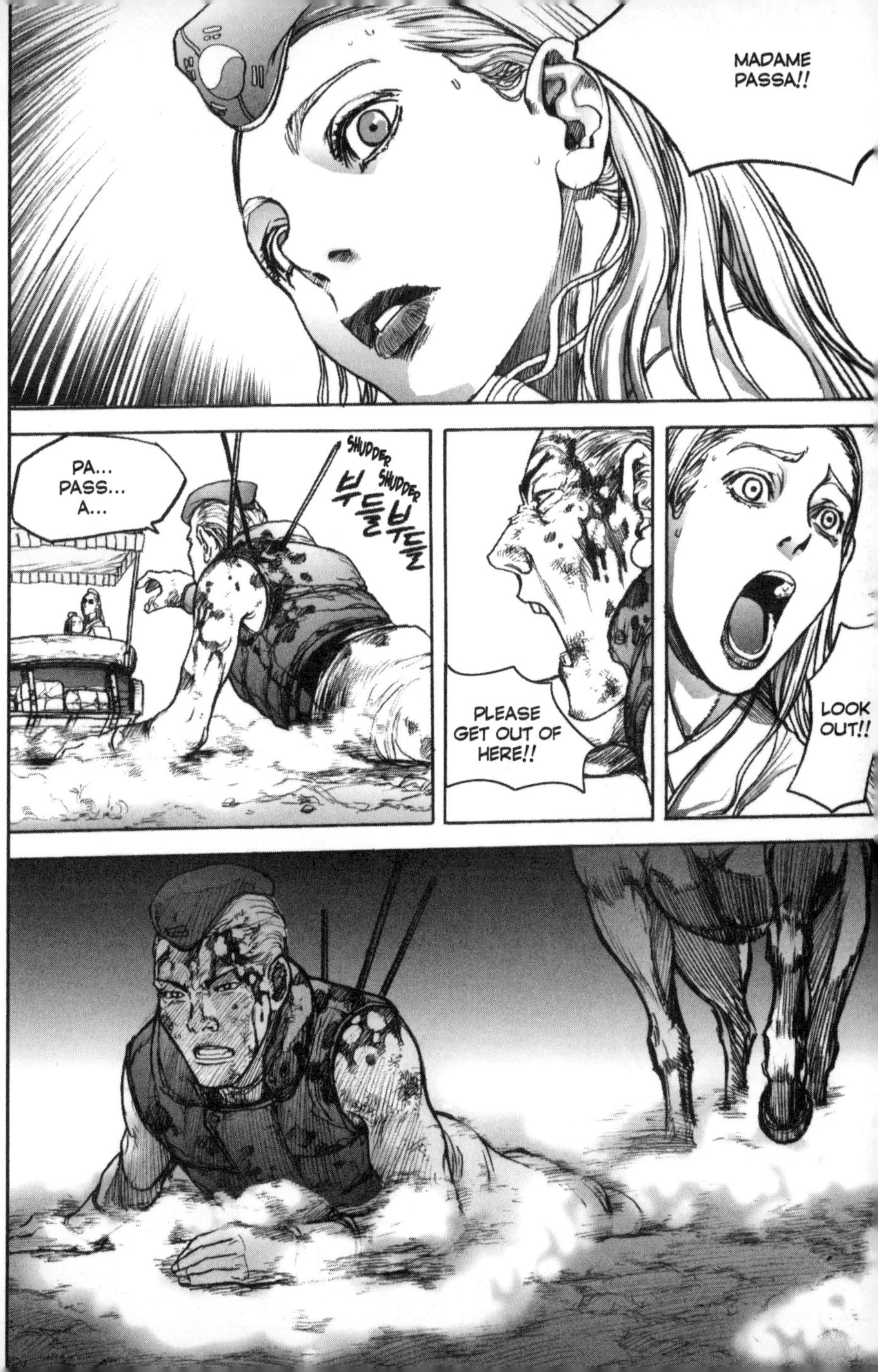
MADAME PASSA!!
PA... PASS... A...
SHUDDER SHUDDER
부들부들
PLEASE GET OUT OF HERE!!
LOOK OUT!!

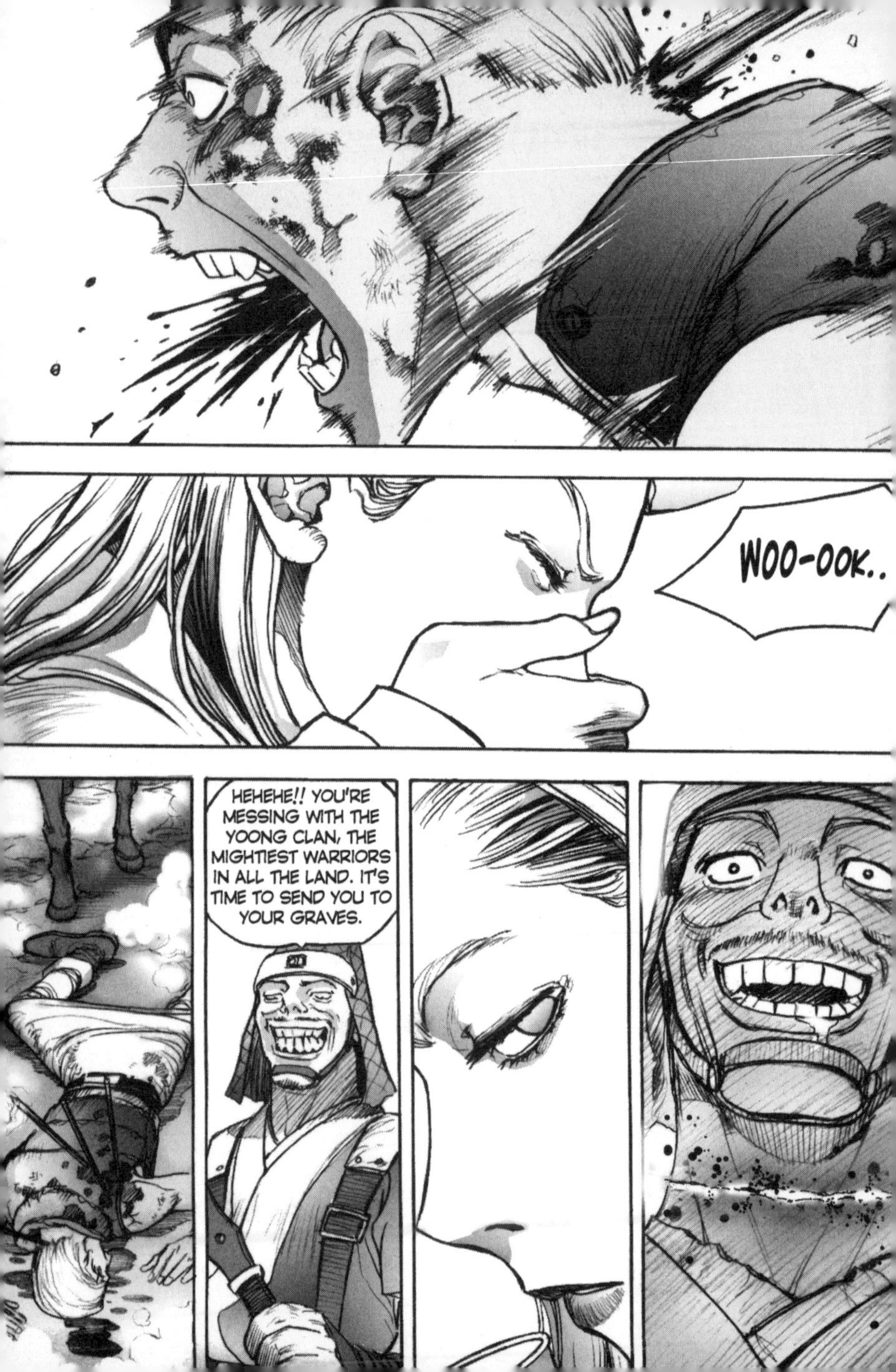
WOO-OOK..
HEHEHE!! YOU'RE MESSING WITH THE YOONG CLAN, THE MIGHTIEST WARRIORS IN ALL THE LAND. IT'S TIME TO SEND YOU TO YOUR GRAVES.

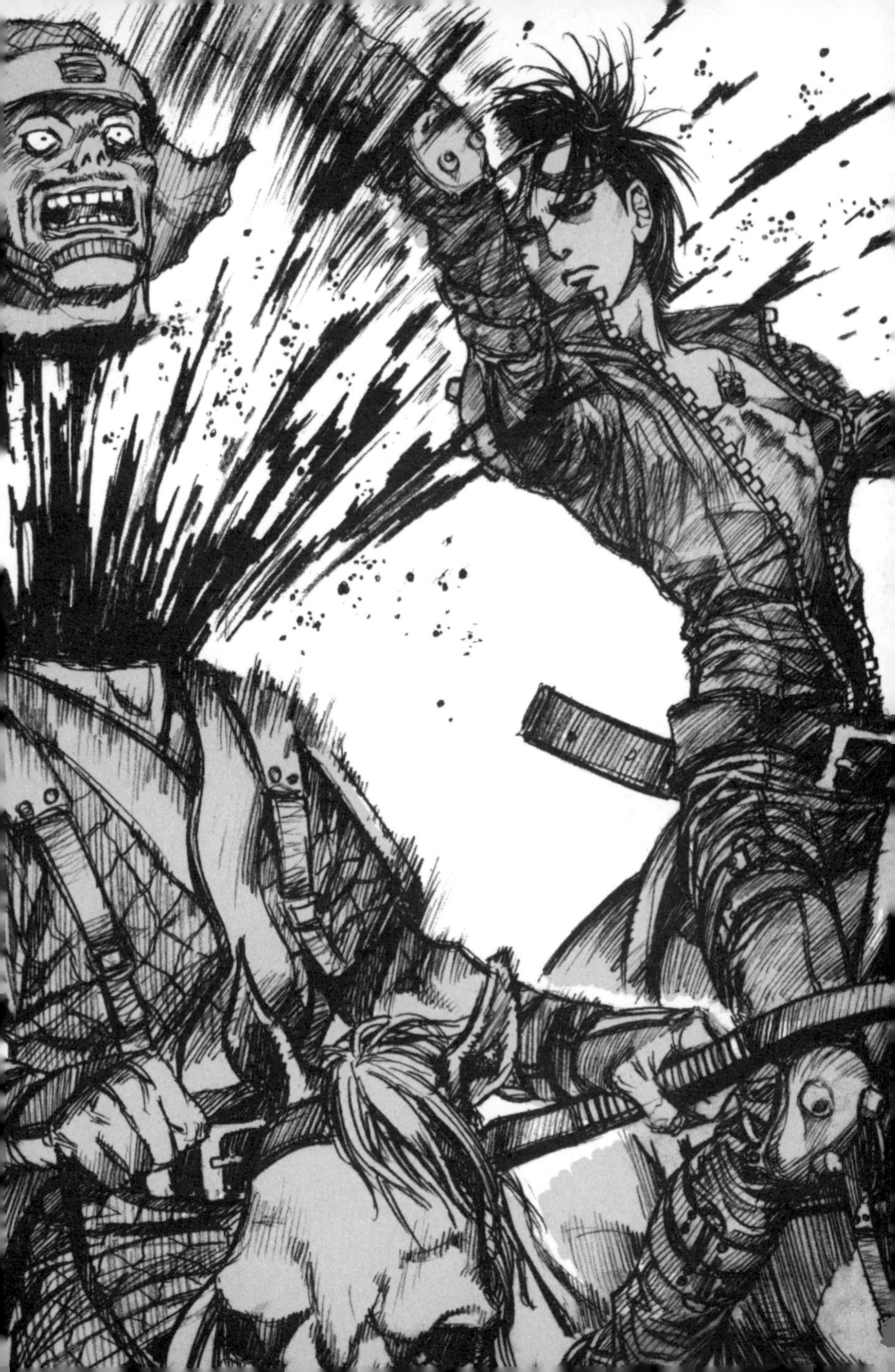

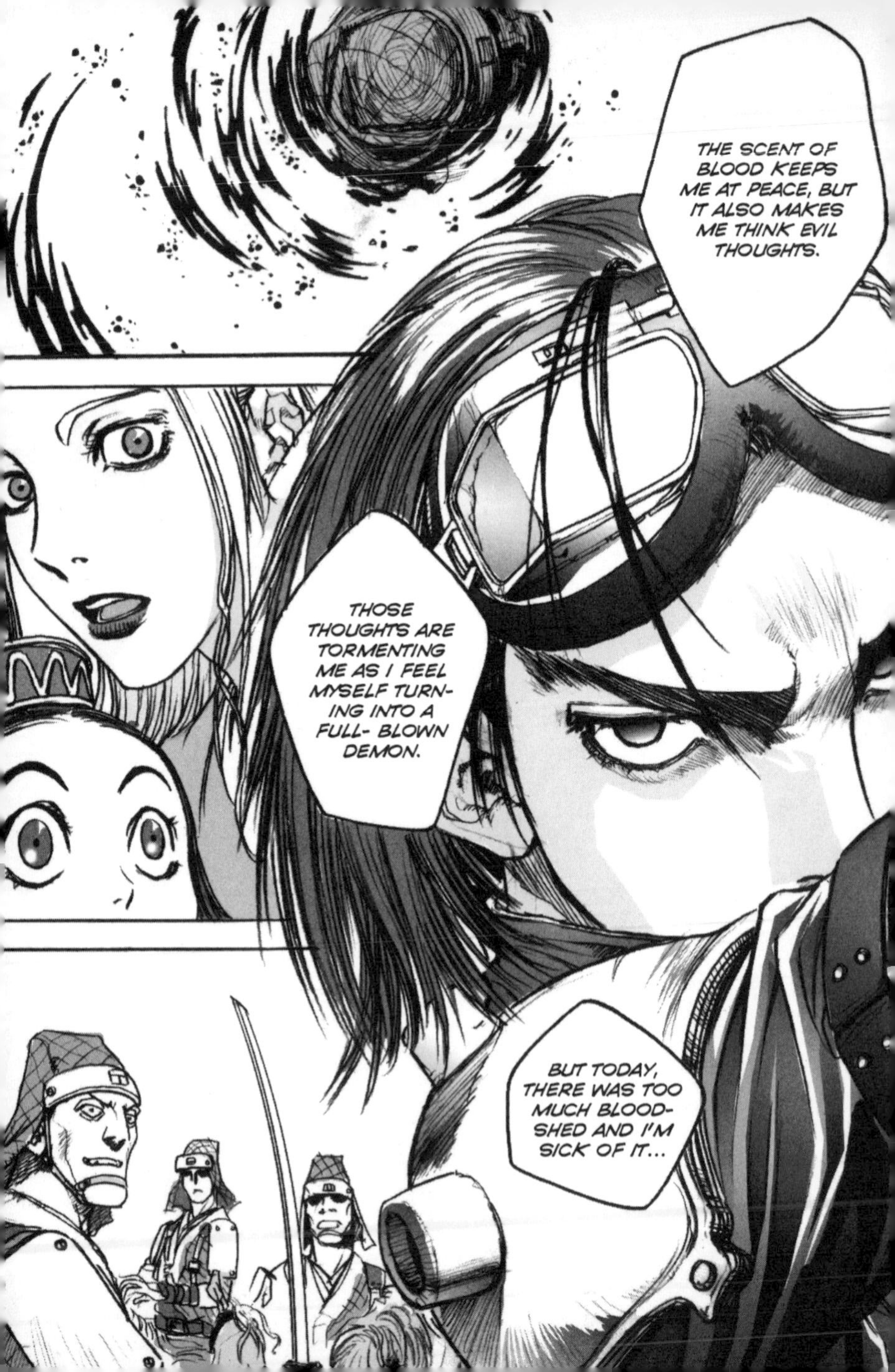
THE SCENT OF BLOOD KEEPS ME AT PEACE, BUT IT ALSO MAKES ME THINK EVIL THOUGHTS.
THOSE THOUGHTS ARE TORMENTING ME AS I FEEL MYSELF TURNING INTO A FULL- BLOWN DEMON.
BUT TODAY, THERE WAS TOO MUCH BLOODSHED AND I'M SICK OF IT...

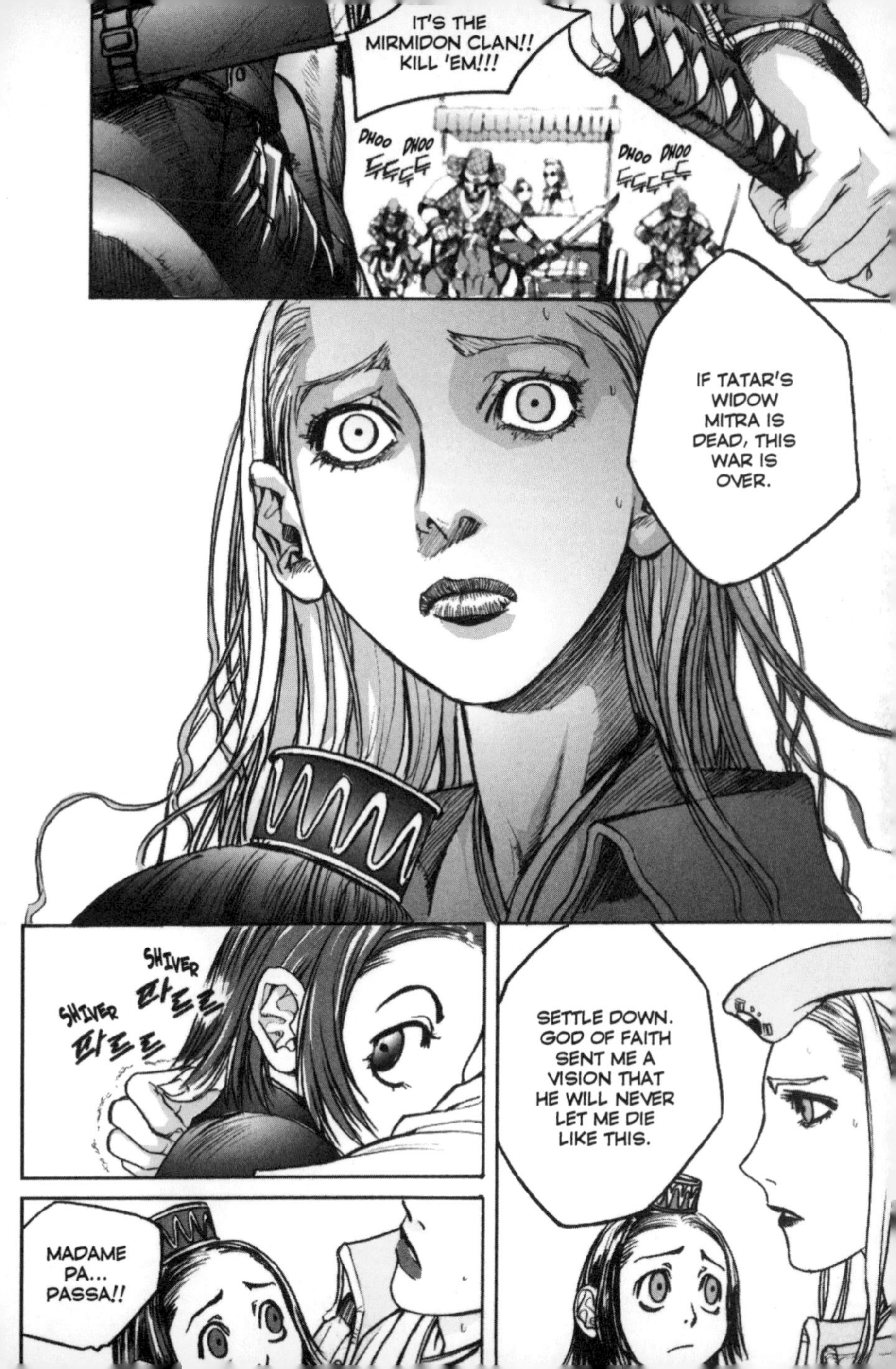
IT'S THE MIRMIDON CLAN!! KILL 'EM!!!
DHOO DHOO
DHOO DHOO
IF TATAR'S WIDOW MITRA IS DEAD, THIS WAR IS OVER.
SHIVER
파르르
SHIVER
파르르
MADAME PA... PASSA!!
SETTLE DOWN. GOD OF FAITH SENT ME A VISION THAT HE WILL NEVER LET ME DIE LIKE THIS.

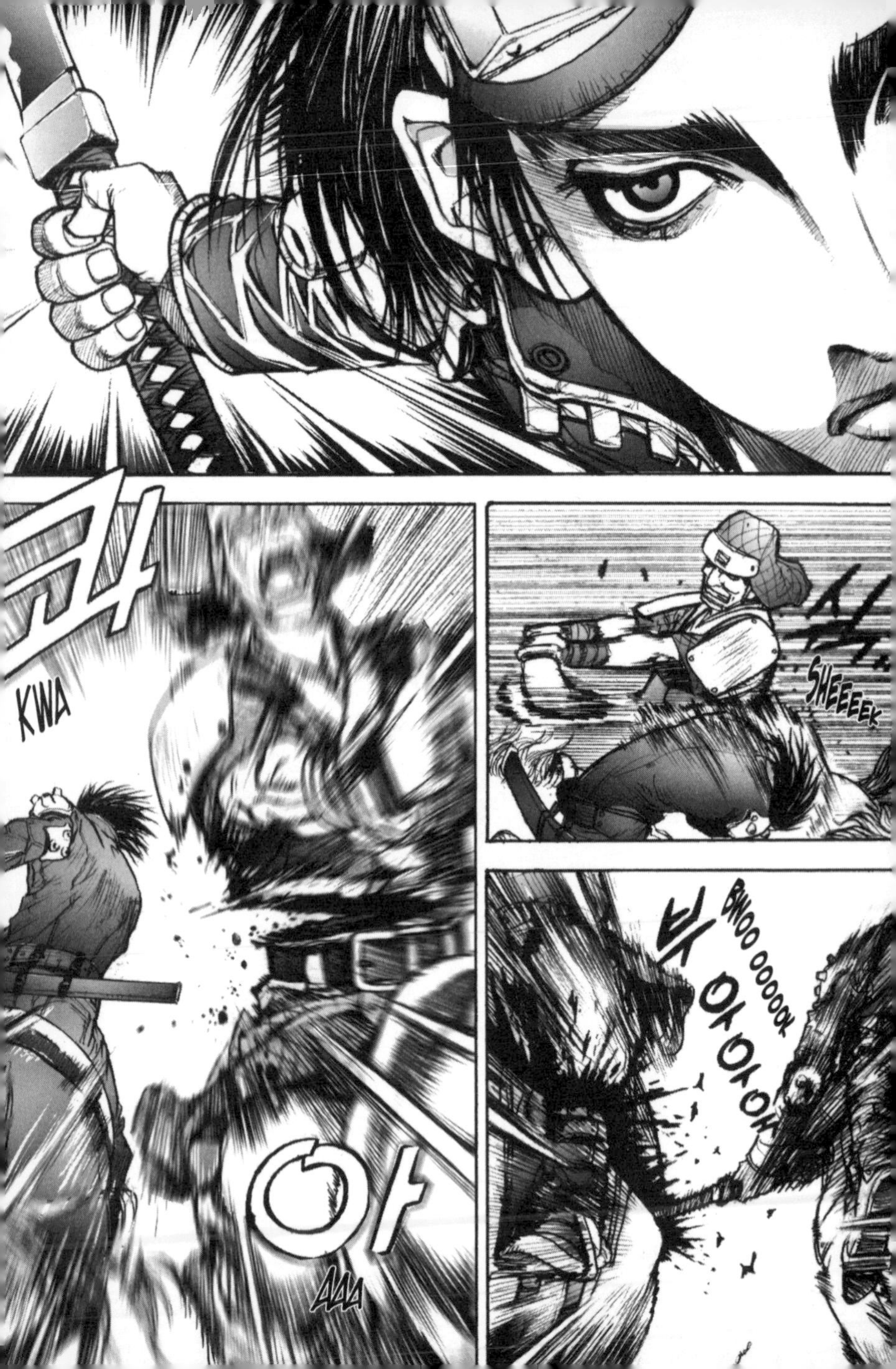
KWA
SHEEEEK
BWOO OOOOOOK
AAA

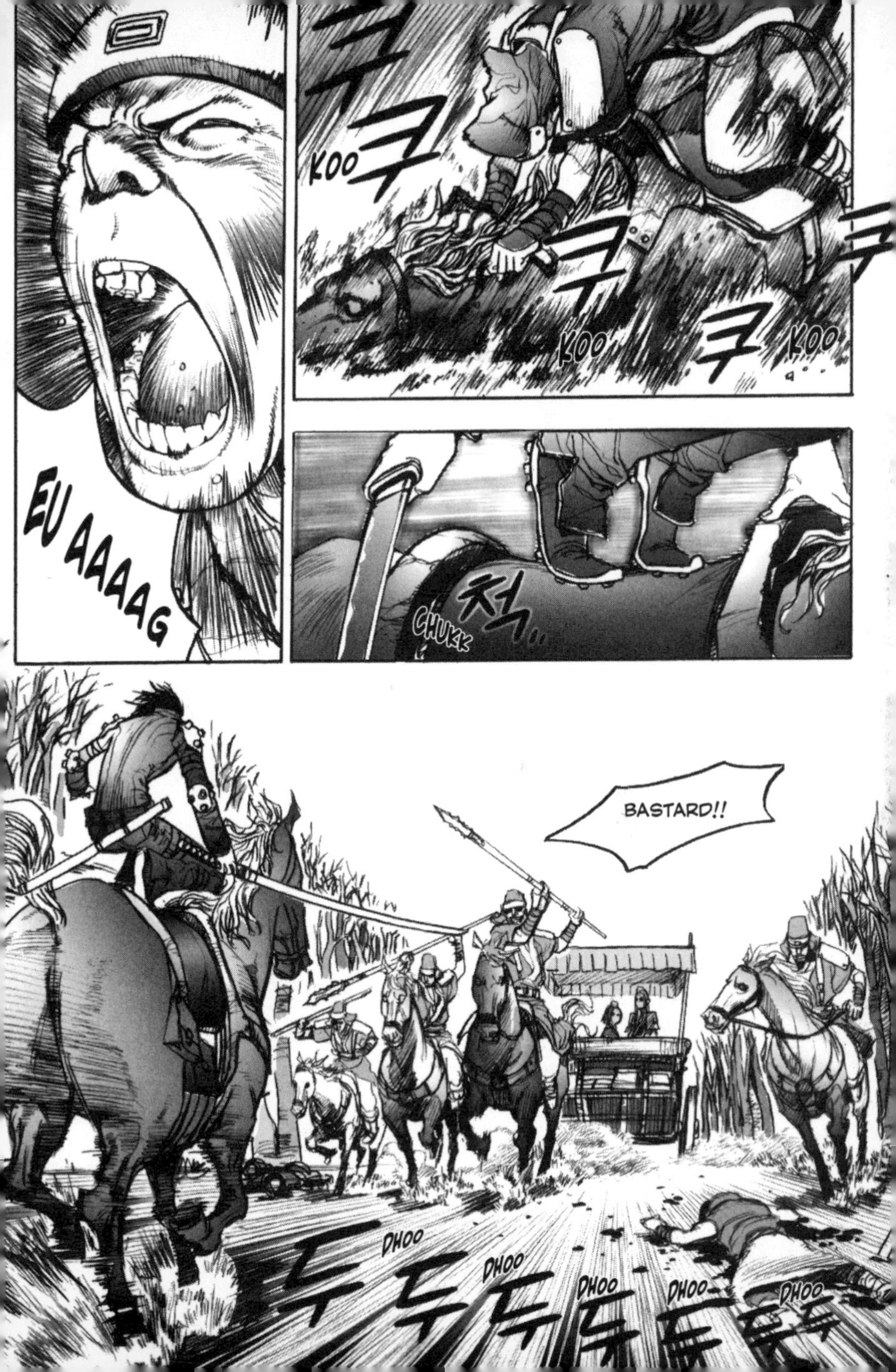

EU AAAAAG
쿠
KOO
쿠
KOO
쿠
KOO
척
CHUKK
BASTARD!!
두
DHOO
두
DHOO
두
DHOO
두
DHOO
두
DHOO

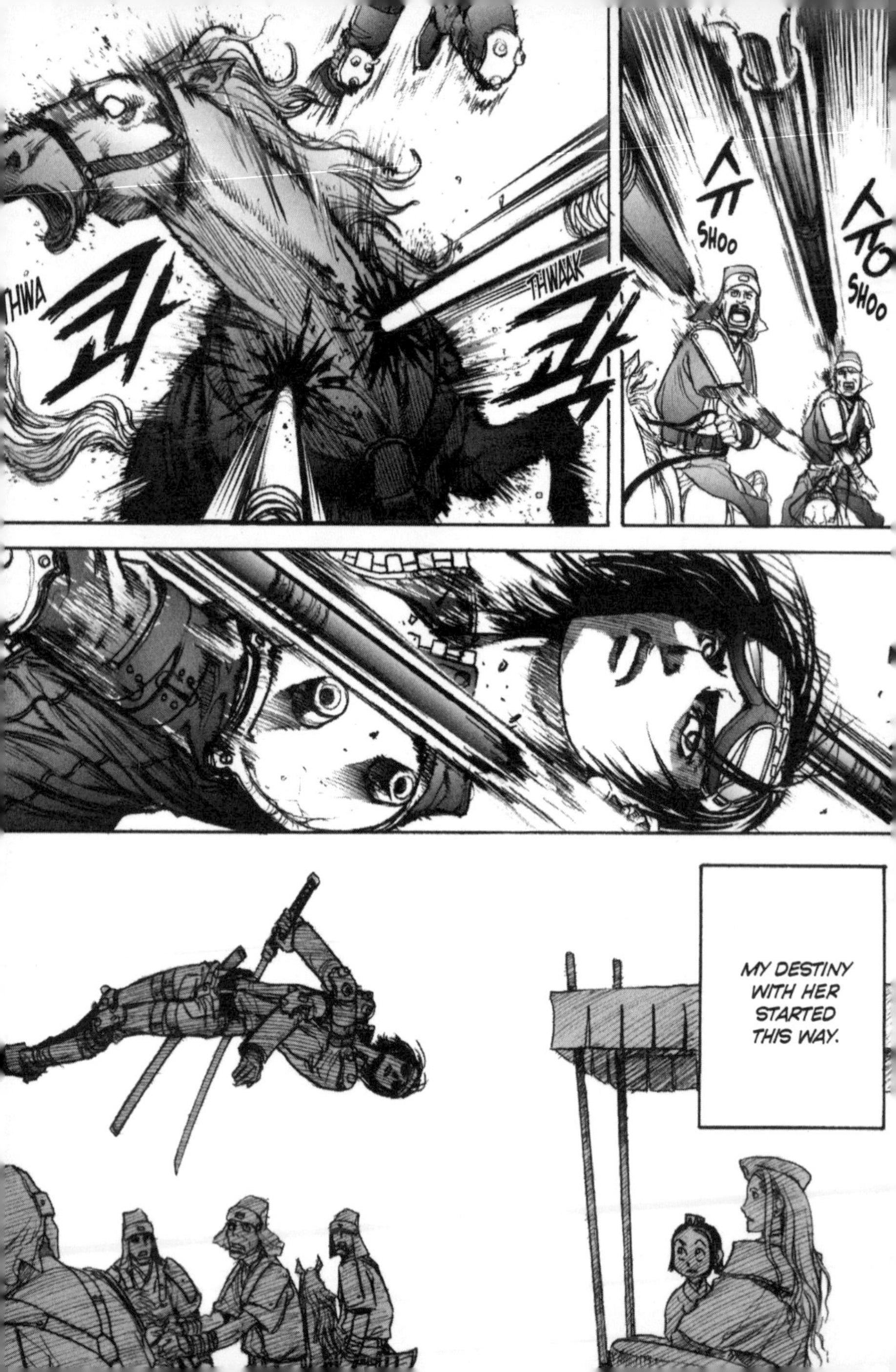

SHOO
SHOO
THWAAK
THWA
MY DESTINY WITH HER STARTED THIS WAY.

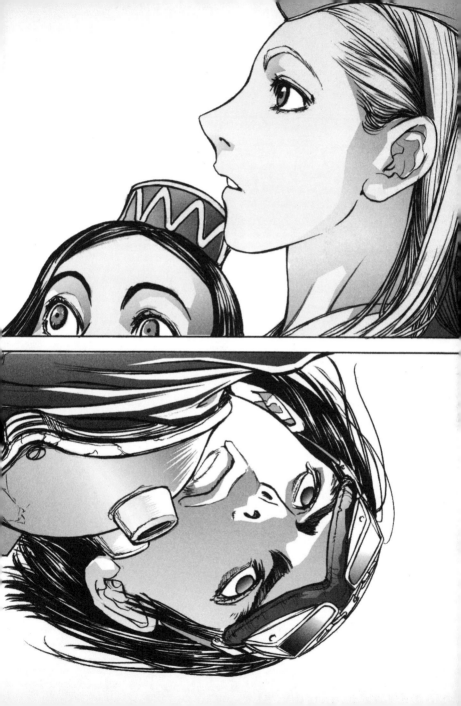

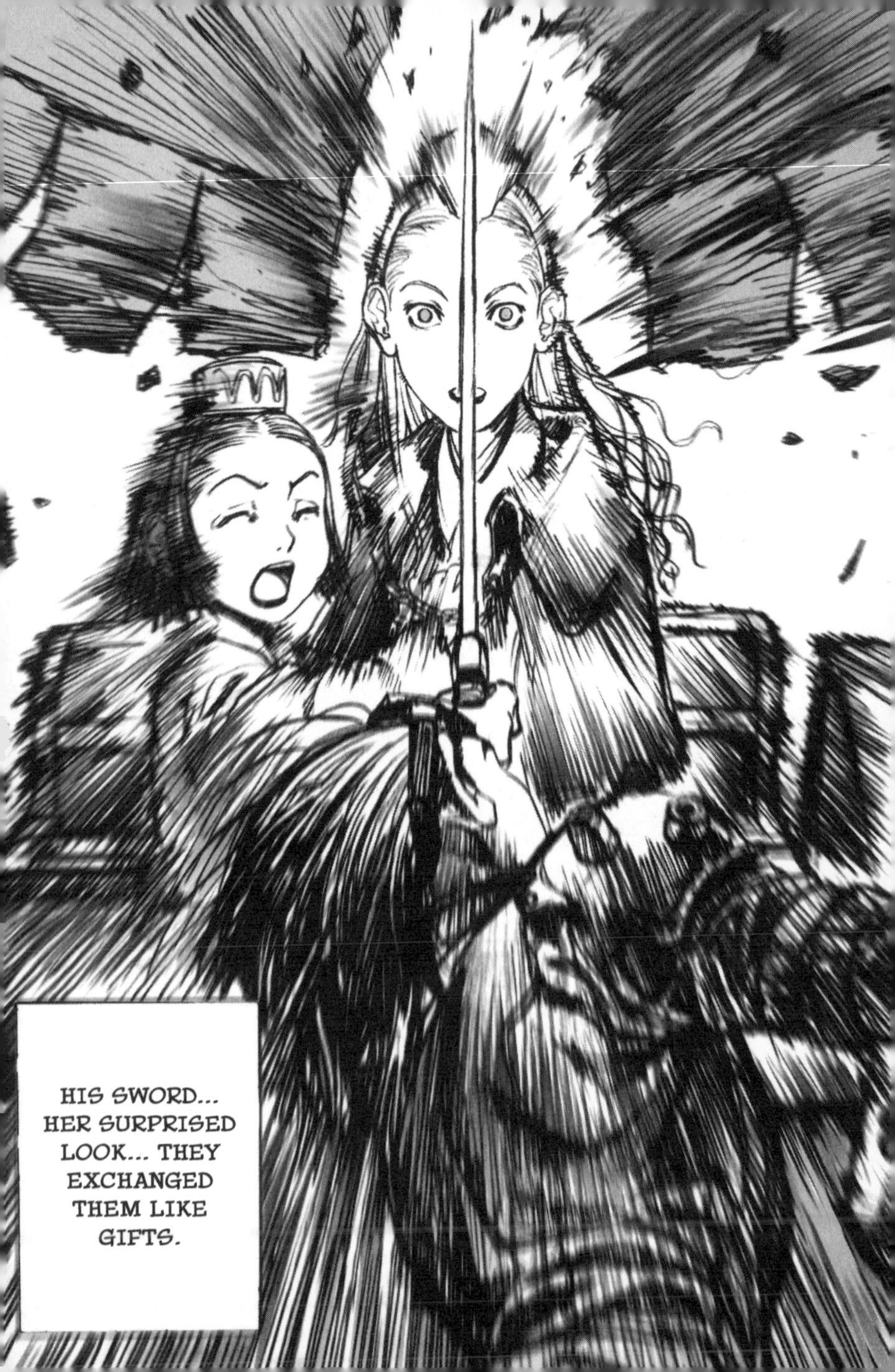
HIS SWORD...
HER SURPRISED
LOOK... THEY
EXCHANGED
THEM LIKE
GIFTS.

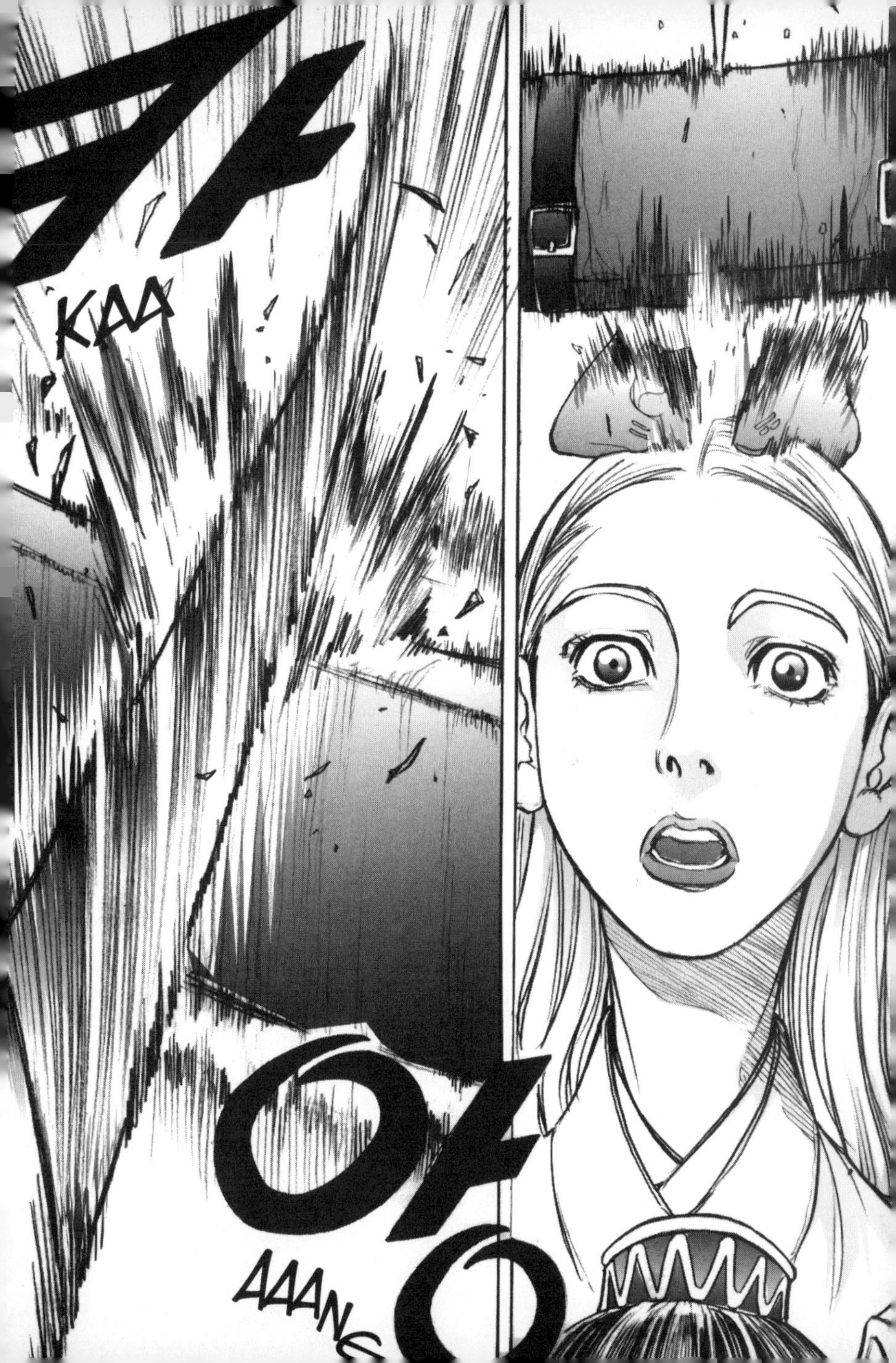
KAA
AAANG

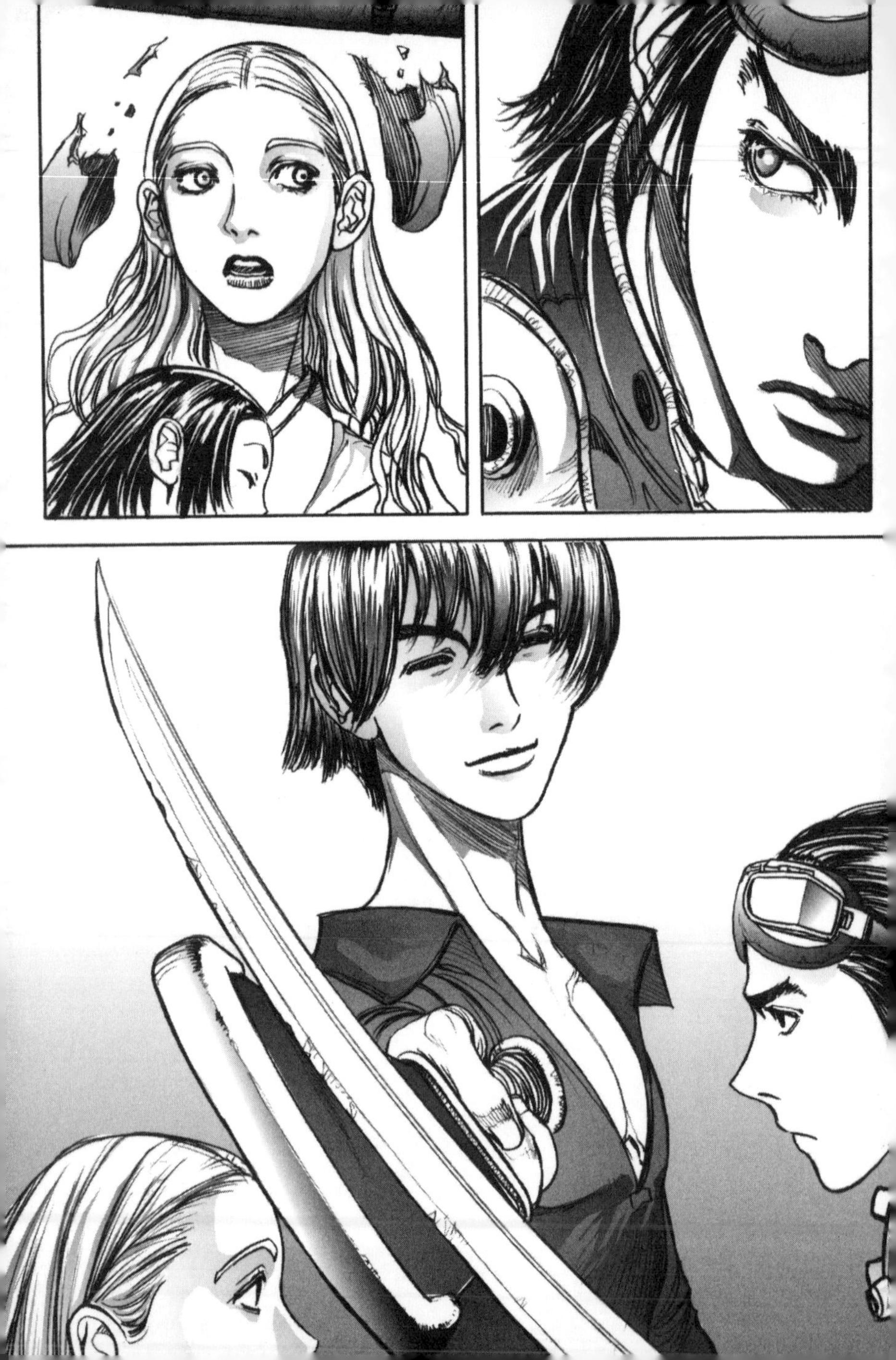

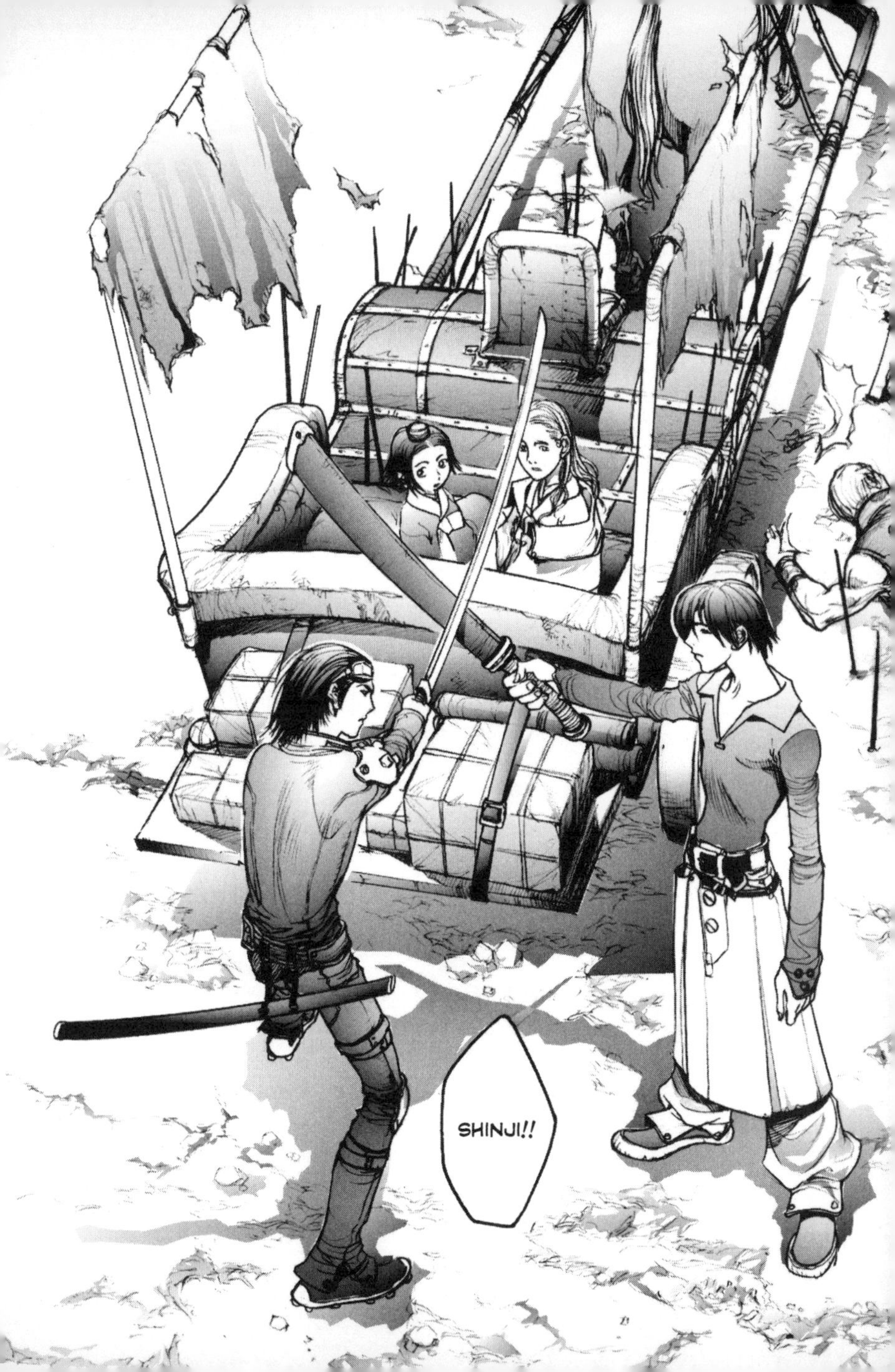
SHINJI!!

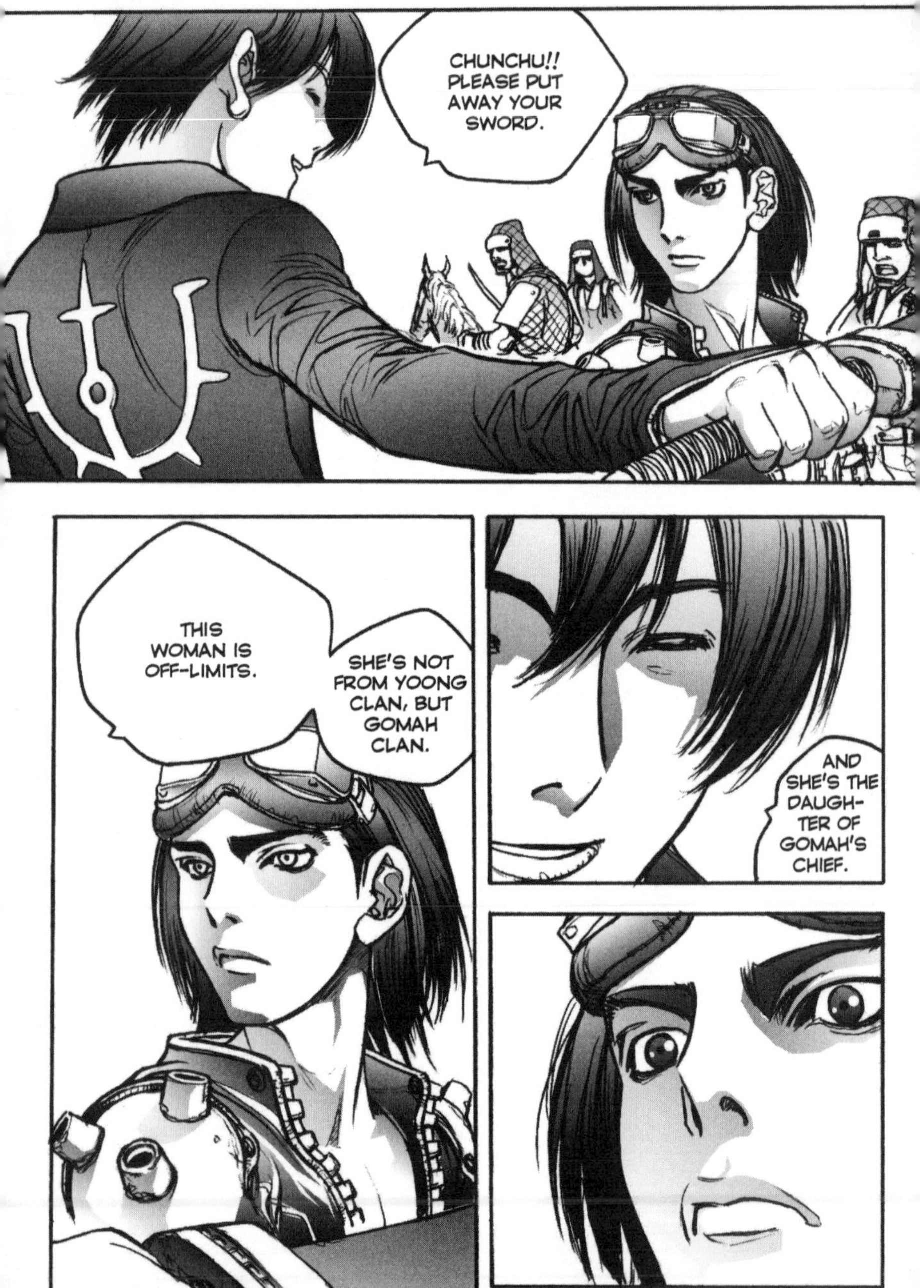
CHUNCHU!! PLEASE PUT AWAY YOUR SWORD.
THIS WOMAN IS OFF-LIMITS.
SHE'S NOT FROM YOONG CLAN, BUT GOMAH CLAN.
AND SHE'S THE DAUGH- TER OF GOMAH'S CHIEF.

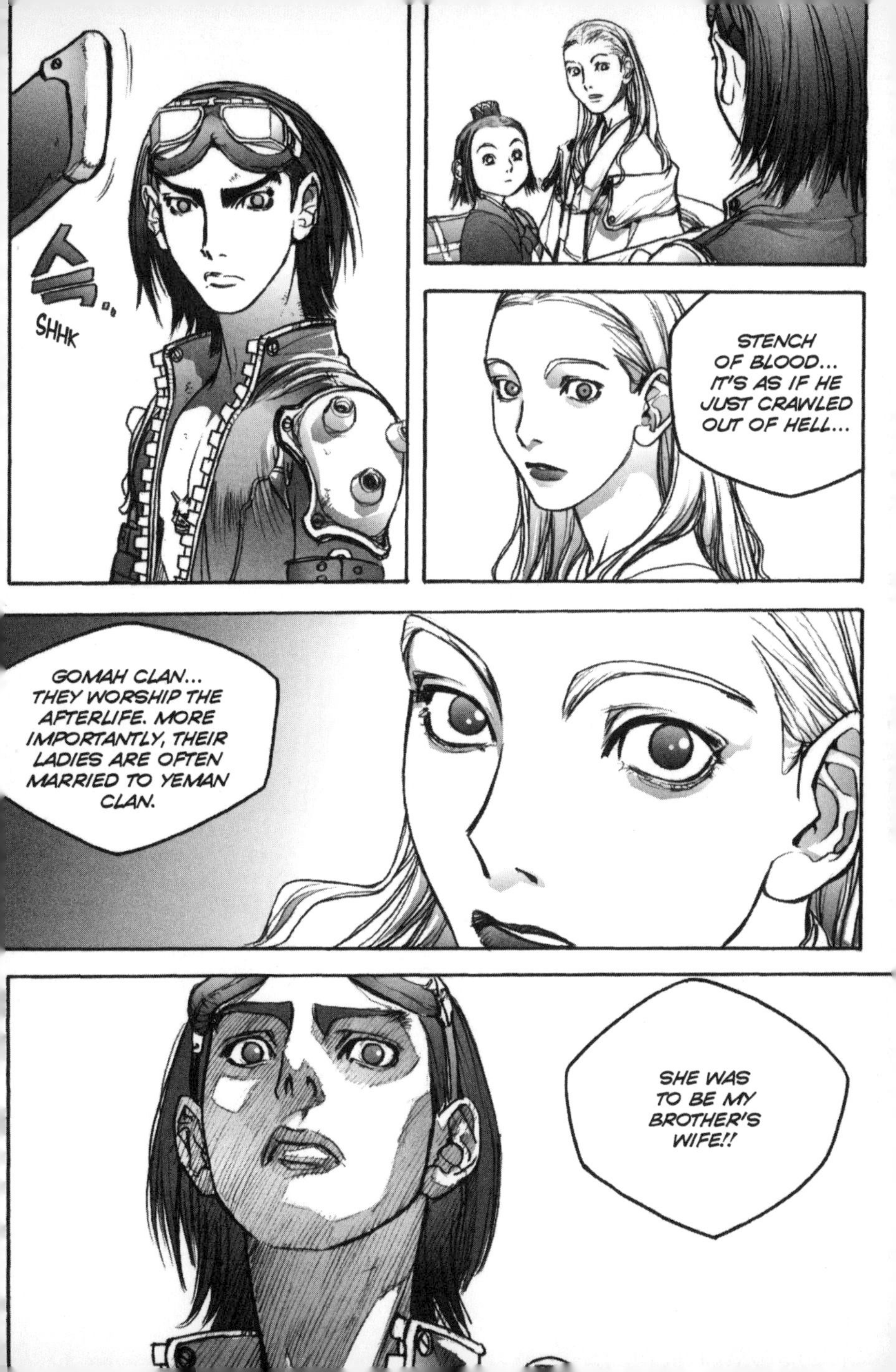
SHHK
STENCH OF BLOOD... IT'S AS IF HE JUST CRAWLED OUT OF HELL...
GOMAH CLAN... THEY WORSHIP THE AFTERLIFE. MORE IMPORTANTLY, THEIR LADIES ARE OFTEN MARRIED TO YEMAN CLAN.
SHE WAS TO BE MY BROTHER'S WIFE!!

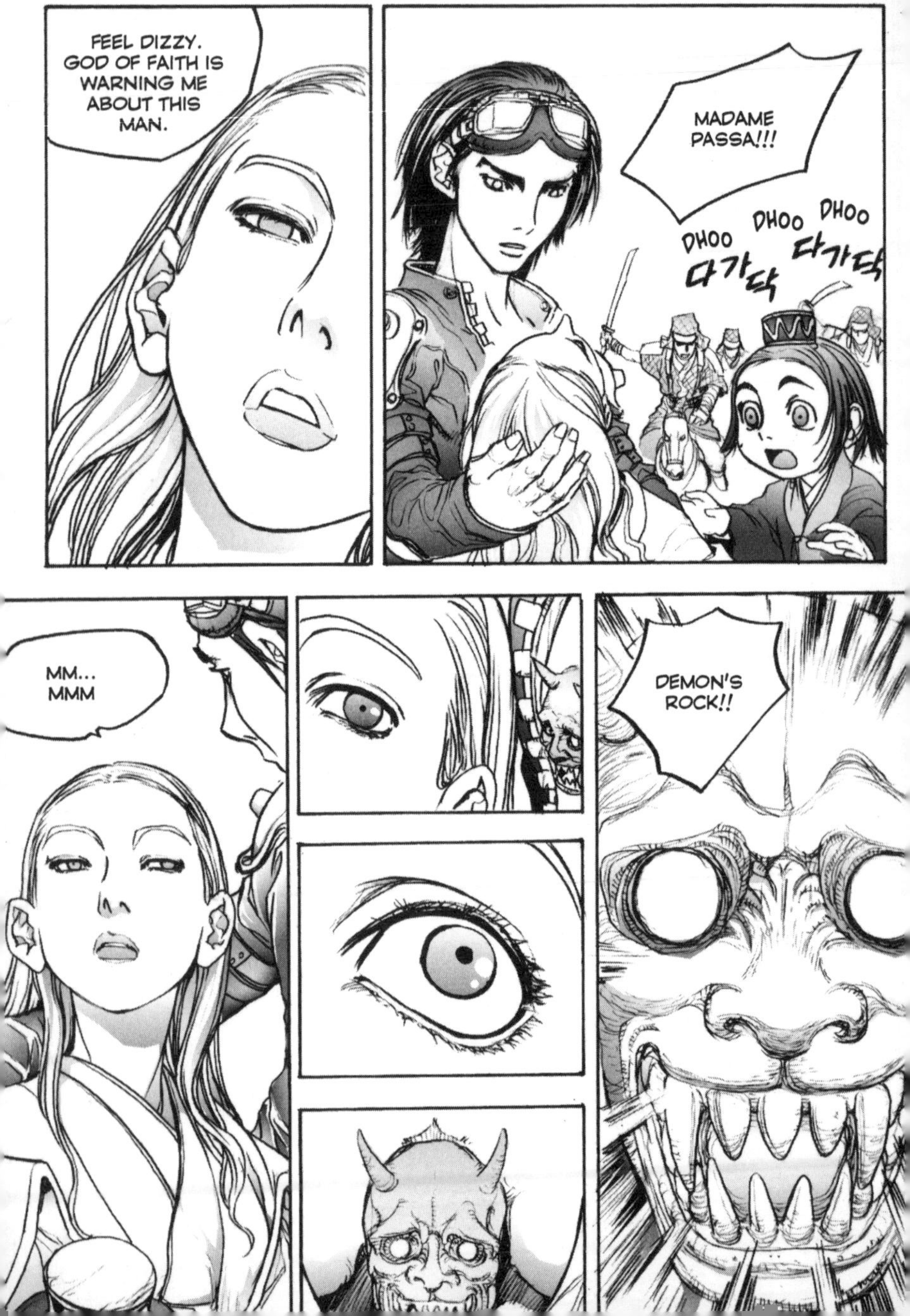
FEEL DIZZY. GOD OF FAITH IS WARNING ME ABOUT THIS MAN.
MADAME PASSA!!!
DHOO DHOO DHOO
다가닥 다가닥
MM... MMM
DEMON'S ROCK!!

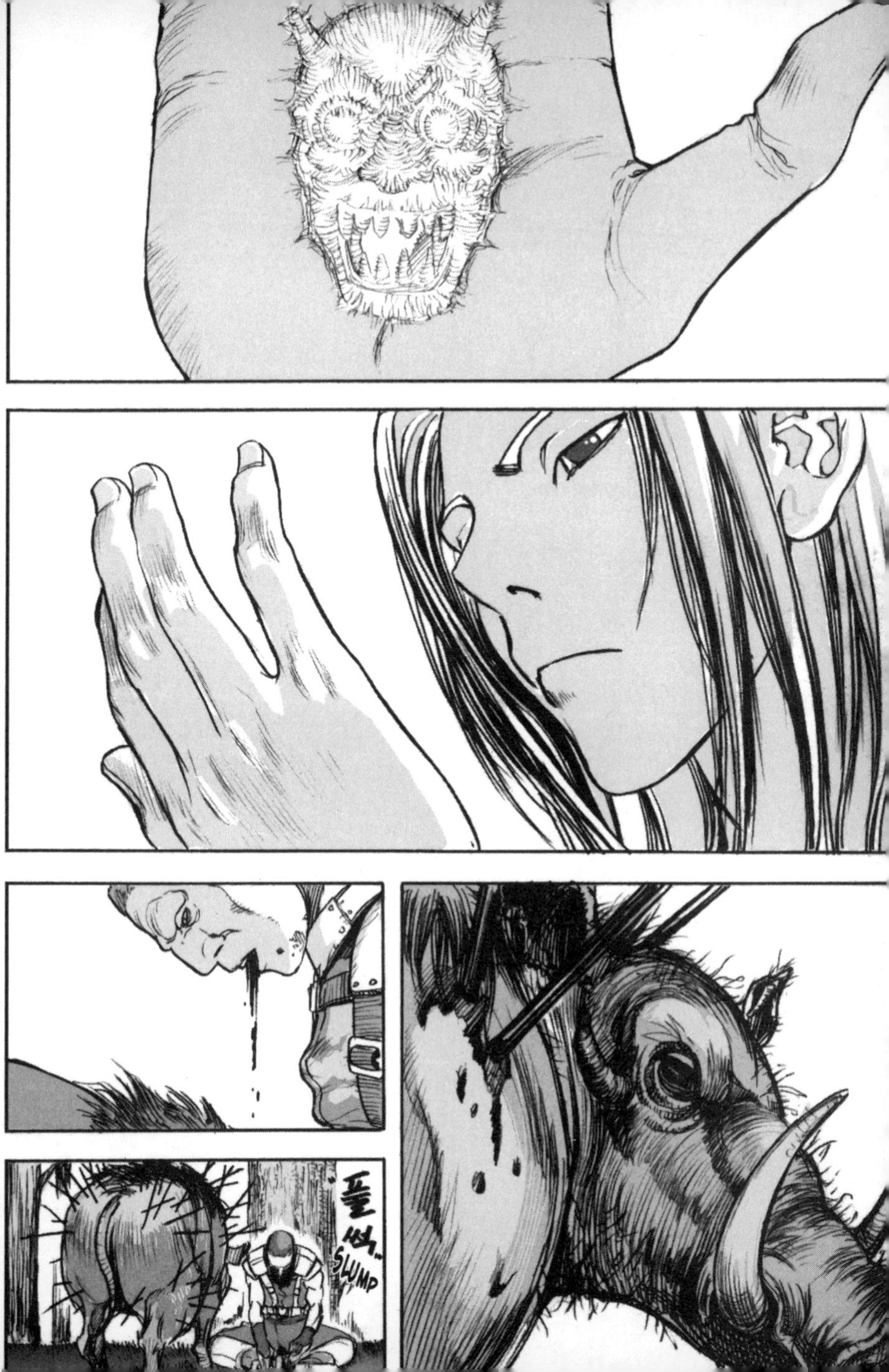
풀썩..
SLUMP

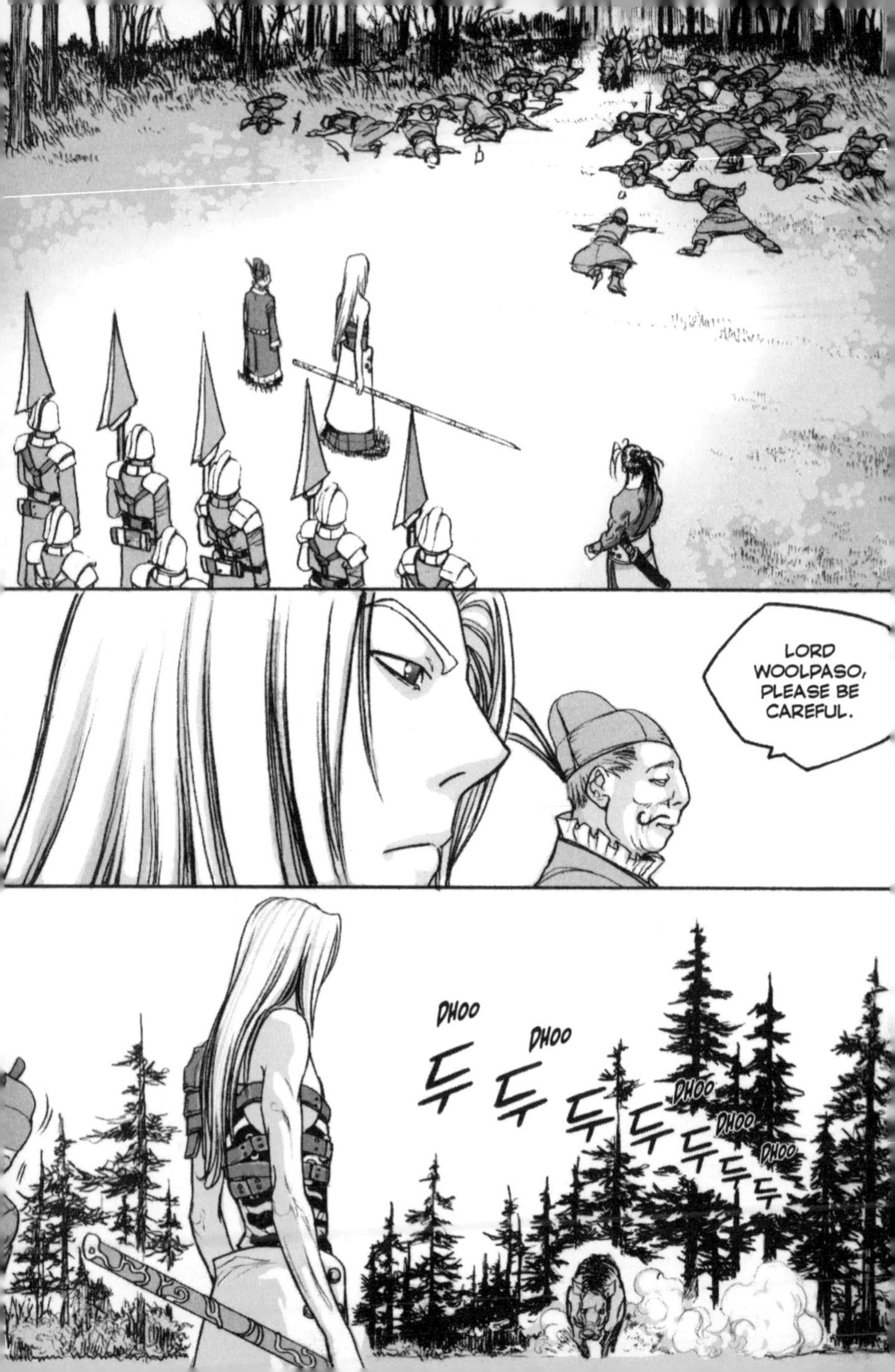
LORD WOOLPASO, PLEASE BE CAREFUL.
DHOO
DHOO
DHOO
DHOO
DHOO

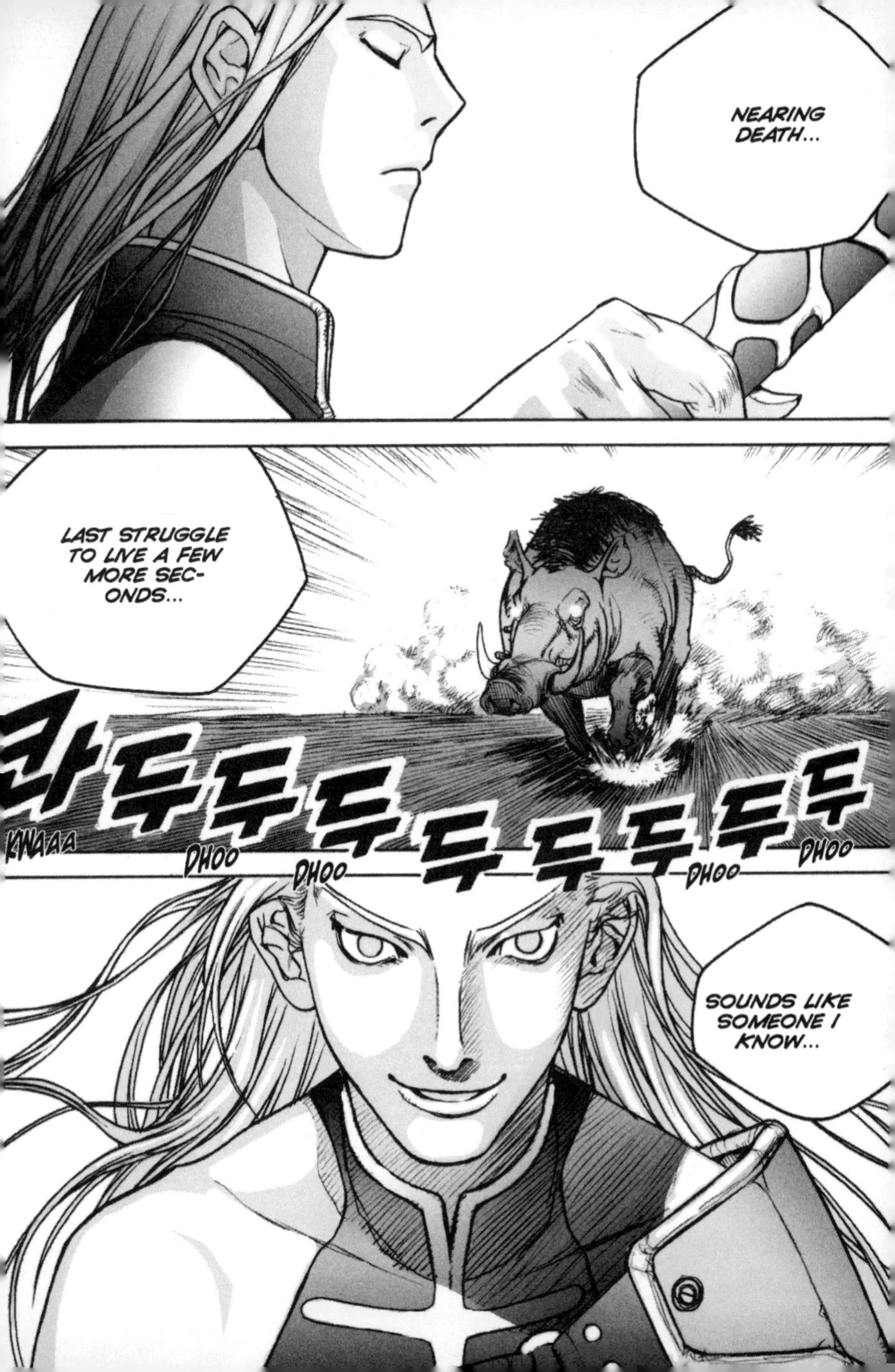
NEARING DEATH...
LAST STRUGGLE TO LIVE A FEW MORE SEC- ONDS...
콰두두두두두두두두
KWAAA
DHOO
DHOO
DHOO
DHOO
SOUNDS LIKE SOMEONE I KNOW...

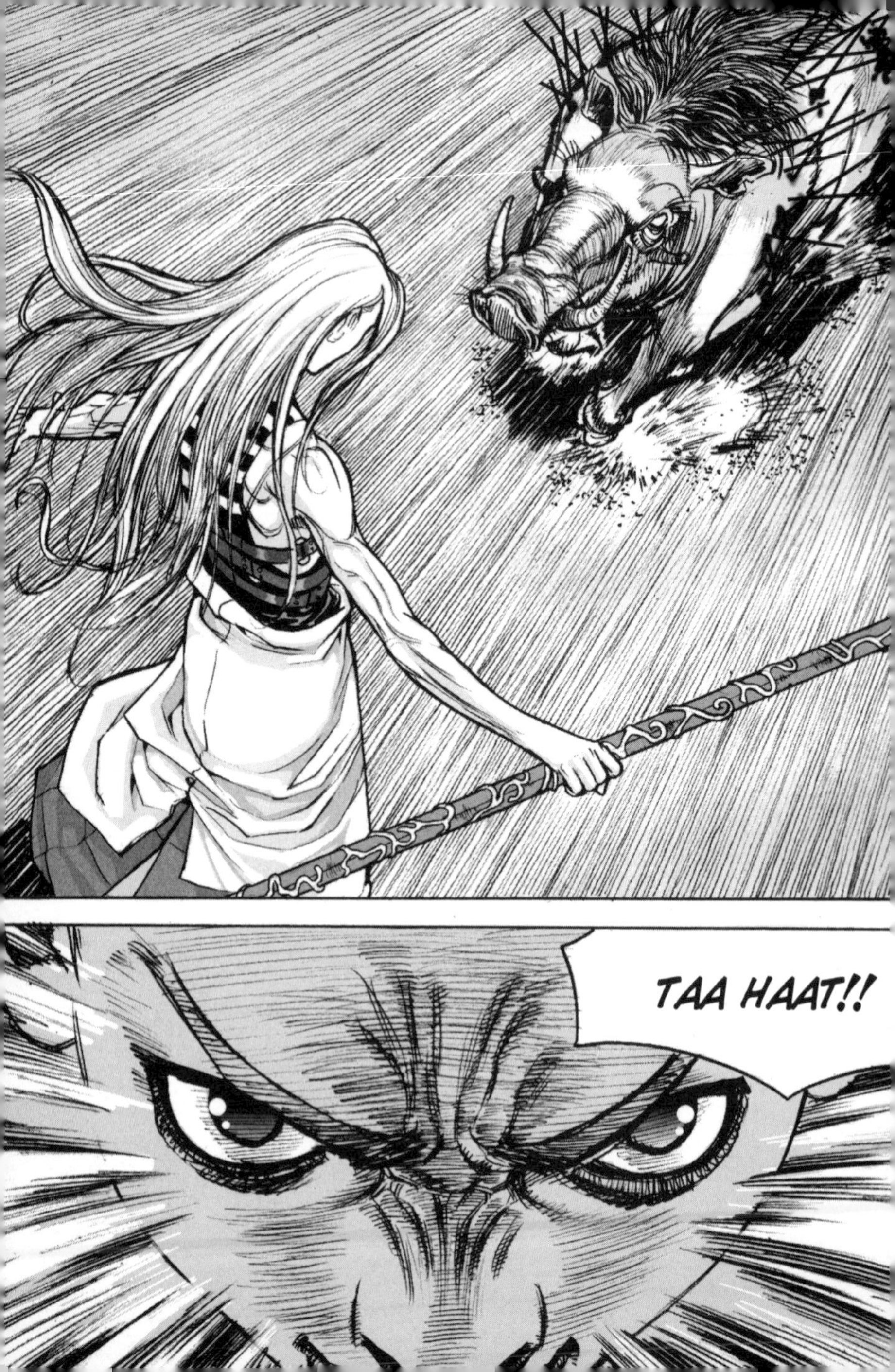
TAA HAAT!!

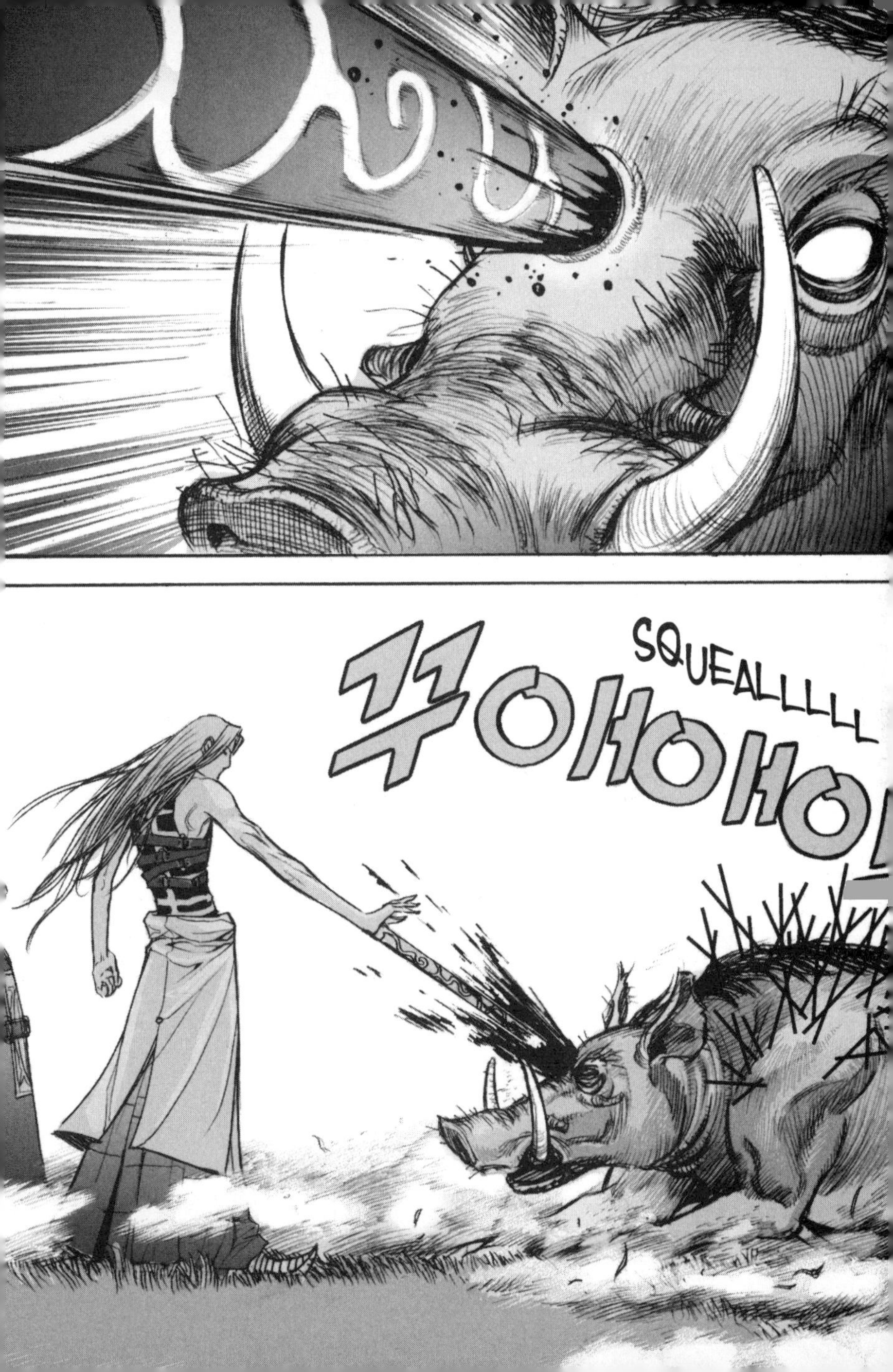
SQUEALLLLL

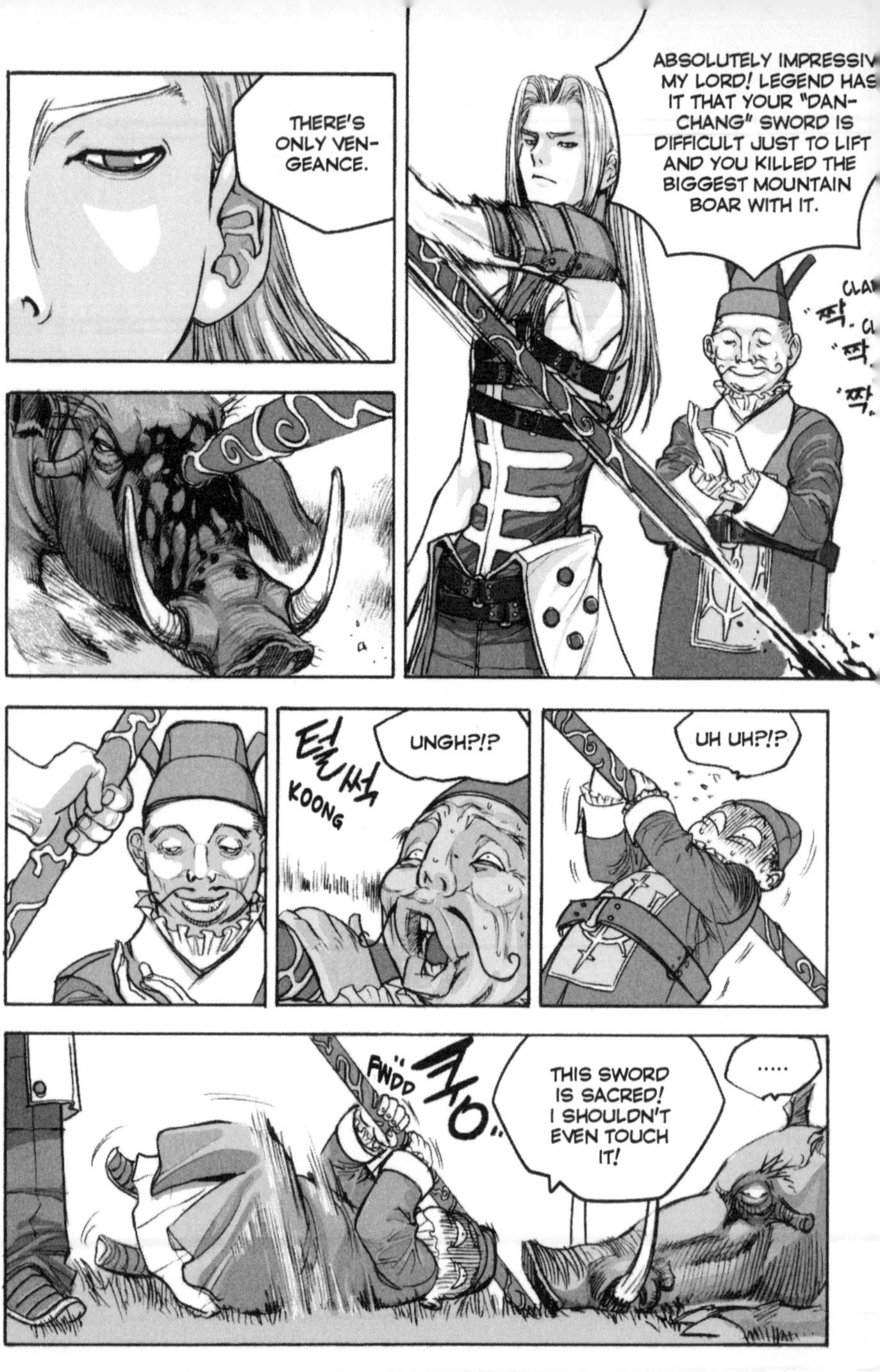
THERE'S ONLY VEN-GEANCE.
ABSOLUTELY IMPRESSIV MY LORD! LEGEND HAS IT THAT YOUR "DAN-CHANG" SWORD IS DIFFICULT JUST TO LIFT AND YOU KILLED THE BIGGEST MOUNTAIN BOAR WITH IT.
CLA
짝
짝
짝
털썩
KOONG
UNGH?!?
UH UH?!?
FWDD
THIS SWORD IS SACRED! I SHOULDN'T EVEN TOUCH IT!
.....

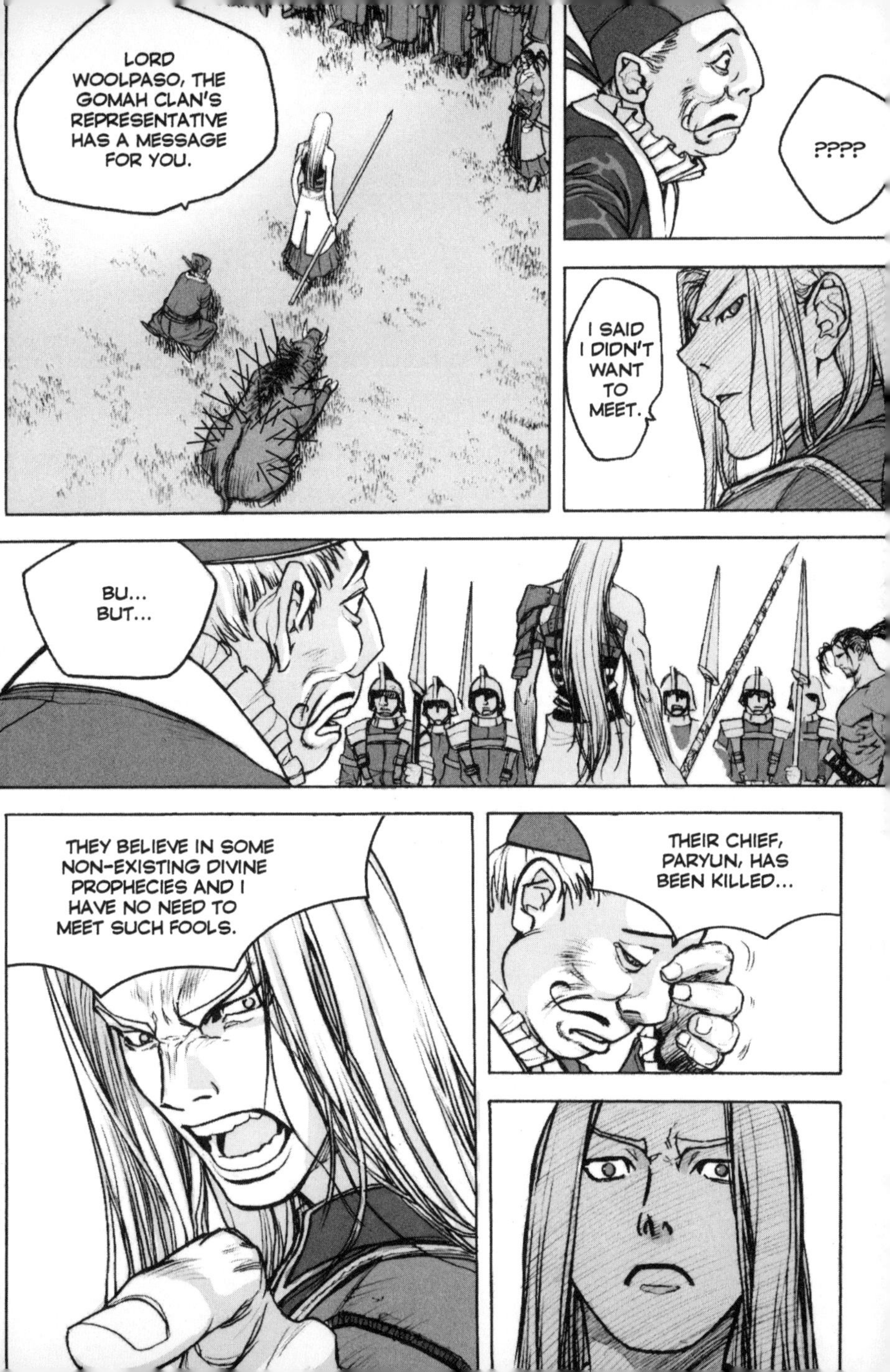
LORD WOOLPASO, THE GOMAH CLAN'S REPRESENTATIVE HAS A MESSAGE FOR YOU.
????
I SAID I DIDN'T WANT TO MEET.
BU... BUT...
THEY BELIEVE IN SOME NON-EXISTING DIVINE PROPHECIES AND I HAVE NO NEED TO MEET SUCH FOOLS.
THEIR CHIEF, PARYUN, HAS BEEN KILLED...

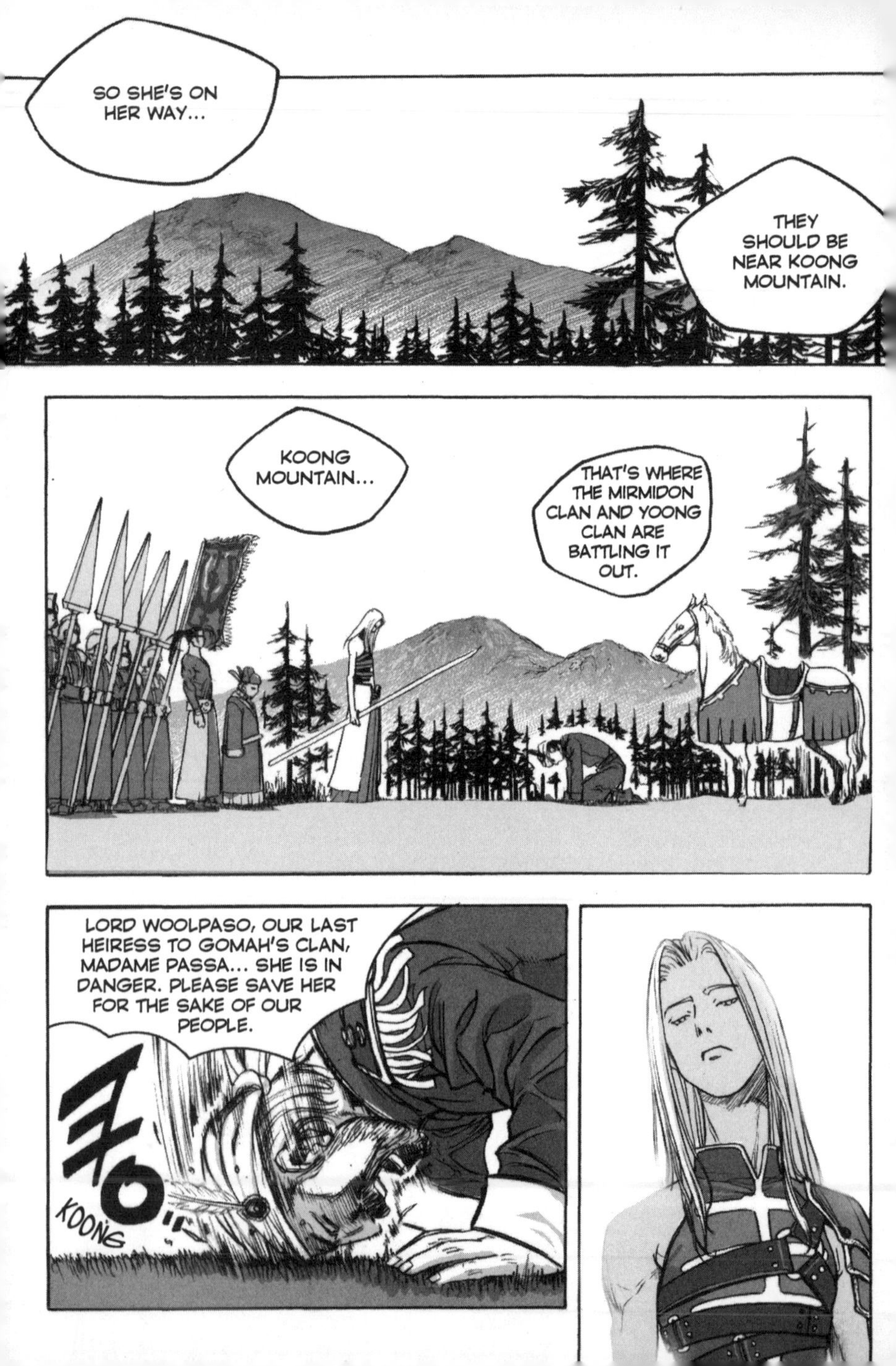
SO SHE'S ON HER WAY...
THEY SHOULD BE NEAR KOONG MOUNTAIN.
KOONG MOUNTAIN...
THAT'S WHERE THE MIRMIDON CLAN AND YOONG CLAN ARE BATTLING IT OUT.
LORD WOOLPASO, OUR LAST HEIRESS TO GOMAH'S CLAN, MADAME PASSA... SHE IS IN DANGER. PLEASE SAVE HER FOR THE SAKE OF OUR PEOPLE.
KOONG

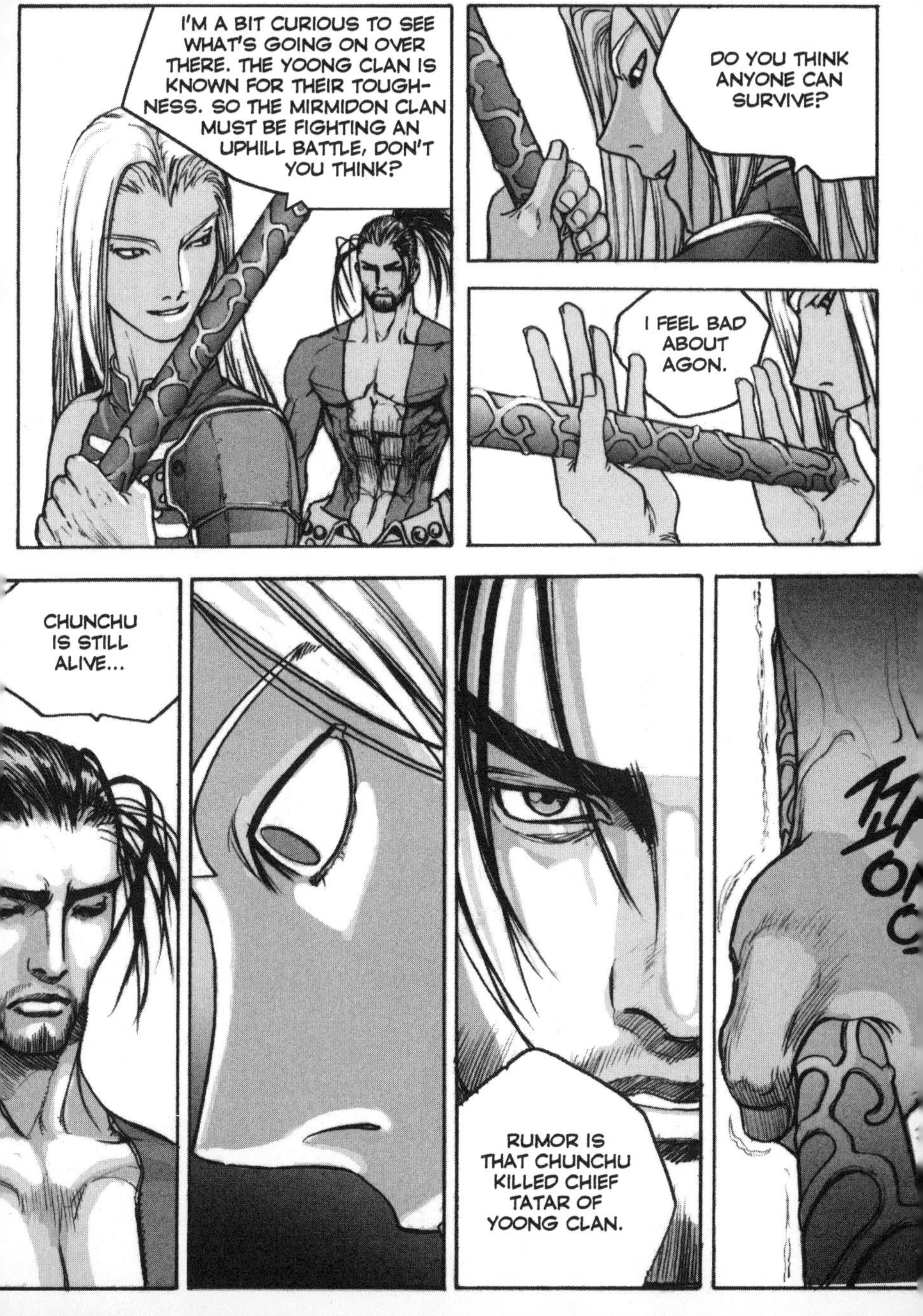
I'M A BIT CURIOUS TO SEE WHAT'S GOING ON OVER THERE. THE YOONG CLAN IS KNOWN FOR THEIR TOUGH-NESS. SO THE MIRMIDON CLAN MUST BE FIGHTING AN UPHILL BATTLE, DON'T YOU THINK?
DO YOU THINK ANYONE CAN SURVIVE?
I FEEL BAD ABOUT AGON.
CHUNCHU IS STILL ALIVE...
RUMOR IS THAT CHUNCHU KILLED CHIEF TATAR OF YOONG CLAN.

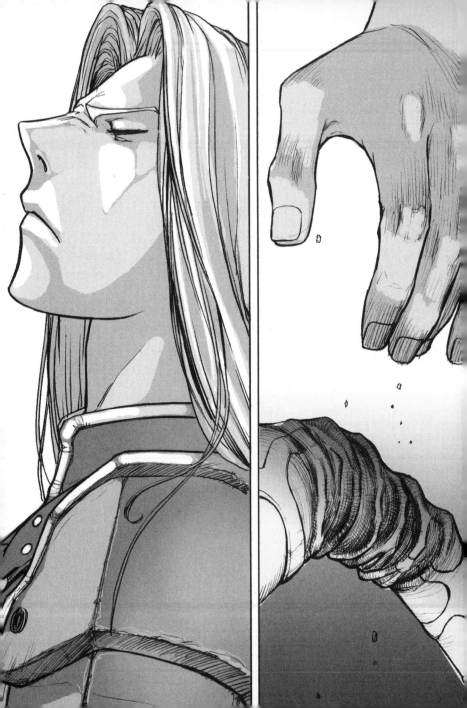

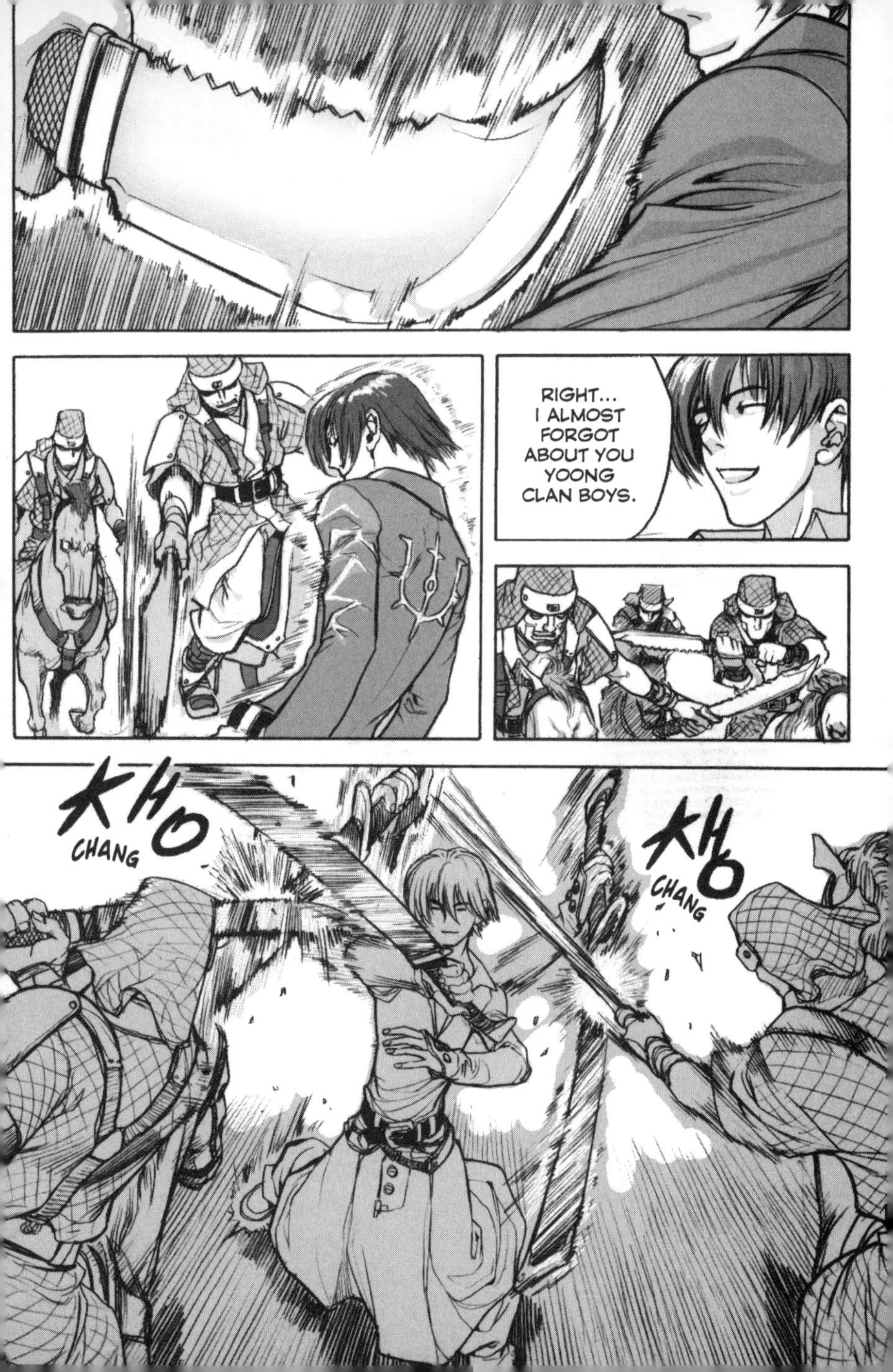
RIGHT... I ALMOST FORGOT ABOUT YOU YOONG CLAN BOYS.
KHO
CHANG
KHO
CHANG

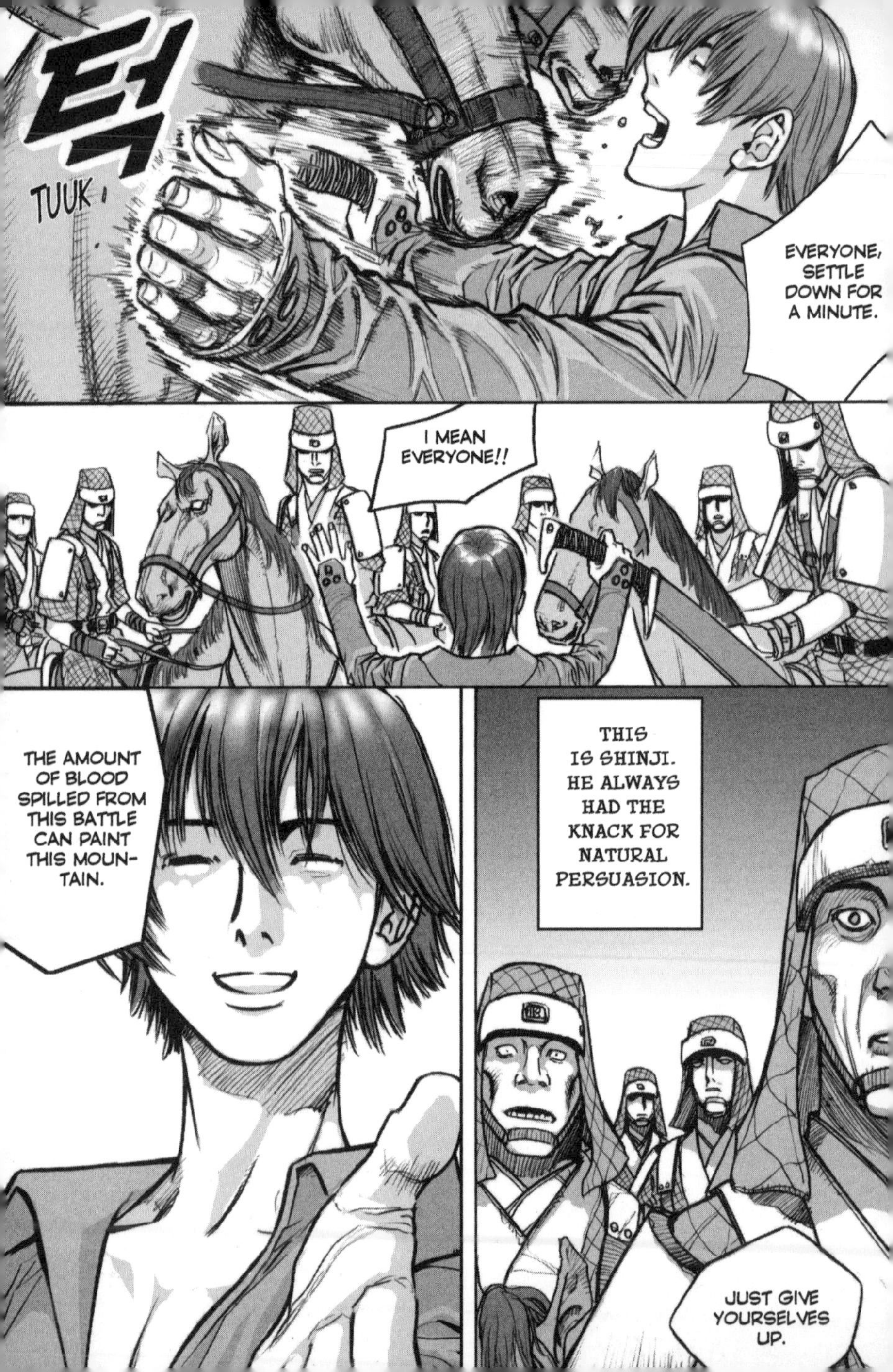

터
TUUK
EVERYONE, SETTLE DOWN FOR A MINUTE.
I MEAN EVERYONE!!
THE AMOUNT OF BLOOD SPILLED FROM THIS BATTLE CAN PAINT THIS MOUN-TAIN.
THIS IS SHINJI. HE ALWAYS HAD THE KNACK FOR NATURAL PERSUASION.
JUST GIVE YOURSELVES UP.

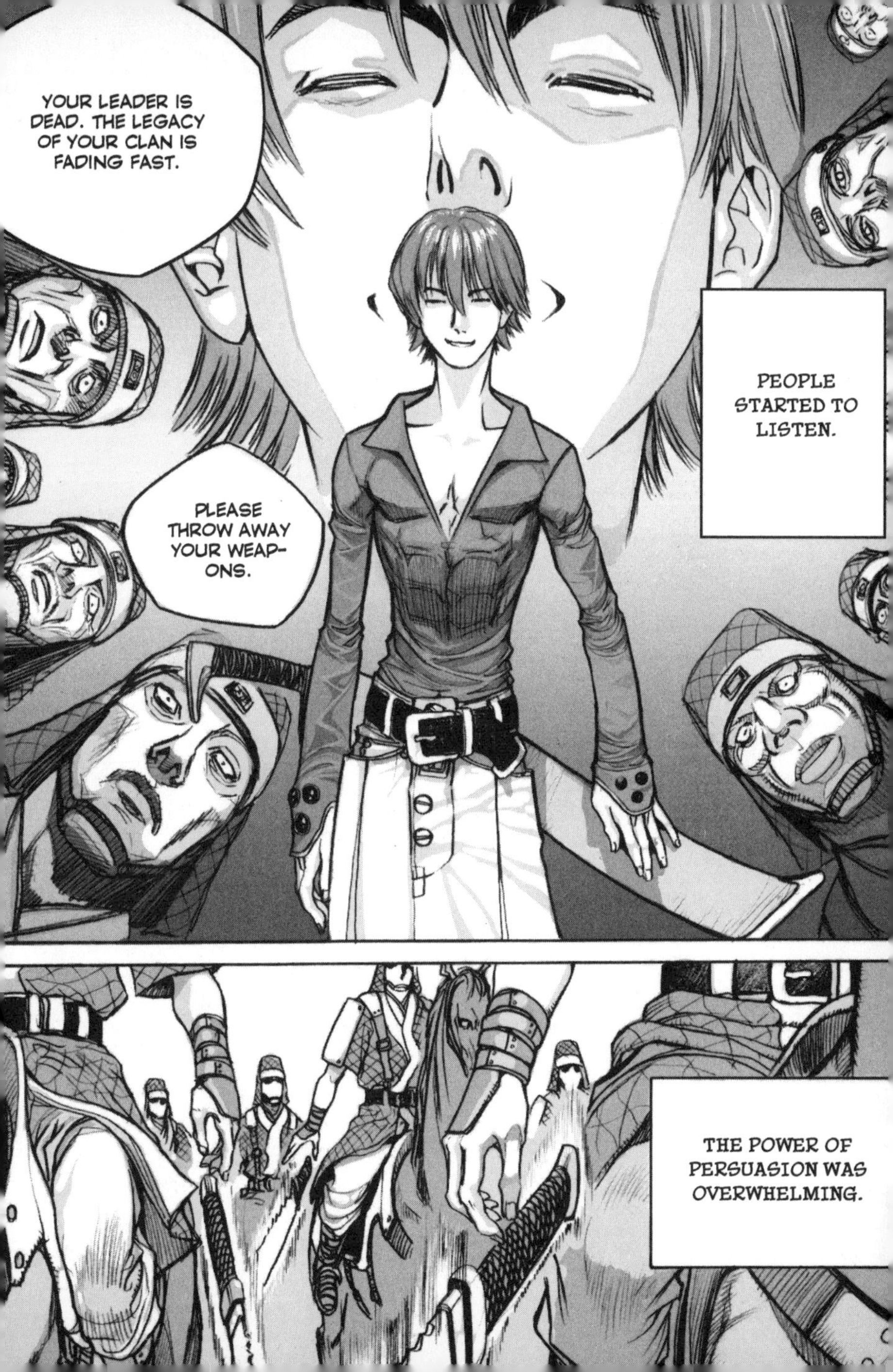
YOUR LEADER IS DEAD. THE LEGACY OF YOUR CLAN IS FADING FAST.
PLEASE THROW AWAY YOUR WEAP-ONS.
PEOPLE STARTED TO LISTEN.
THE POWER OF PERSUASION WAS OVERWHELMING.

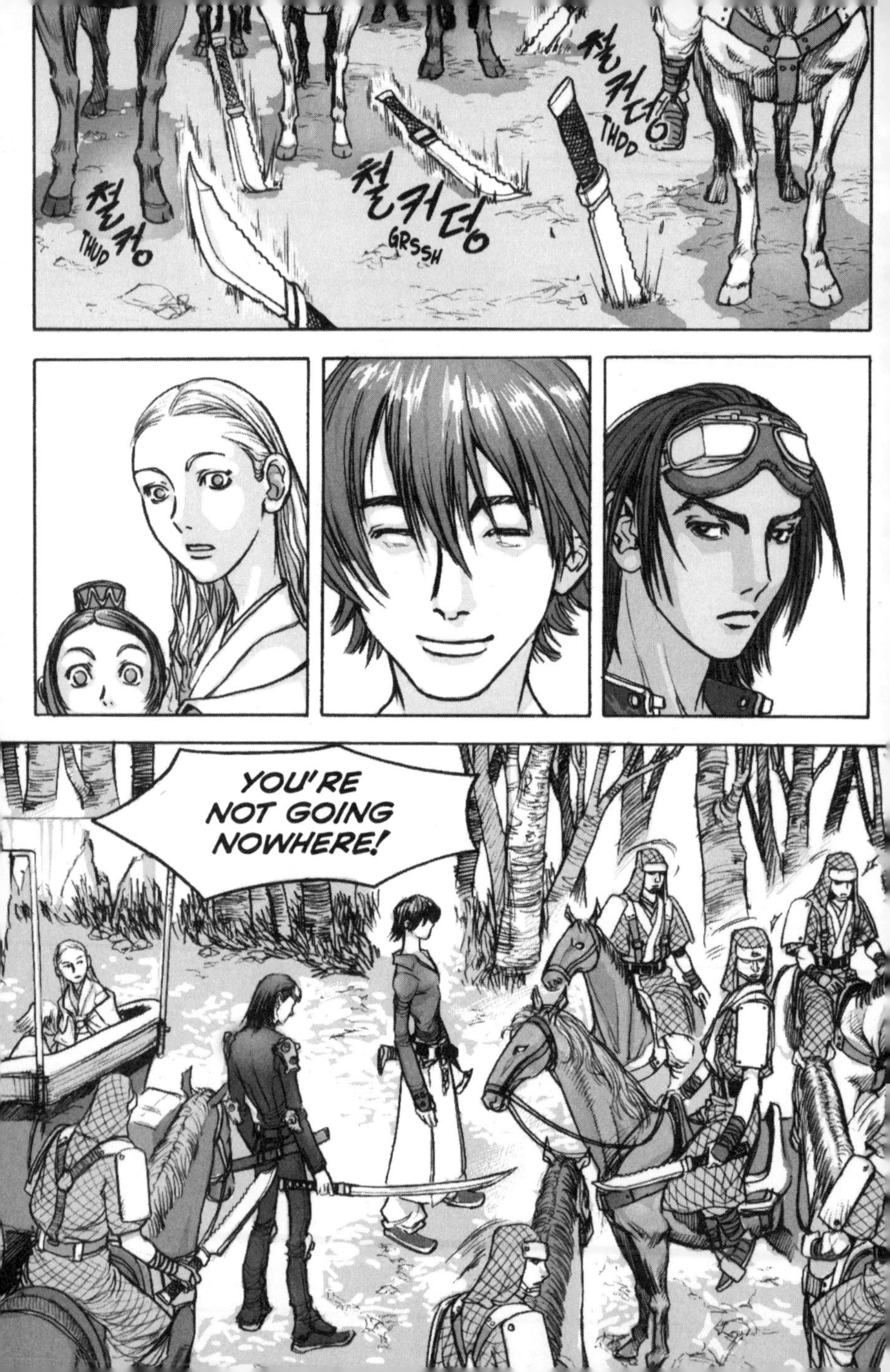
철컹
THUD
철커덩
GRSSH
철커덩
THDD
YOU'RE NOT GOING NOWHERE!

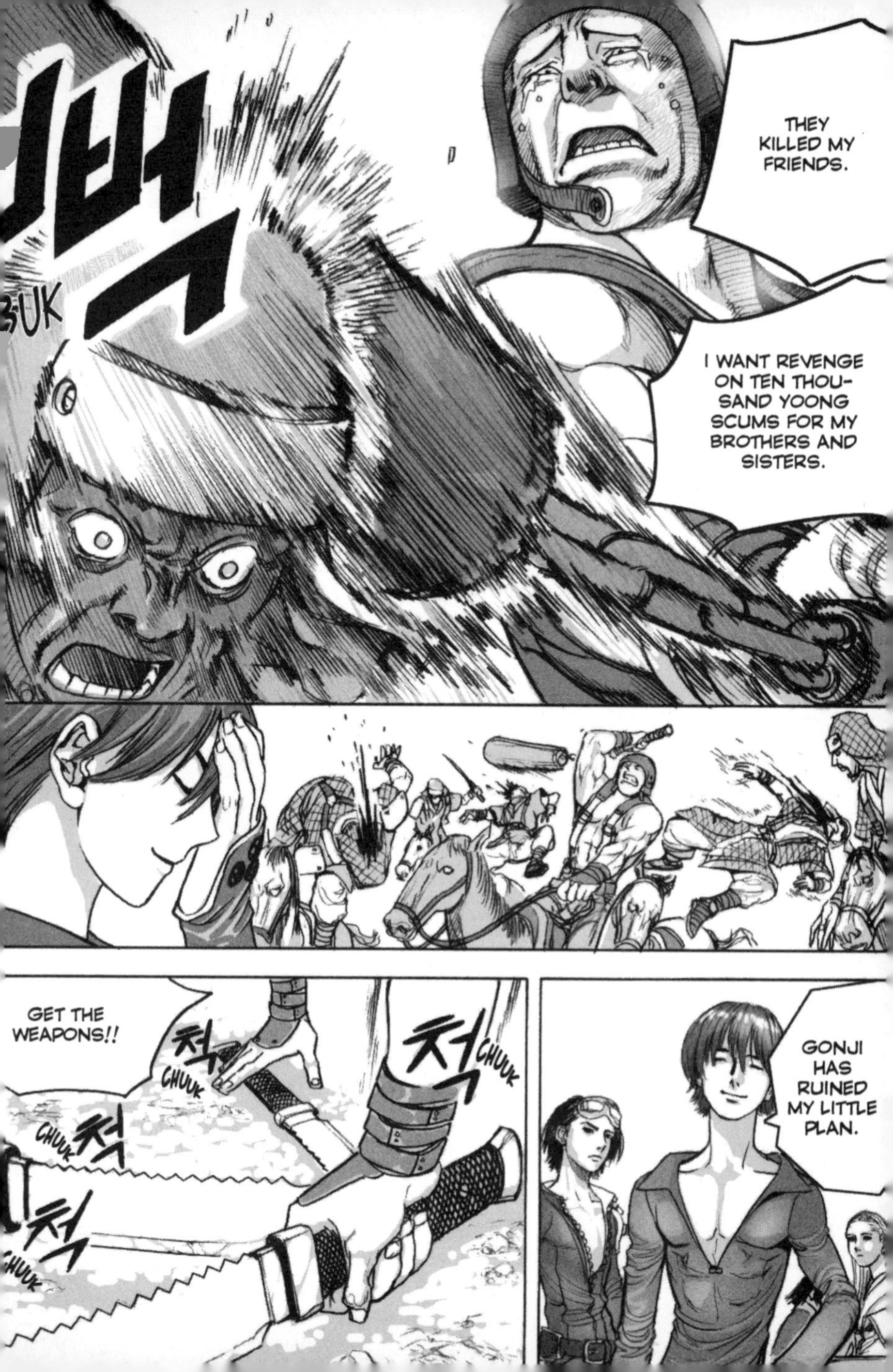

퍽
BUK
THEY KILLED MY FRIENDS.
I WANT REVENGE ON TEN THOU-SAND YOONG SCUMS FOR MY BROTHERS AND SISTERS.
GONJI HAS RUINED MY LITTLE PLAN.
GET THE WEAPONS!!
척
CHUUK
척
CHUUK
척
CHUUK
척
CHUUK

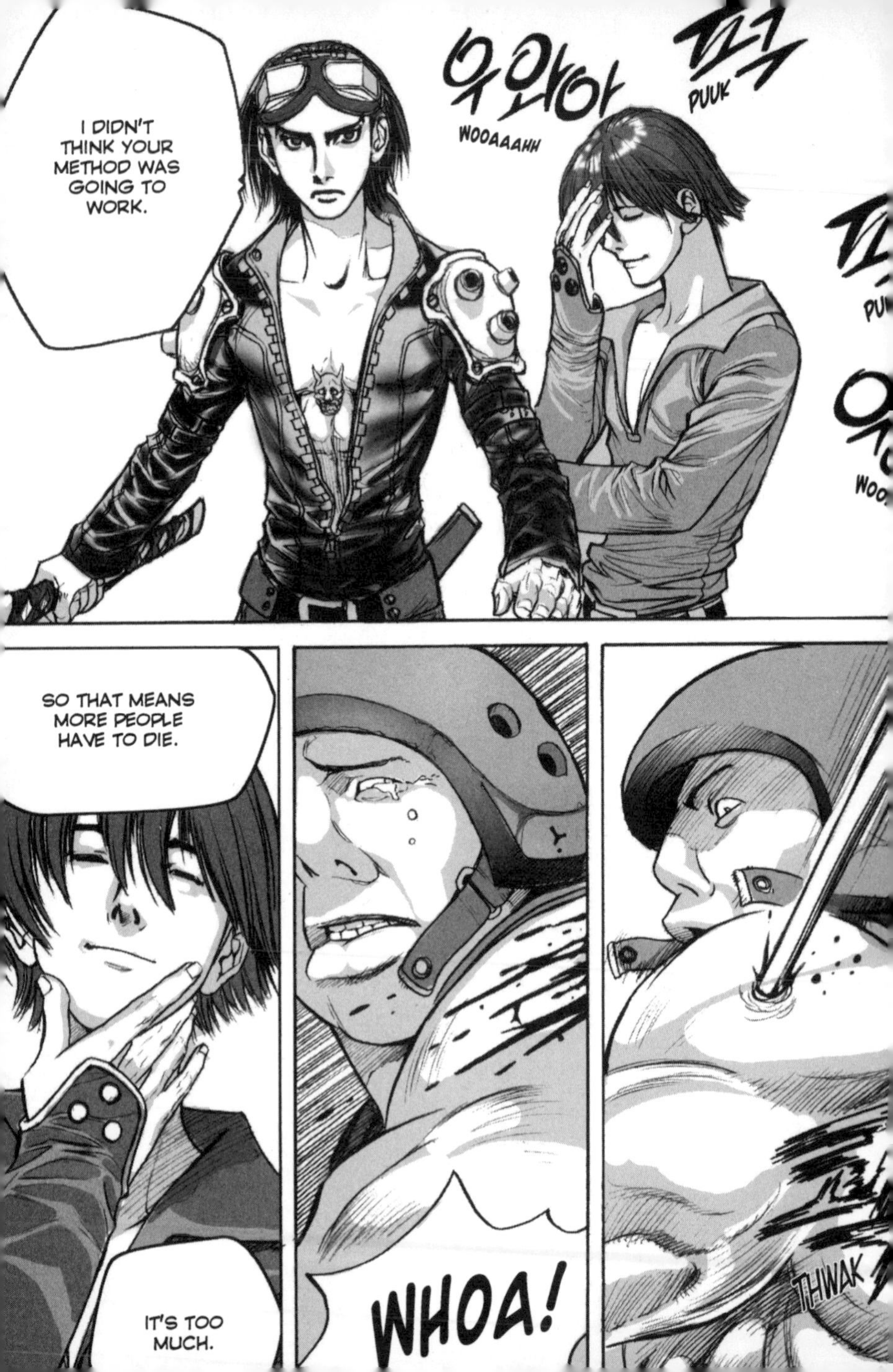
I DIDN'T THINK YOUR METHOD WAS GOING TO WORK.
WOOAAAHH
PUUK
SO THAT MEANS MORE PEOPLE HAVE TO DIE.
IT'S TOO MUCH.
WHOA!
THWAK

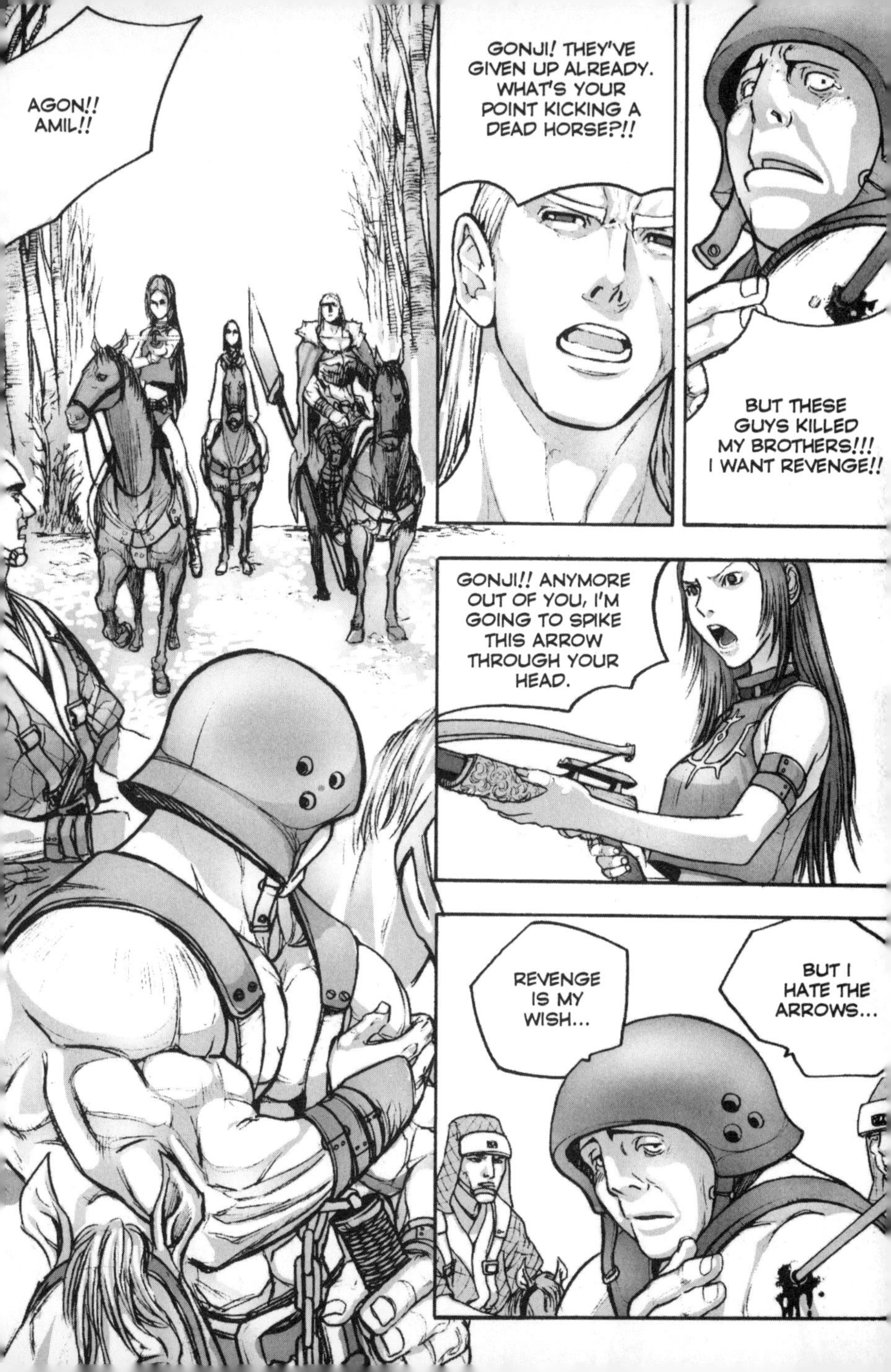
AGON!! AMIL!!
GONJI! THEY'VE GIVEN UP ALREADY. WHAT'S YOUR POINT KICKING A DEAD HORSE?!!
BUT THESE GUYS KILLED MY BROTHERS!!! I WANT REVENGE!!
GONJI!! ANYMORE OUT OF YOU, I'M GOING TO SPIKE THIS ARROW THROUGH YOUR HEAD.
REVENGE IS MY WISH...
BUT I HATE THE ARROWS...

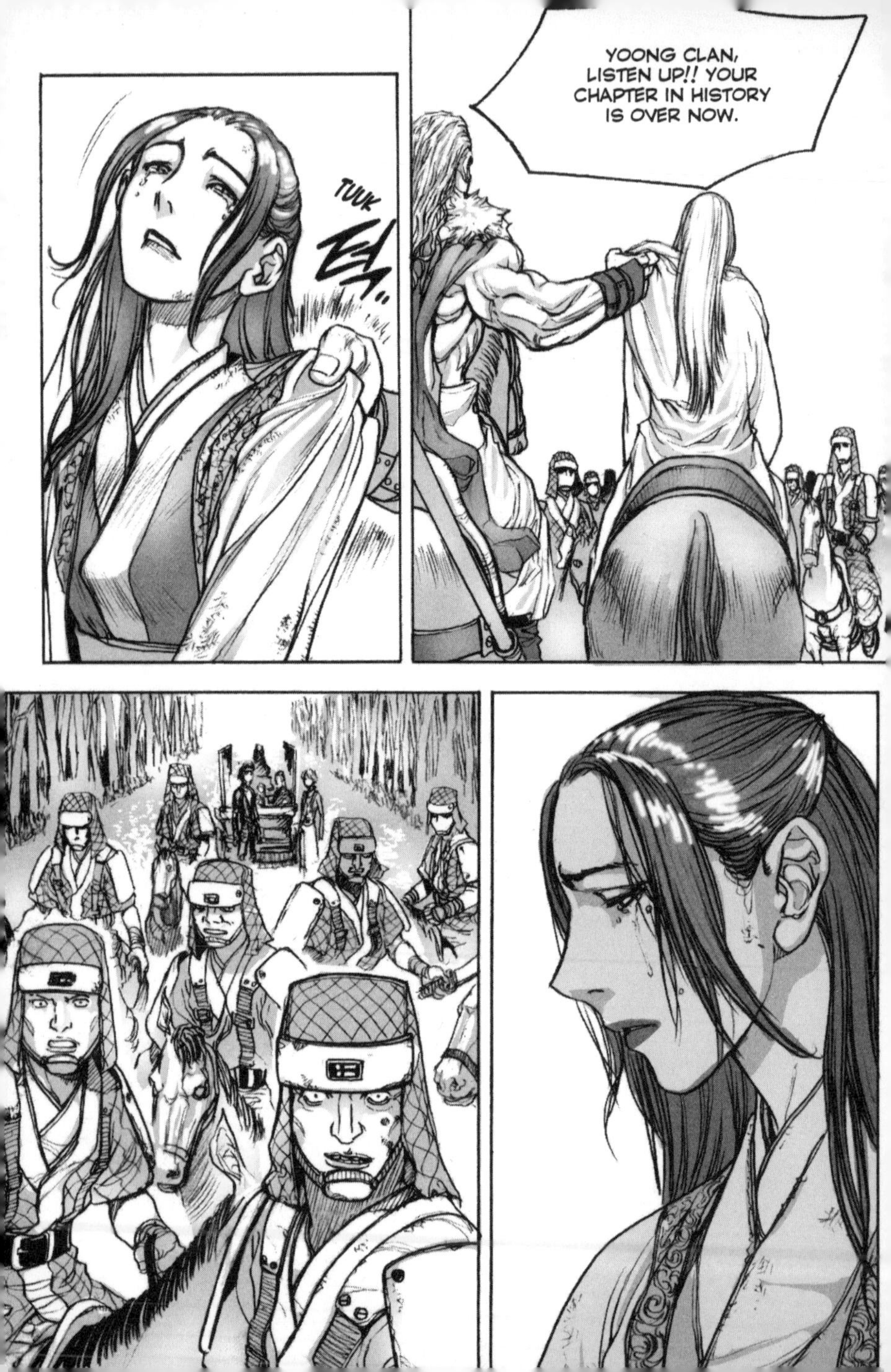
TUUK
YOONG CLAN, LISTEN UP!! YOUR CHAPTER IN HISTORY IS OVER NOW.

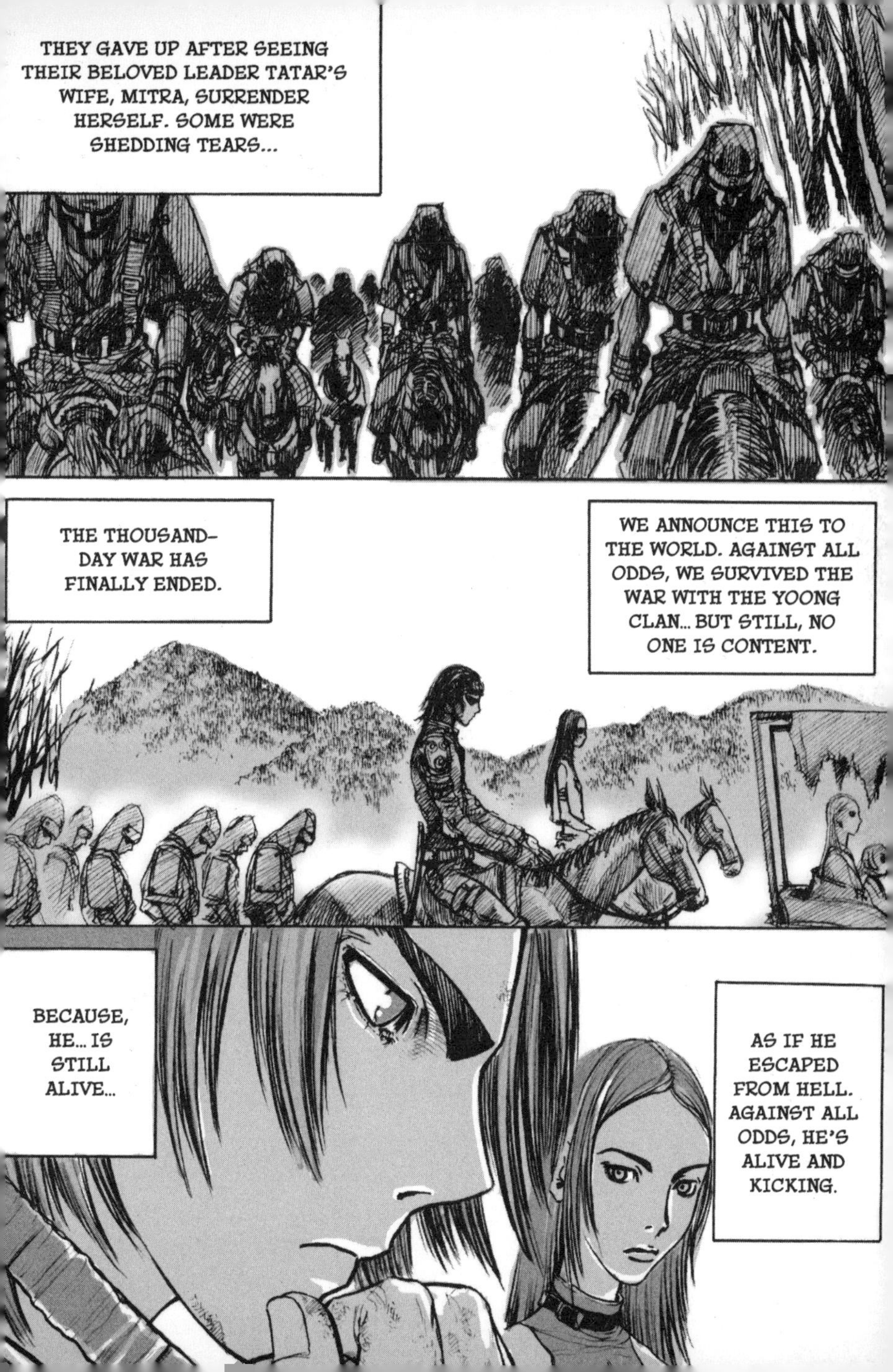
THEY GAVE UP AFTER SEEING THEIR BELOVED LEADER TATAR'S WIFE, MITRA, SURRENDER HERSELF. SOME WERE SHEDDING TEARS...
THE THOUSAND-DAY WAR HAS FINALLY ENDED.
WE ANNOUNCE THIS TO THE WORLD. AGAINST ALL ODDS, WE SURVIVED THE WAR WITH THE YOONG CLAN... BUT STILL, NO ONE IS CONTENT.
BECAUSE, HE... IS STILL ALIVE...
AS IF HE ESCAPED FROM HELL. AGAINST ALL ODDS, HE'S ALIVE AND KICKING.

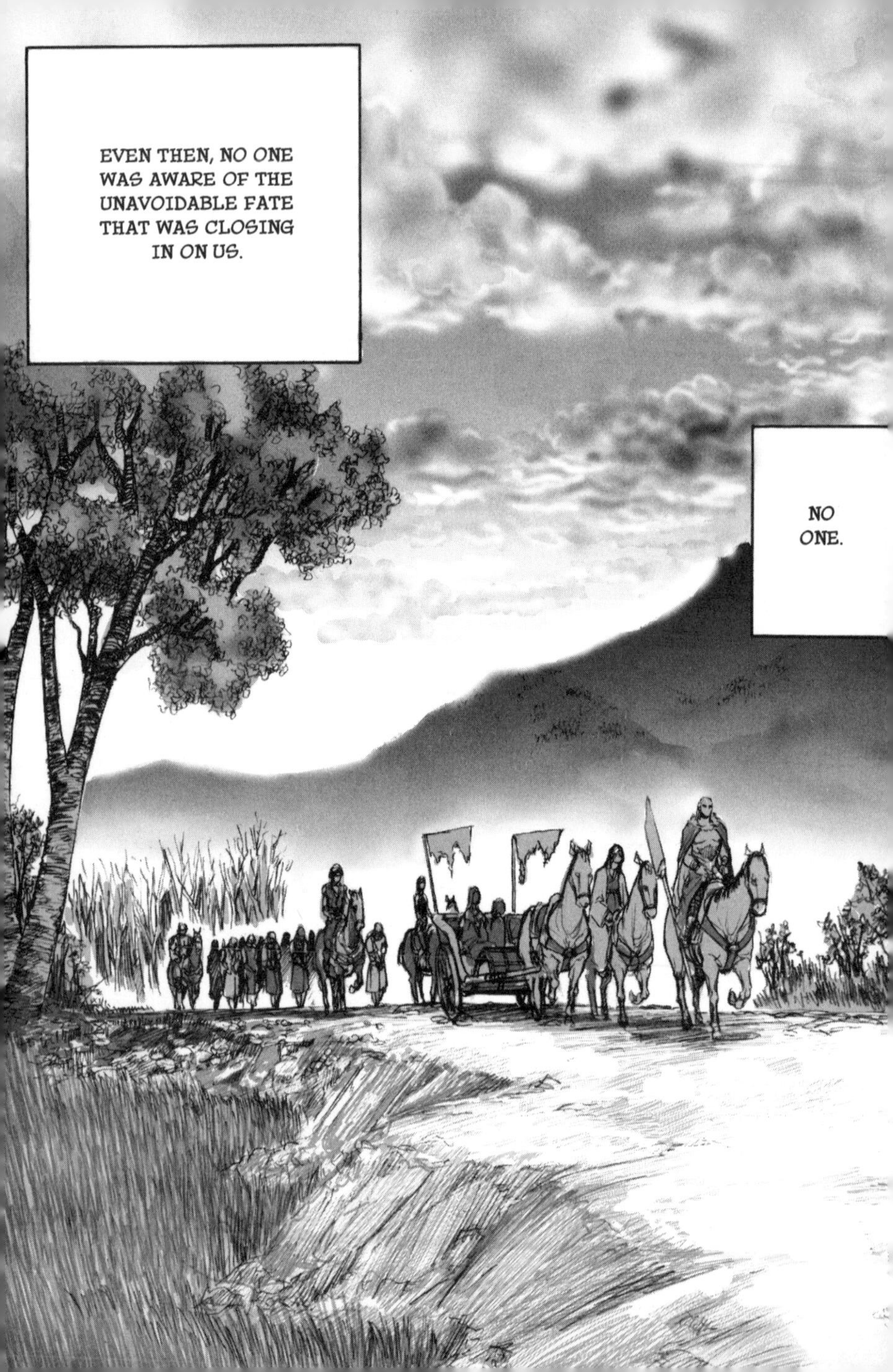
EVEN THEN, NO ONE WAS AWARE OF THE UNAVOIDABLE FATE THAT WAS CLOSING IN ON US.
NO ONE.

천추

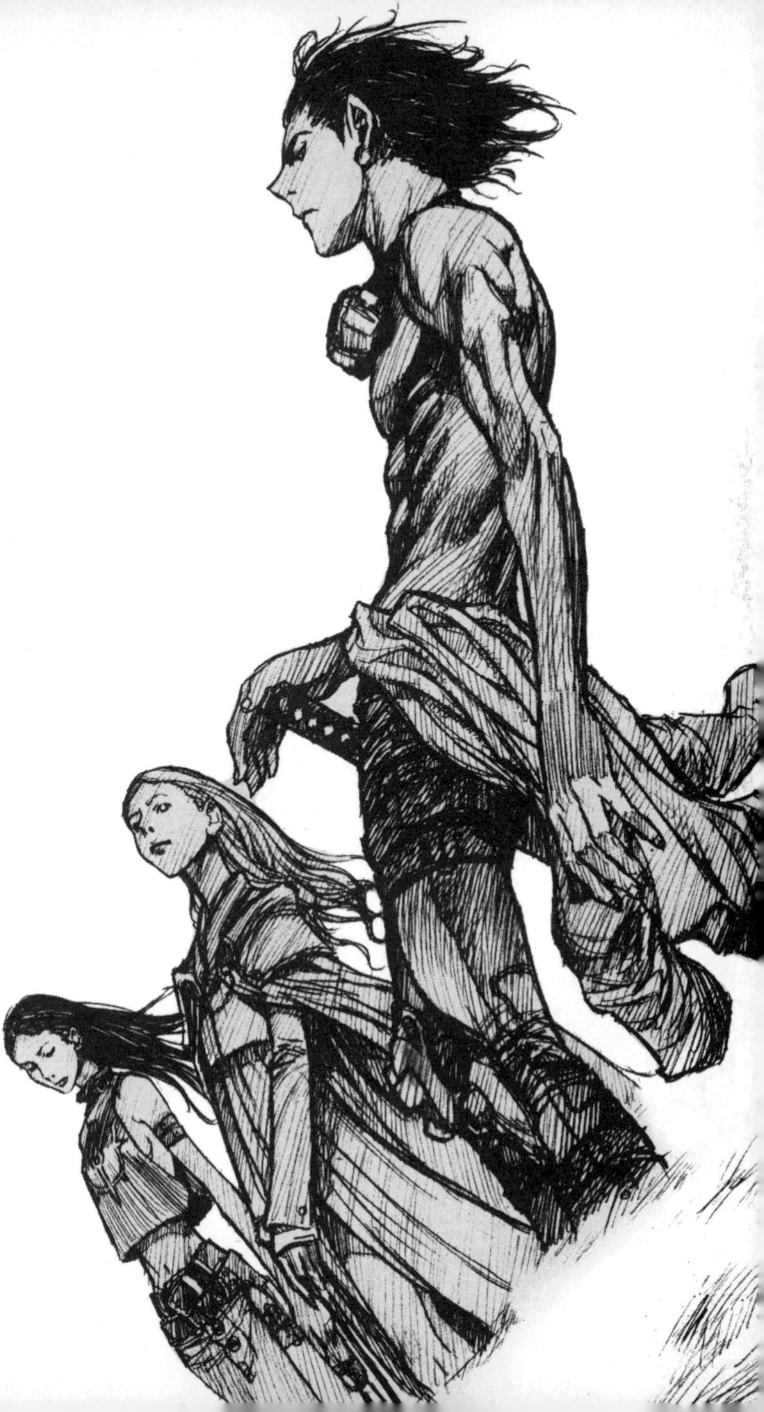

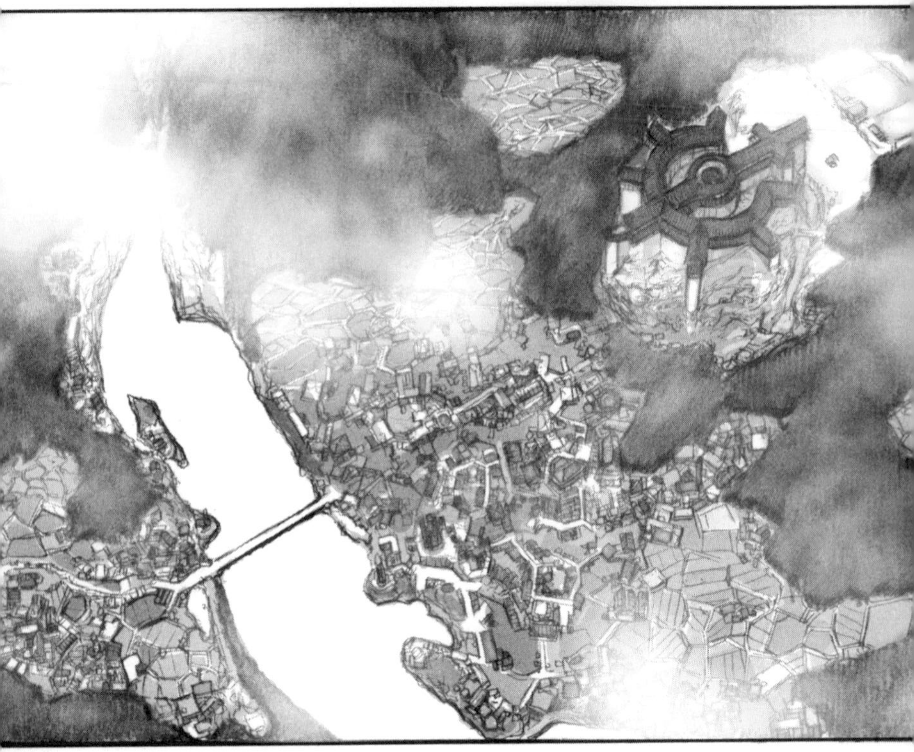

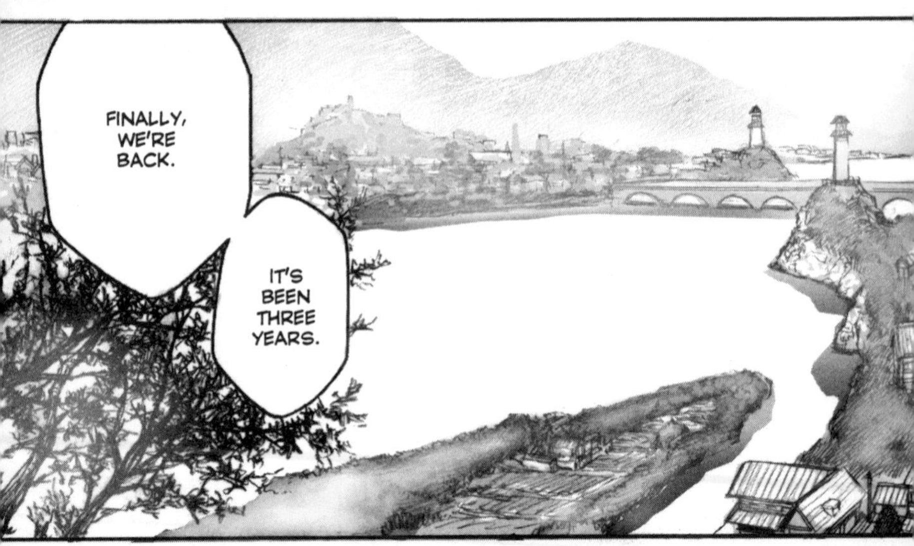
FINALLY, WE'RE BACK.
IT'S BEEN THREE YEARS.

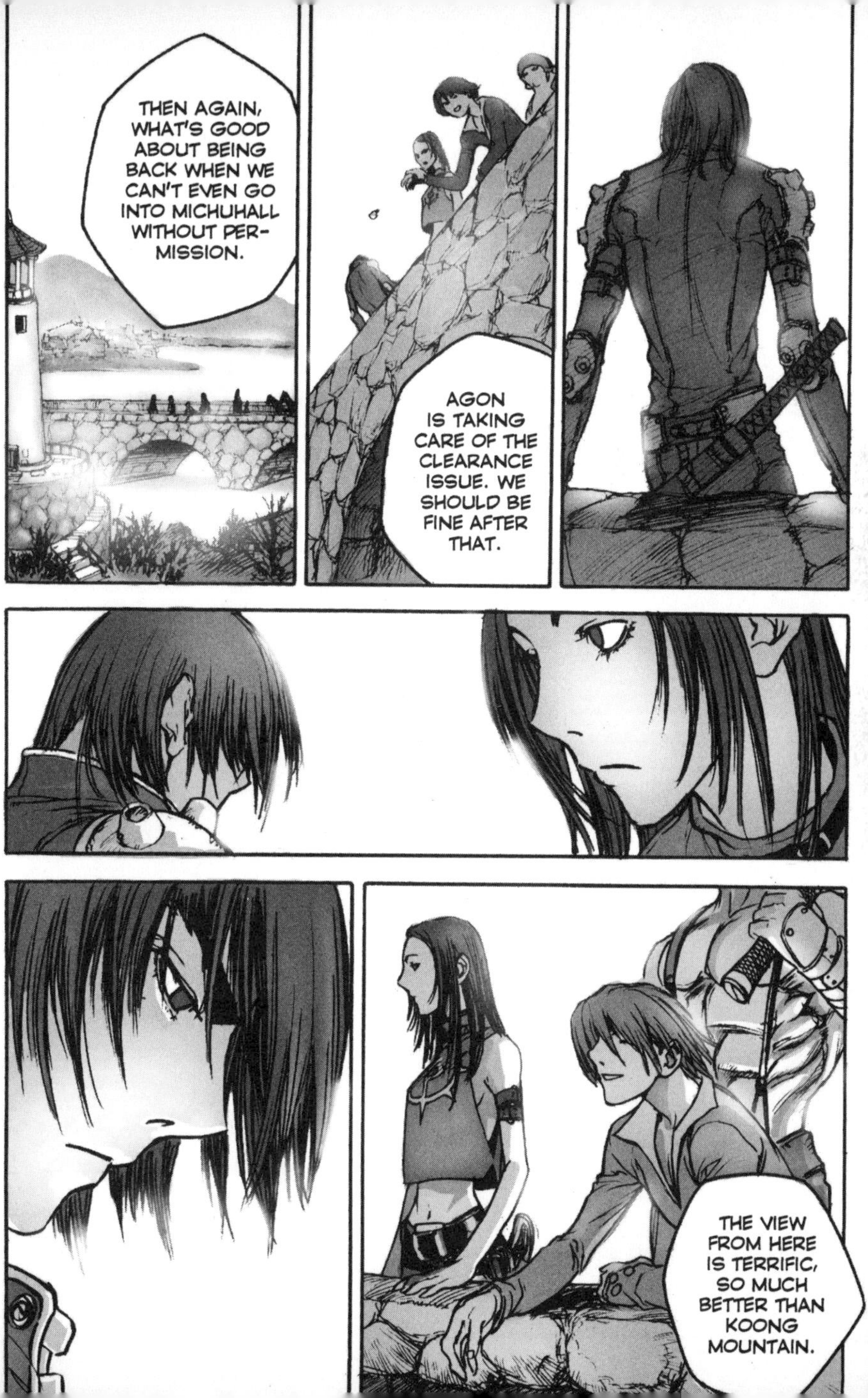
THEN AGAIN, WHAT'S GOOD ABOUT BEING BACK WHEN WE CAN'T EVEN GO INTO MICHUHALL WITHOUT PER-MISSION.
AGON IS TAKING CARE OF THE CLEARANCE ISSUE. WE SHOULD BE FINE AFTER THAT.
THE VIEW FROM HERE IS TERRIFIC, SO MUCH BETTER THAN KOONG MOUNTAIN.

HYUNG=HONORIFIC FROM YOUNGER TO OLDER MALES.

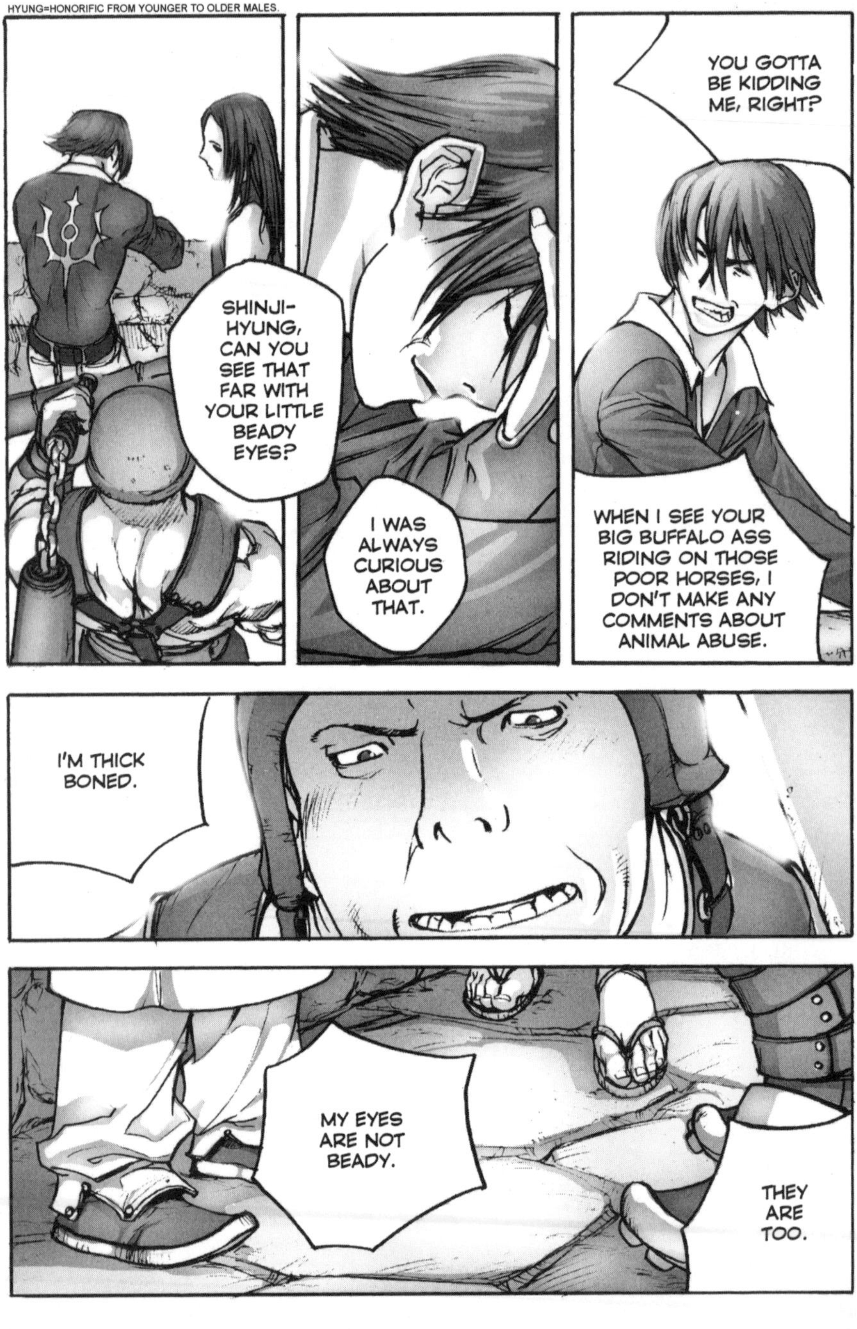
SHINJI-HYUNG, CAN YOU SEE THAT FAR WITH YOUR LITTLE BEADY EYES?
I WAS ALWAYS CURIOUS ABOUT THAT.
YOU GOTTA BE KIDDING ME, RIGHT?
WHEN I SEE YOUR BIG BUFFALO ASS RIDING ON THOSE POOR HORSES, I DON'T MAKE ANY COMMENTS ABOUT ANIMAL ABUSE.
I'M THICK BONED.
MY EYES ARE NOT BEADY.
THEY ARE TOO.

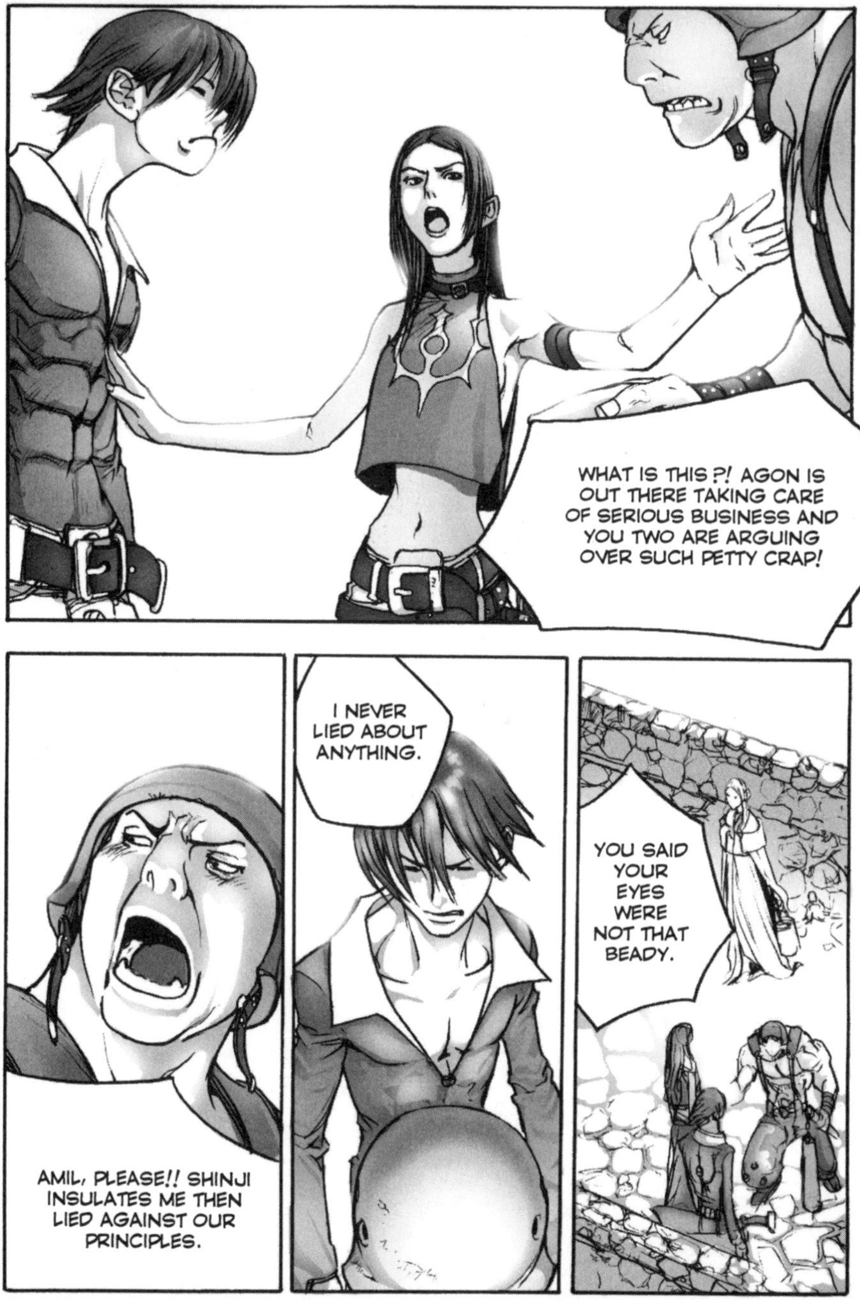
WHAT IS THIS ?! AGON IS OUT THERE TAKING CARE OF SERIOUS BUSINESS AND YOU TWO ARE ARGUING OVER SUCH PETTY CRAP!
AMIL, PLEASE!! SHINJI INSULATES ME THEN LIED AGAINST OUR PRINCIPLES.
I NEVER LIED ABOUT ANYTHING.
YOU SAID YOUR EYES WERE NOT THAT BEADY.

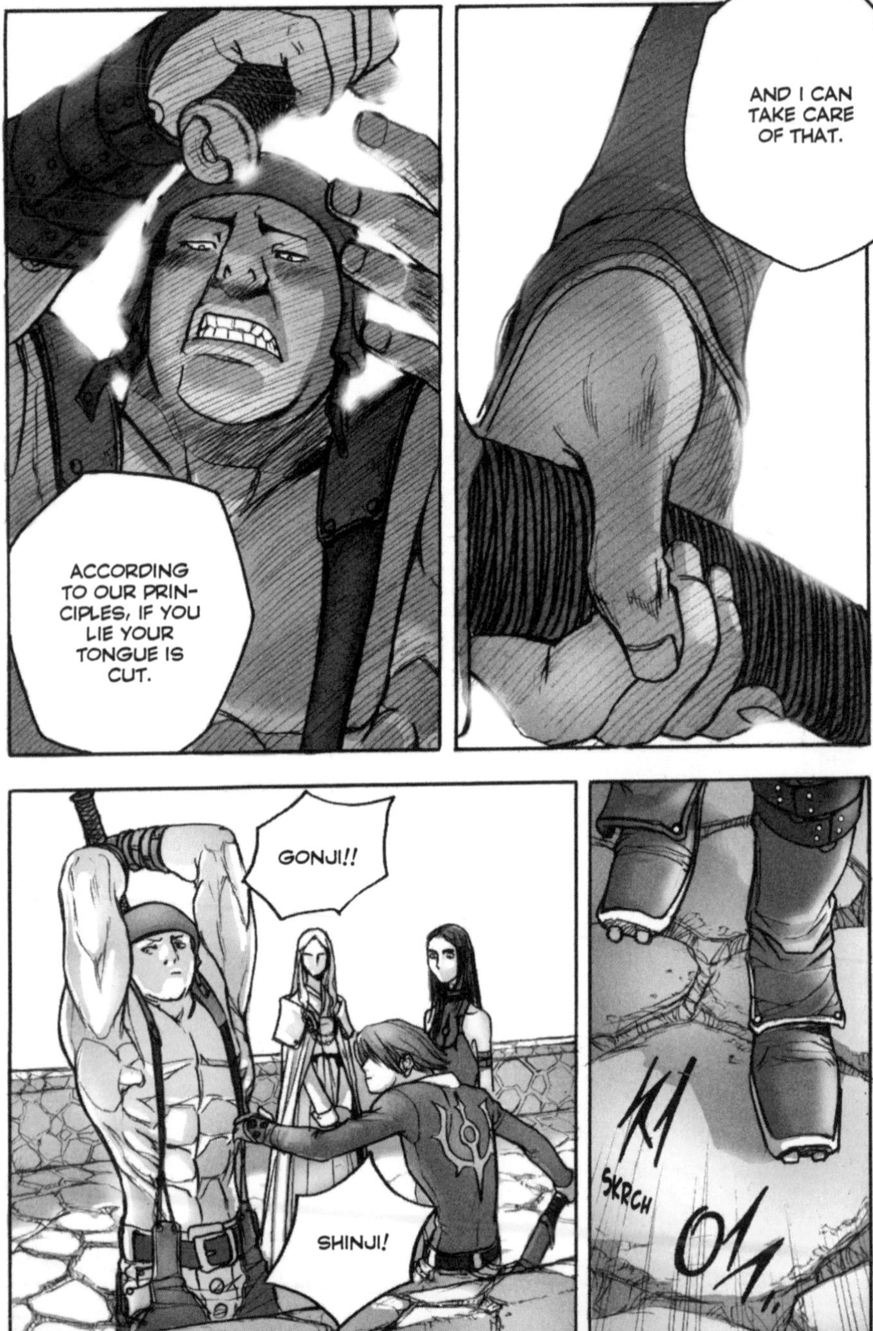
ACCORDING TO OUR PRINCIPLES, IF YOU LIE YOUR TONGUE IS CUT.
AND I CAN TAKE CARE OF THAT.
GONJI!!
SHINJI!
SKRCH

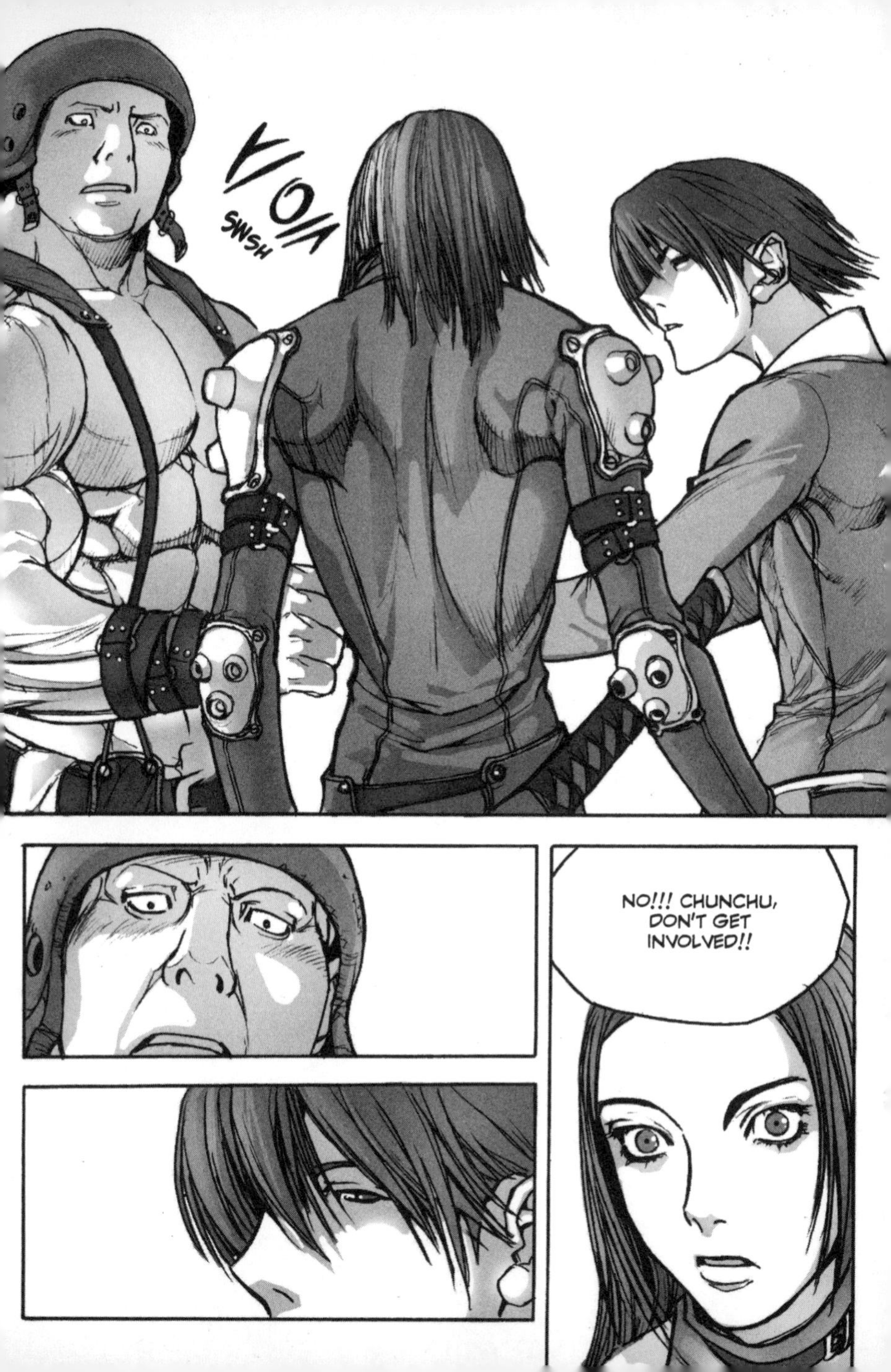
SWSH
NO!!! CHUNCHU, DON'T GET INVOLVED!!

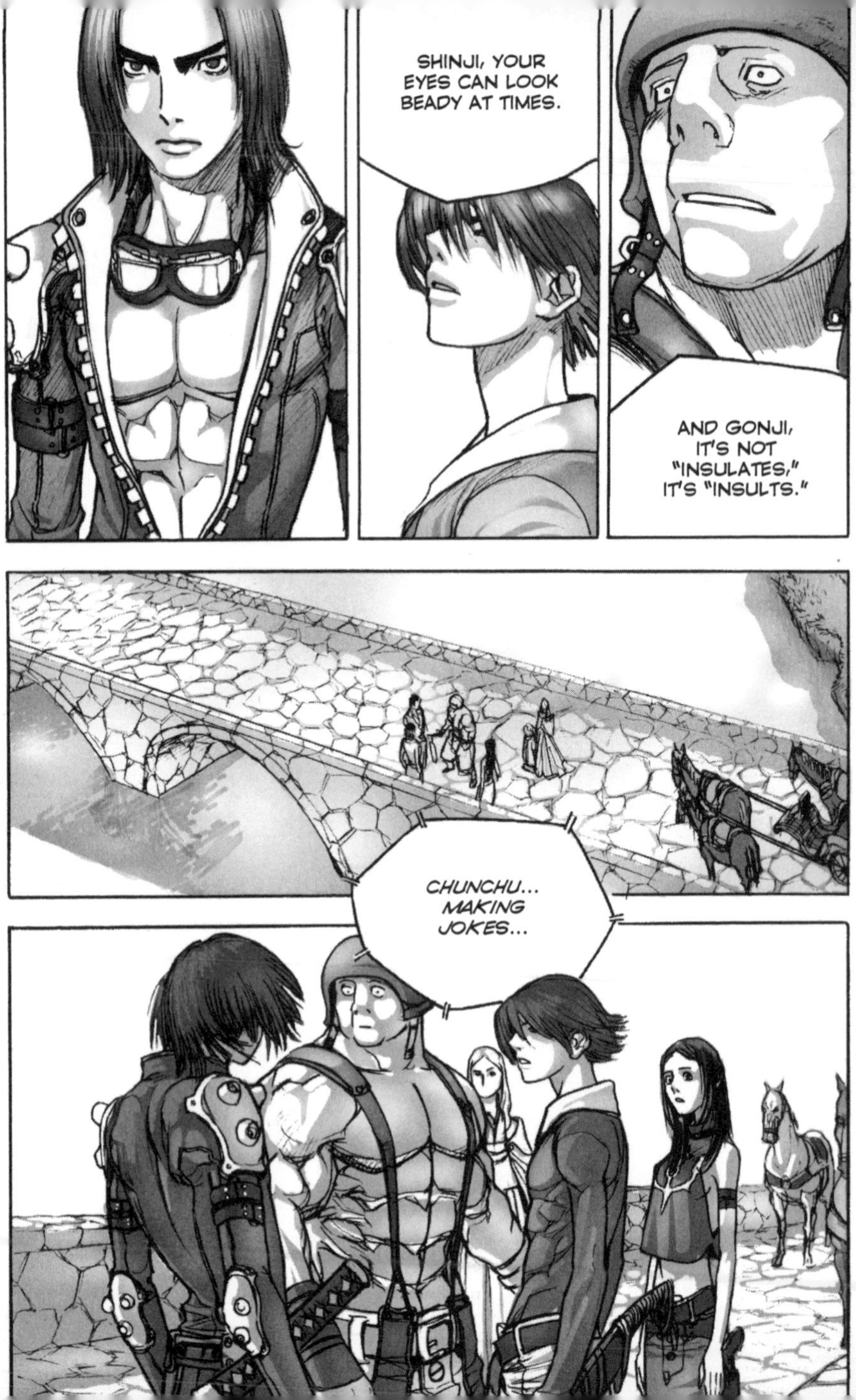
SHINJI, YOUR EYES CAN LOOK BEADY AT TIMES.
AND GONJI, IT'S NOT "INSULATES," IT'S "INSULTS."
CHUNCHU... MAKING JOKES...

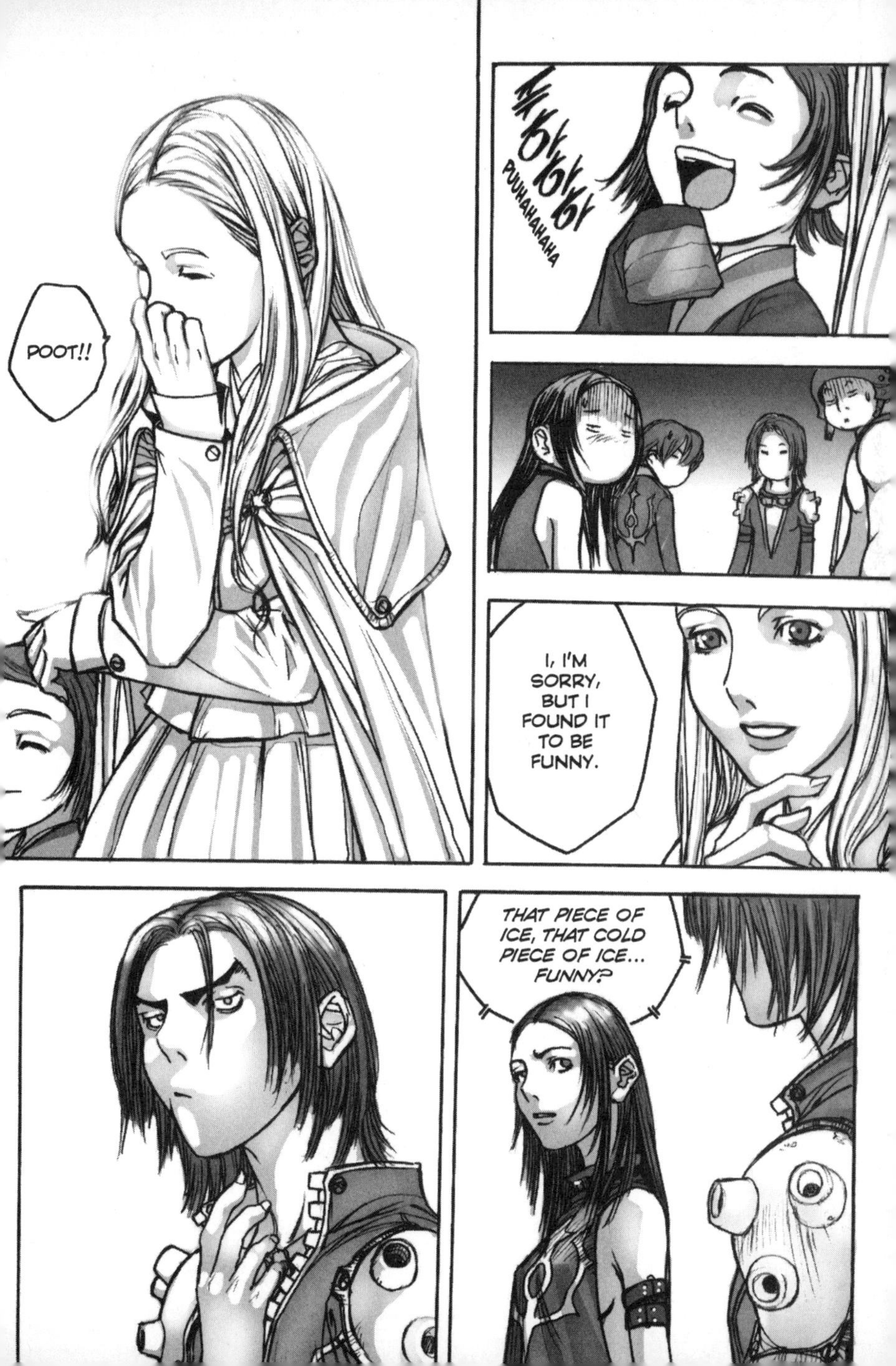

POOT!!
PUUHAHAHAHA
I, I'M SORRY, BUT I FOUND IT TO BE FUNNY.
THAT PIECE OF ICE, THAT COLD PIECE OF ICE... FUNNY?

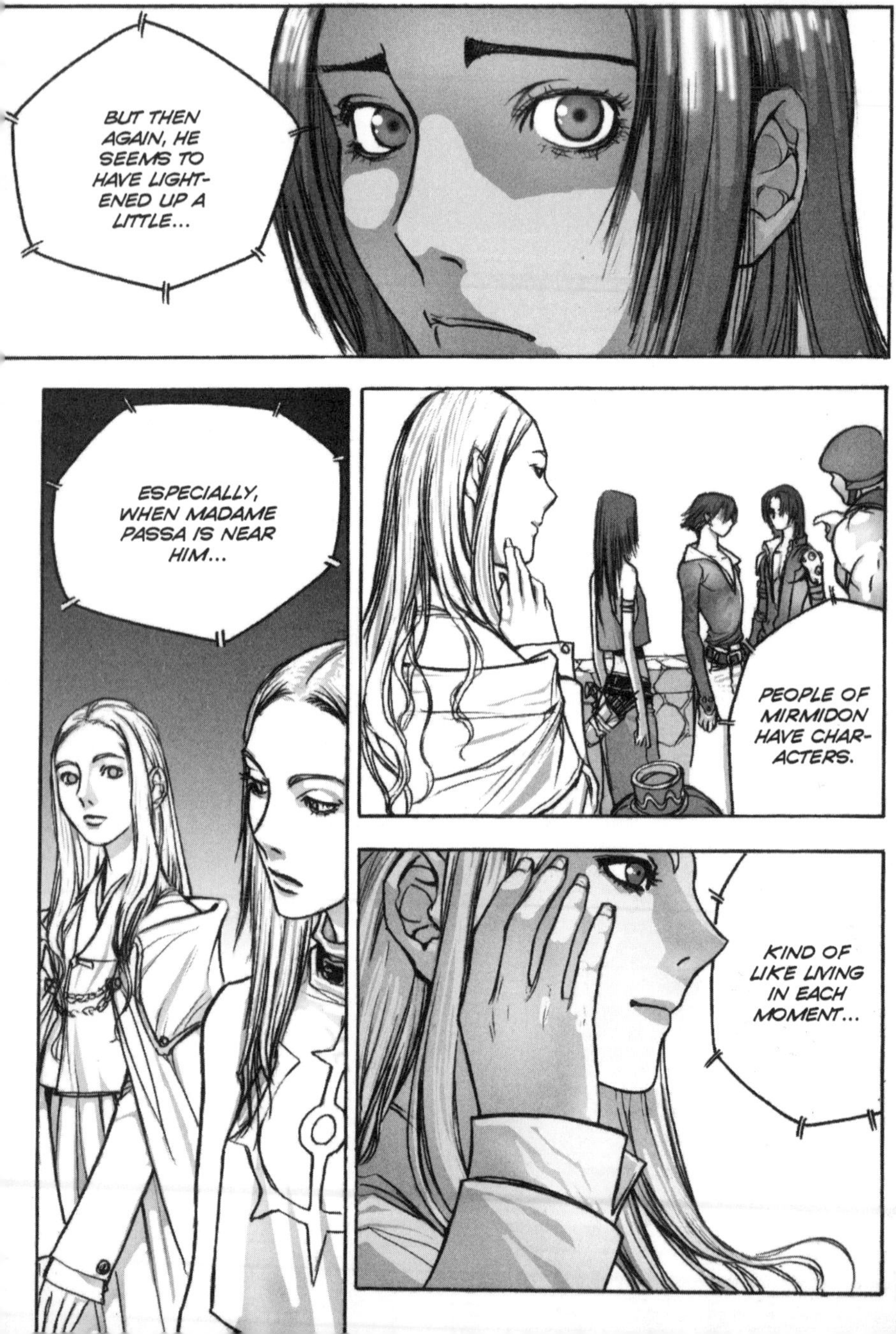
BUT THEN AGAIN, HE SEEMS TO HAVE LIGHT-ENED UP A LITTLE...
ESPECIALLY, WHEN MADAME PASSA IS NEAR HIM...
PEOPLE OF MIRMIDON HAVE CHAR-ACTERS.
KIND OF LIKE LIVING IN EACH MOMENT...

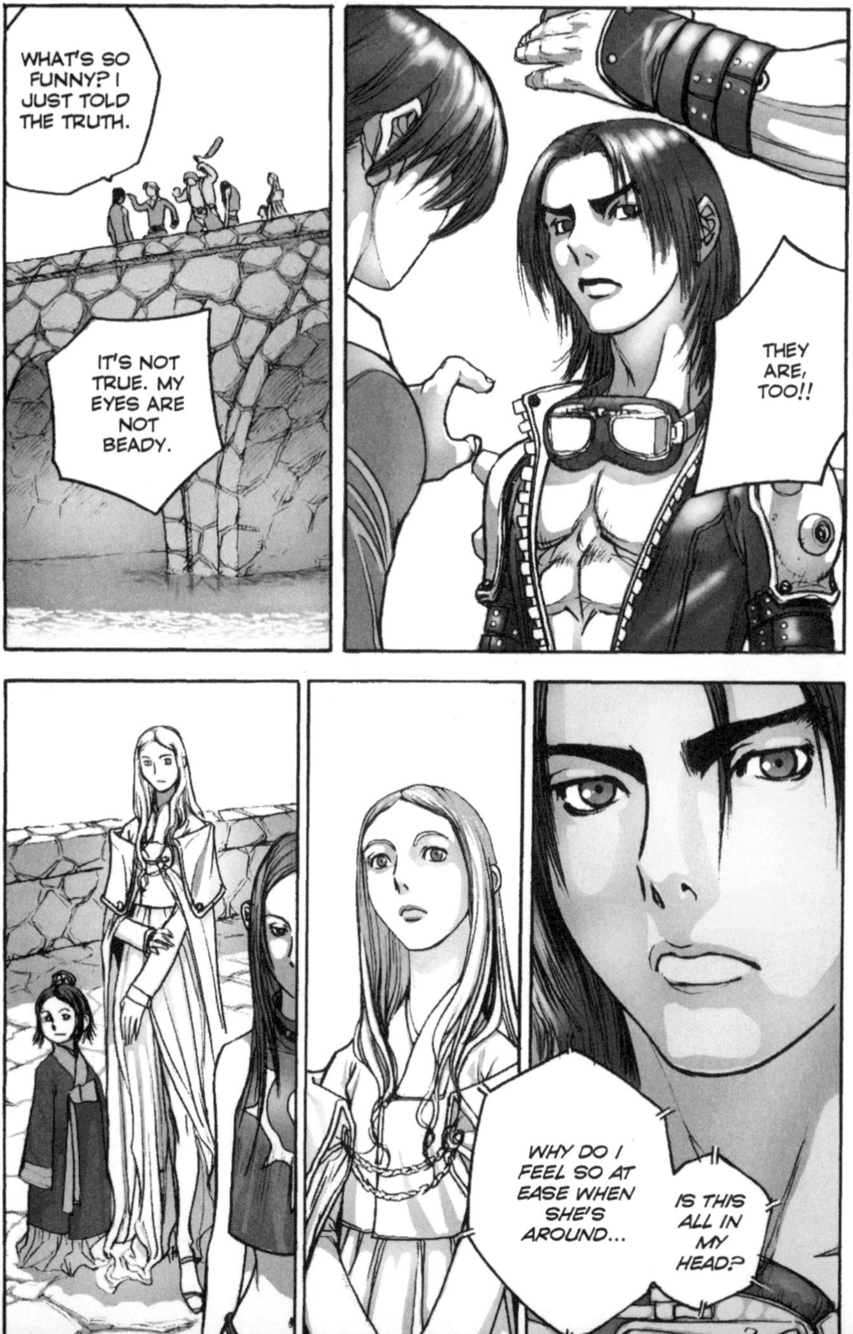
WHAT'S SO FUNNY? I JUST TOLD THE TRUTH.
IT'S NOT TRUE. MY EYES ARE NOT BEADY.
THEY ARE, TOO!!
WHY DO I FEEL SO AT EASE WHEN SHE'S AROUND...
IS THIS ALL IN MY HEAD?

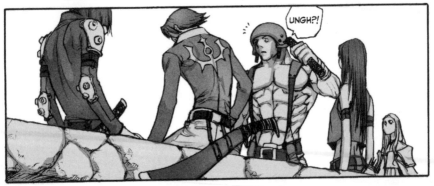

UNGH?!

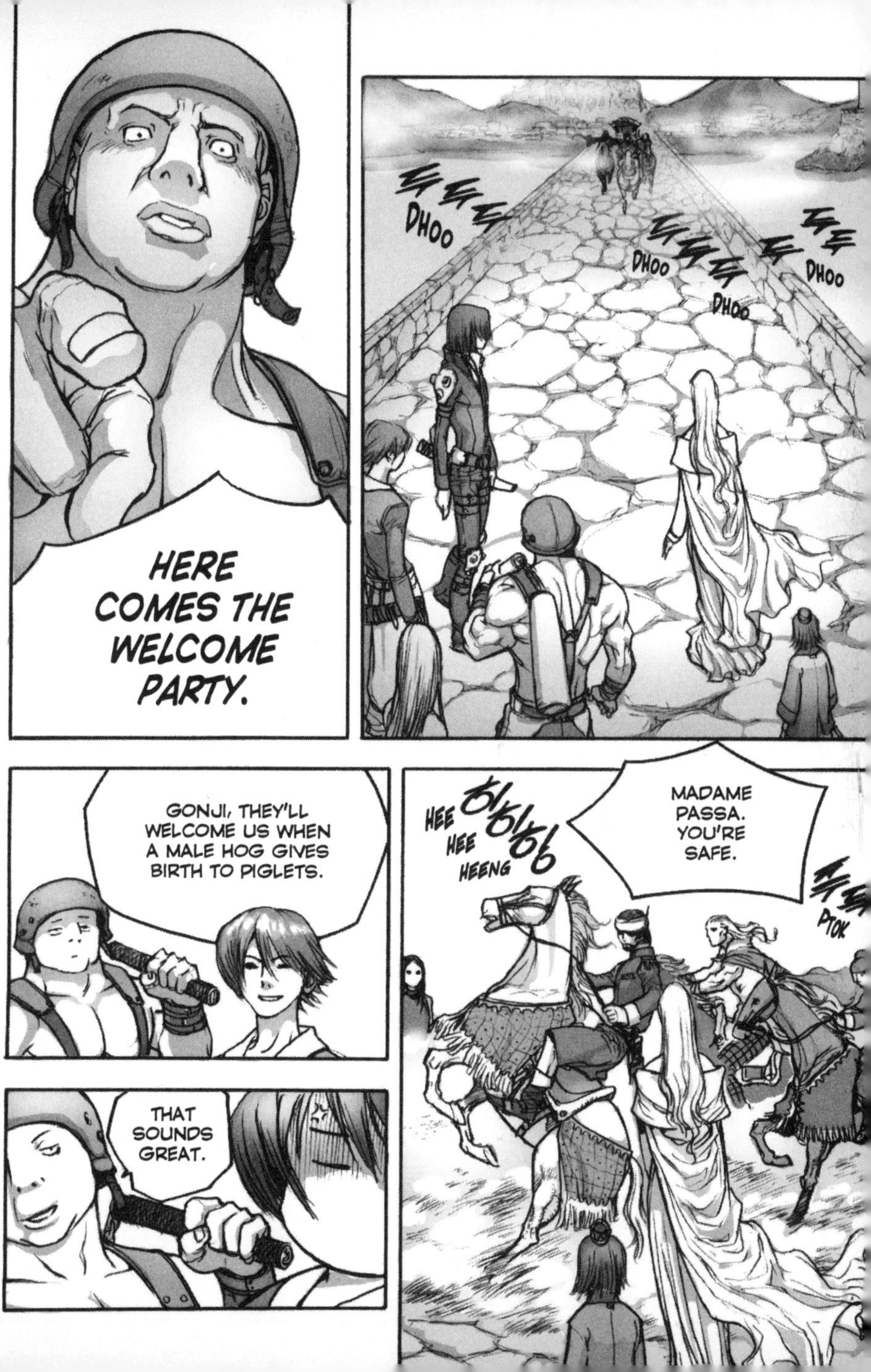
HERE COMES THE WELCOME PARTY.
DHOO
DHOO
DHOO
DHOO
GONJI, THEY'LL WELCOME US WHEN A MALE HOG GIVES BIRTH TO PIGLETS.
THAT SOUNDS GREAT.
히히힝
HEE HEE HEENG
MADAME PASSA. YOU'RE SAFE.
PTOK

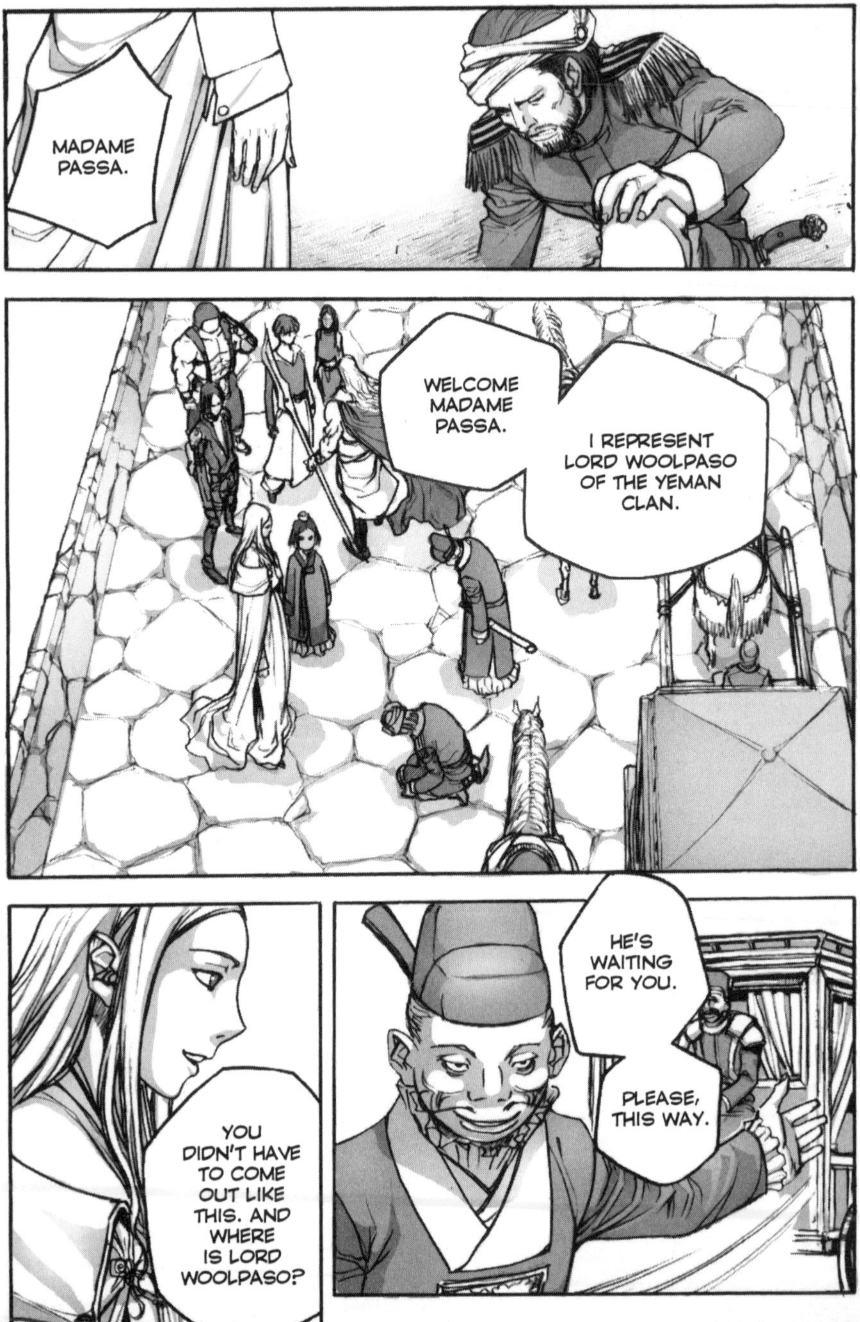
MADAME PASSA.
WELCOME MADAME PASSA.
I REPRESENT LORD WOOLPASO OF THE YEMAN CLAN.
HE'S WAITING FOR YOU.
PLEASE, THIS WAY.
YOU DIDN'T HAVE TO COME OUT LIKE THIS. AND WHERE IS LORD WOOLPASO?

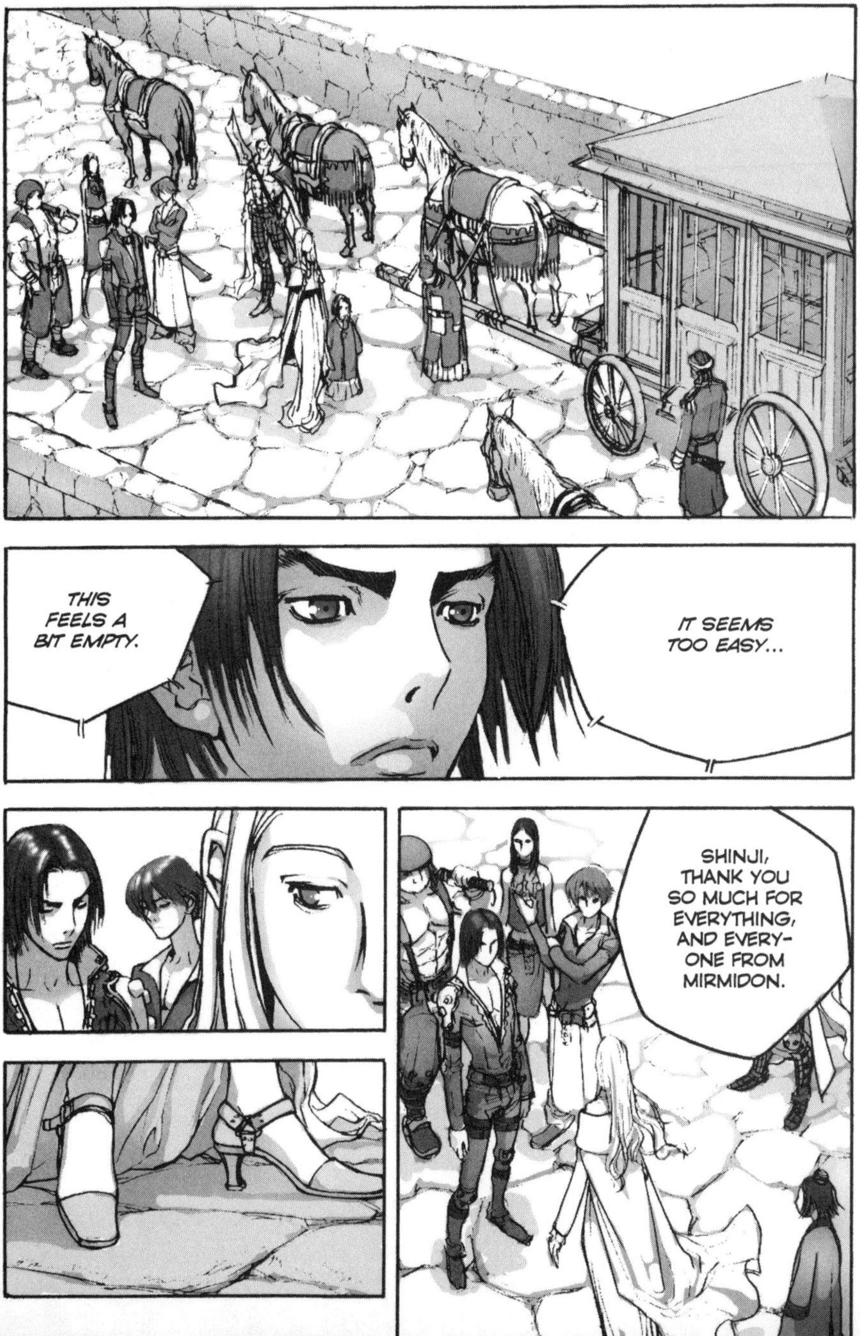

THIS FEELS A BIT EMPTY.
IT SEEMS TOO EASY...
SHINJI, THANK YOU SO MUCH FOR EVERYTHING, AND EVERY-ONE FROM MIRMIDON.

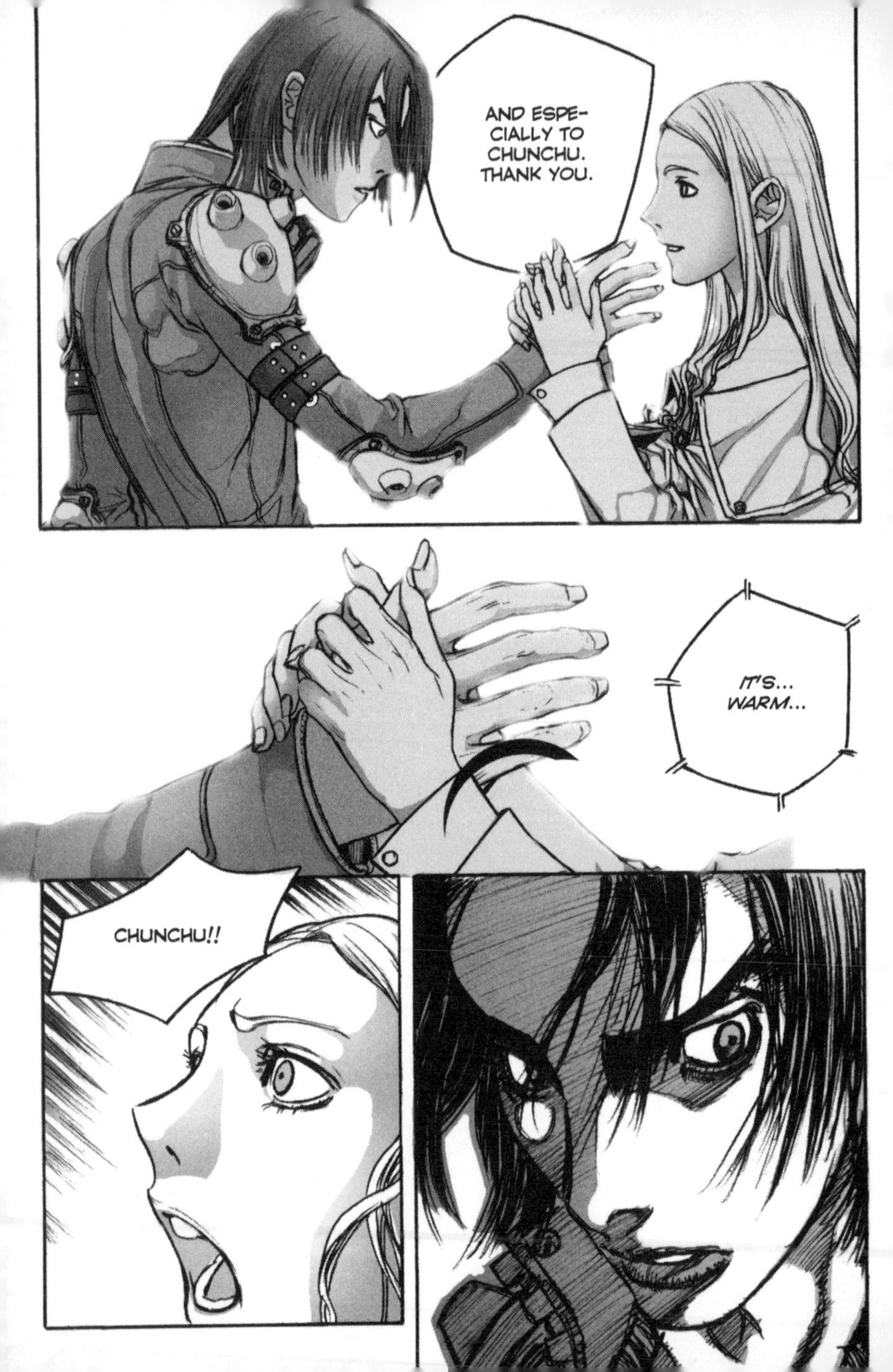
AND ESPE-
CIALLY TO
CHUNCHU.
THANK YOU.
IT'S...
WARM...
CHUNCHU!!

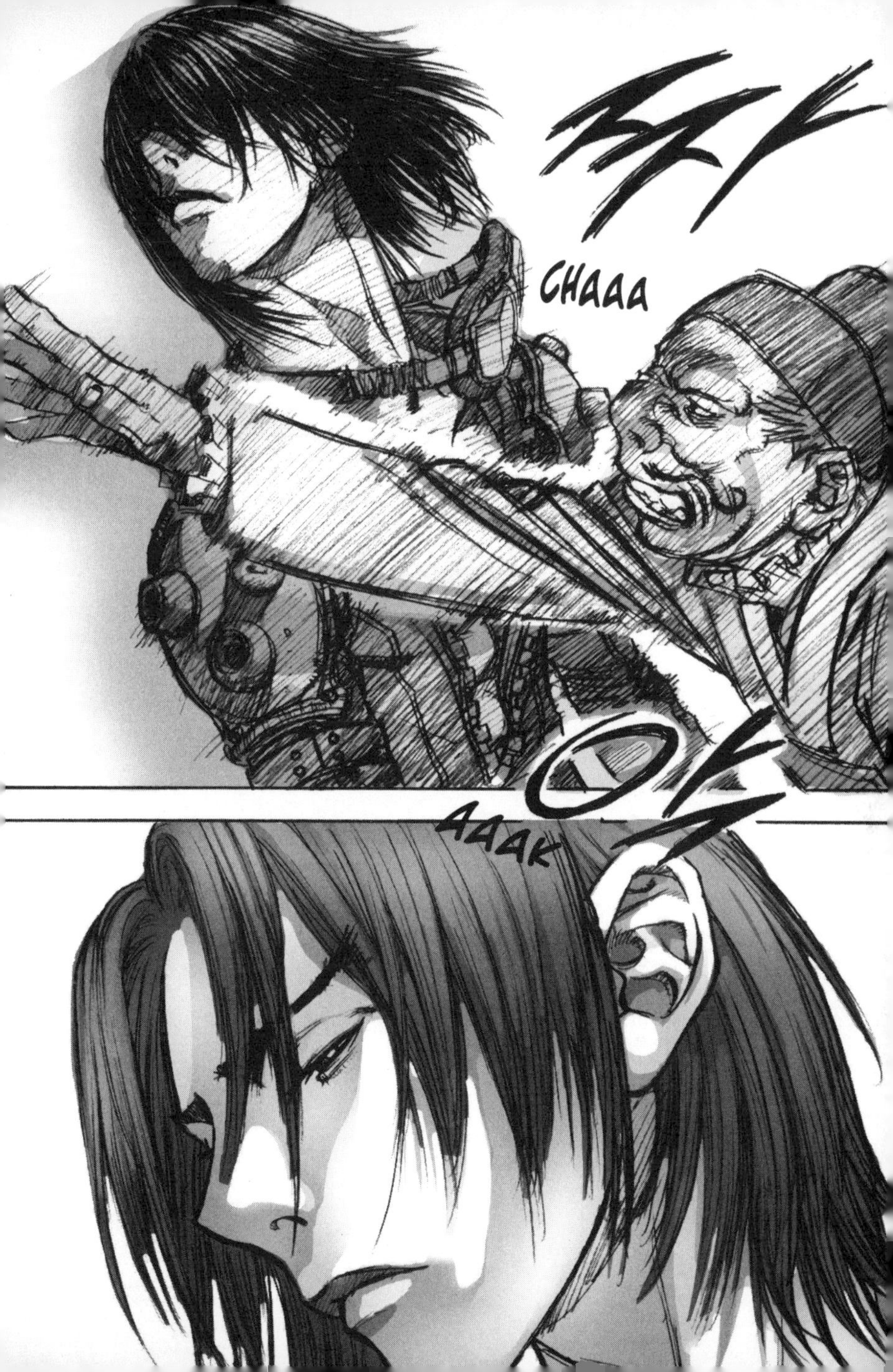
CHAAA
AAAK

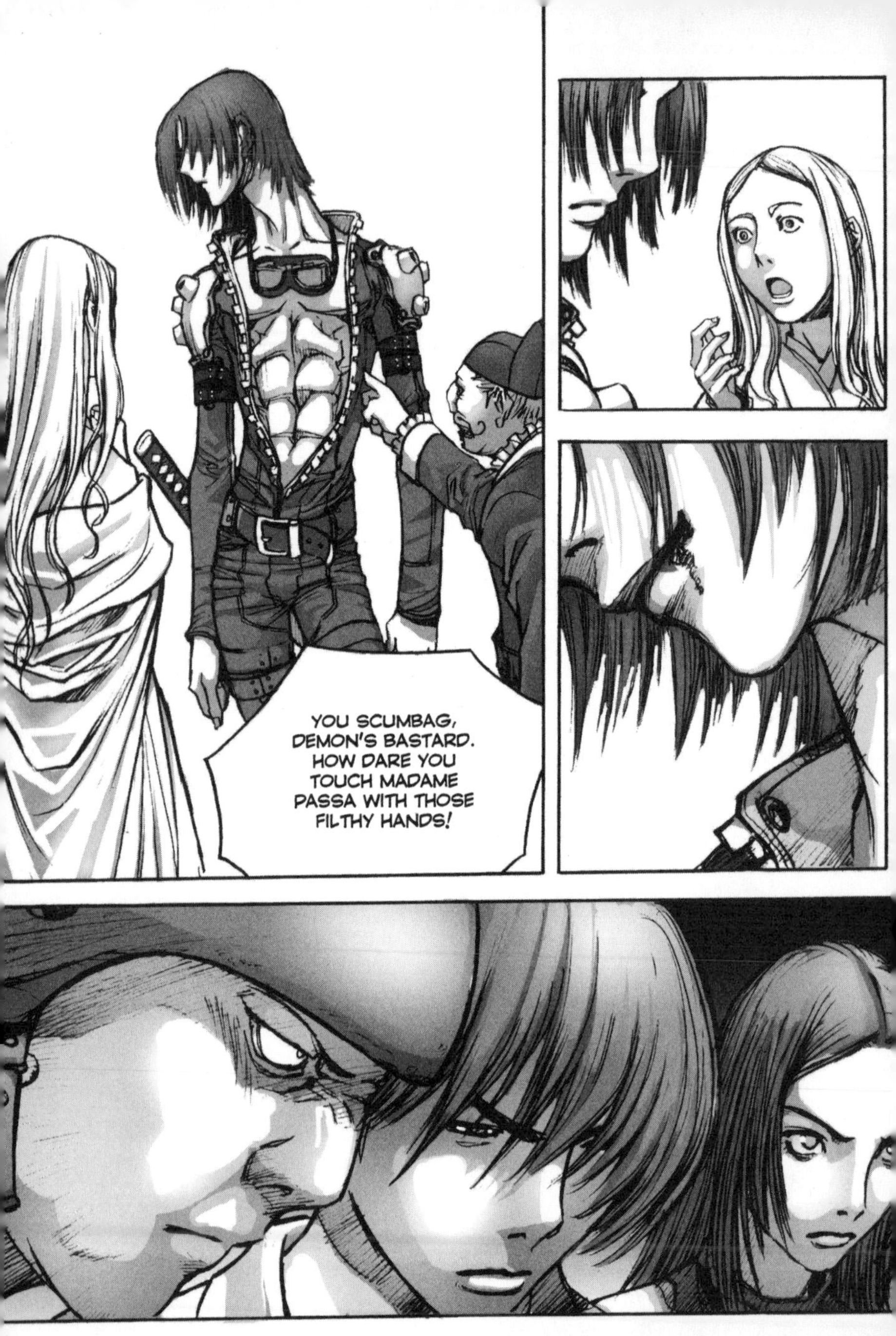
YOU SCUMBAG, DEMON'S BASTARD. HOW DARE YOU TOUCH MADAME PASSA WITH THOSE FILTHY HANDS!

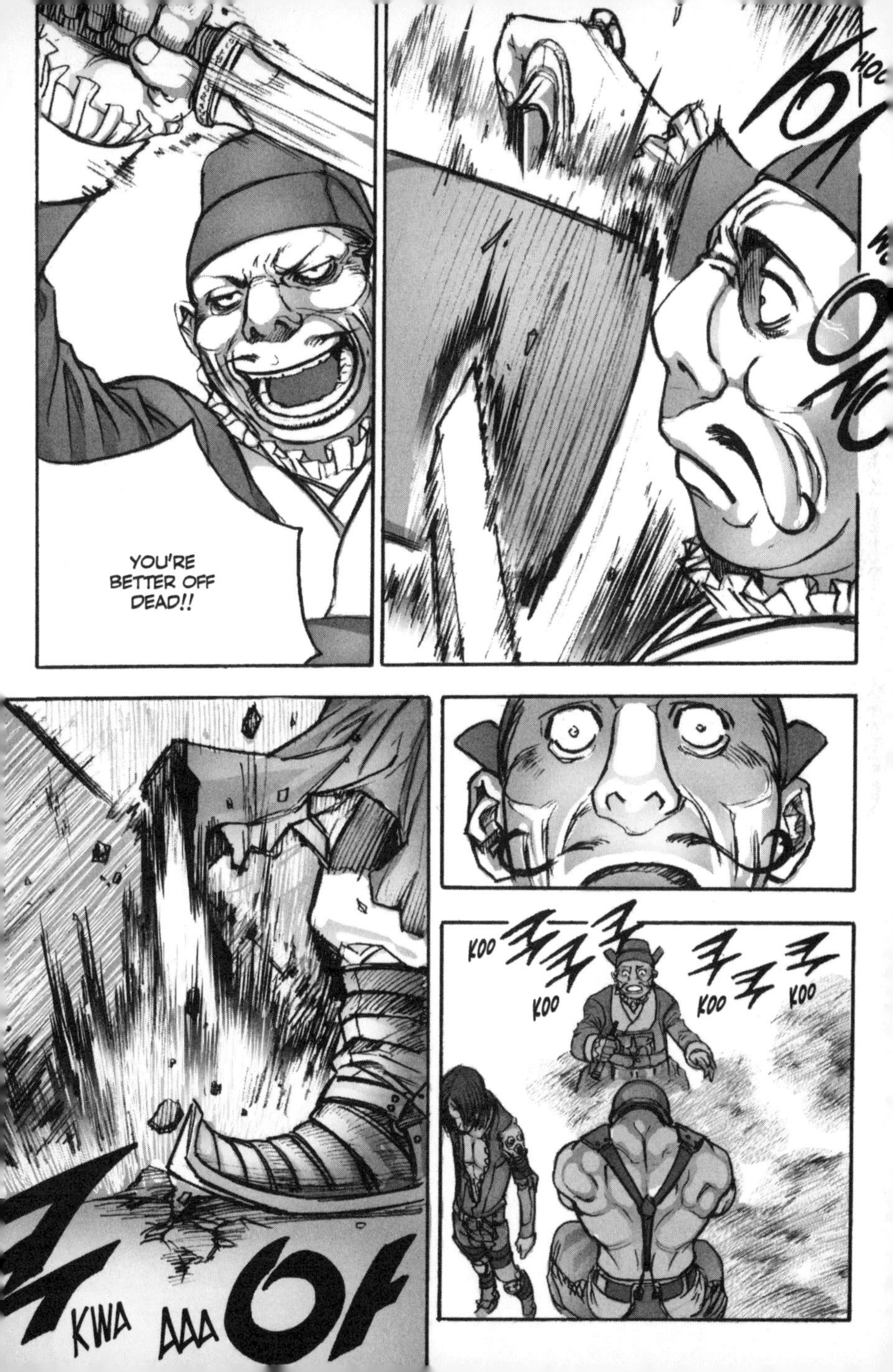
YOU'RE BETTER OFF DEAD!!
HOO
KWA AAA
KOO
KOO
KOO
KOO

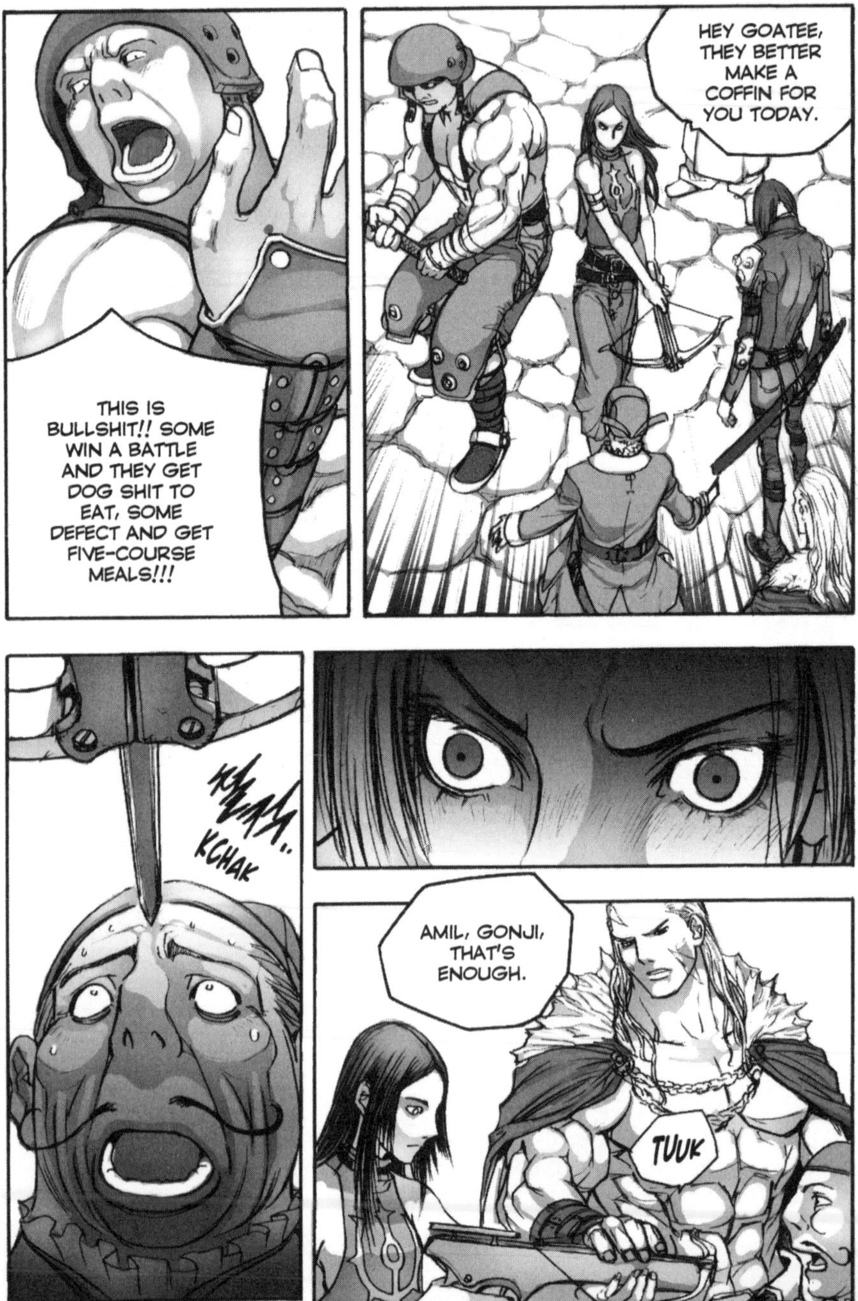
THIS IS BULLSHIT!! SOME WIN A BATTLE AND THEY GET DOG SHIT TO EAT, SOME DEFECT AND GET FIVE-COURSE MEALS!!!
HEY GOATEE, THEY BETTER MAKE A COFFIN FOR YOU TODAY.
KCHAK
AMIL, GONJI, THAT'S ENOUGH.
TUUK

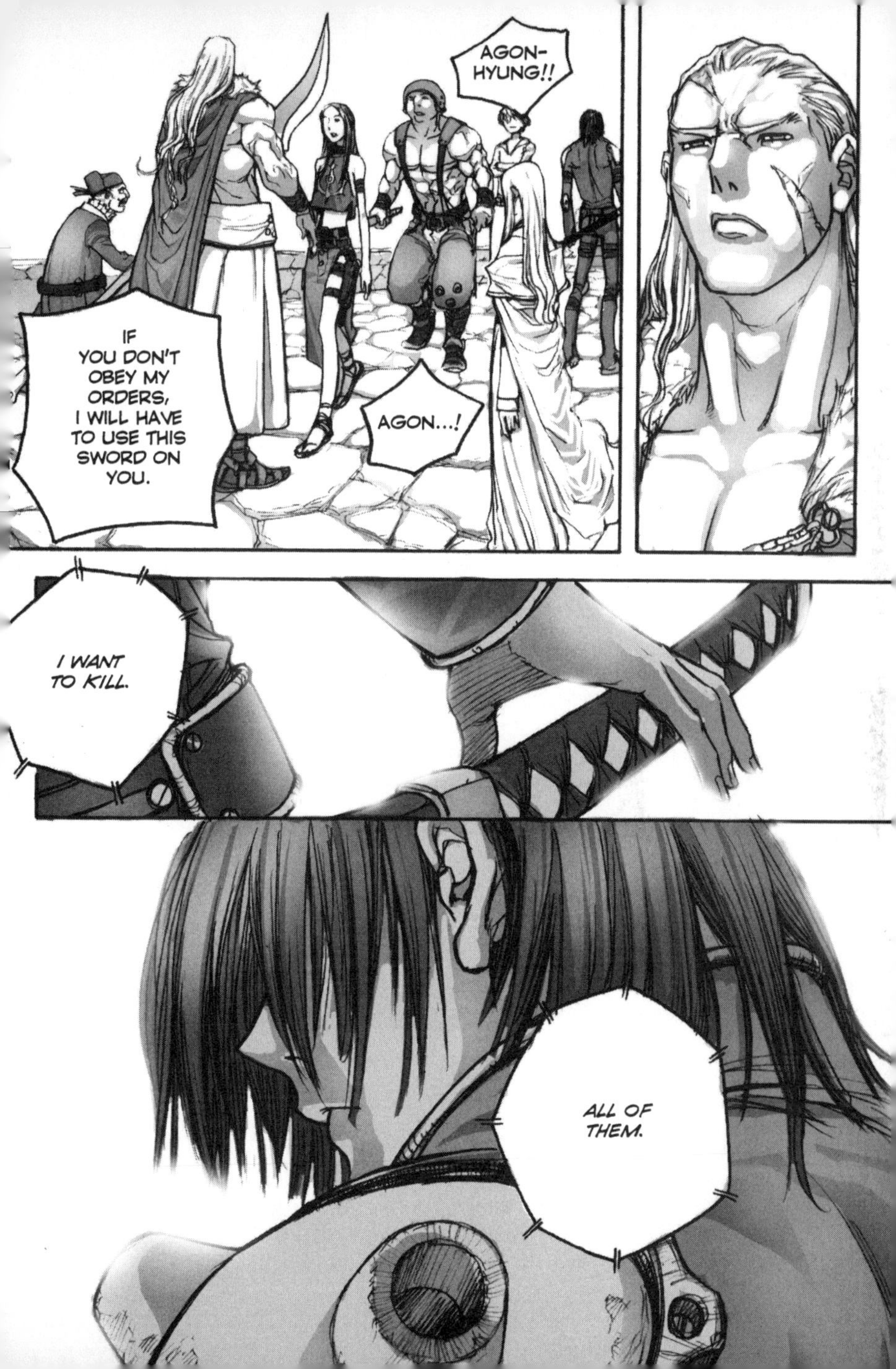
AGON-HYUNG!!
IF YOU DON'T OBEY MY ORDERS, I WILL HAVE TO USE THIS SWORD ON YOU.
AGON...!
I WANT TO KILL.
ALL OF THEM.

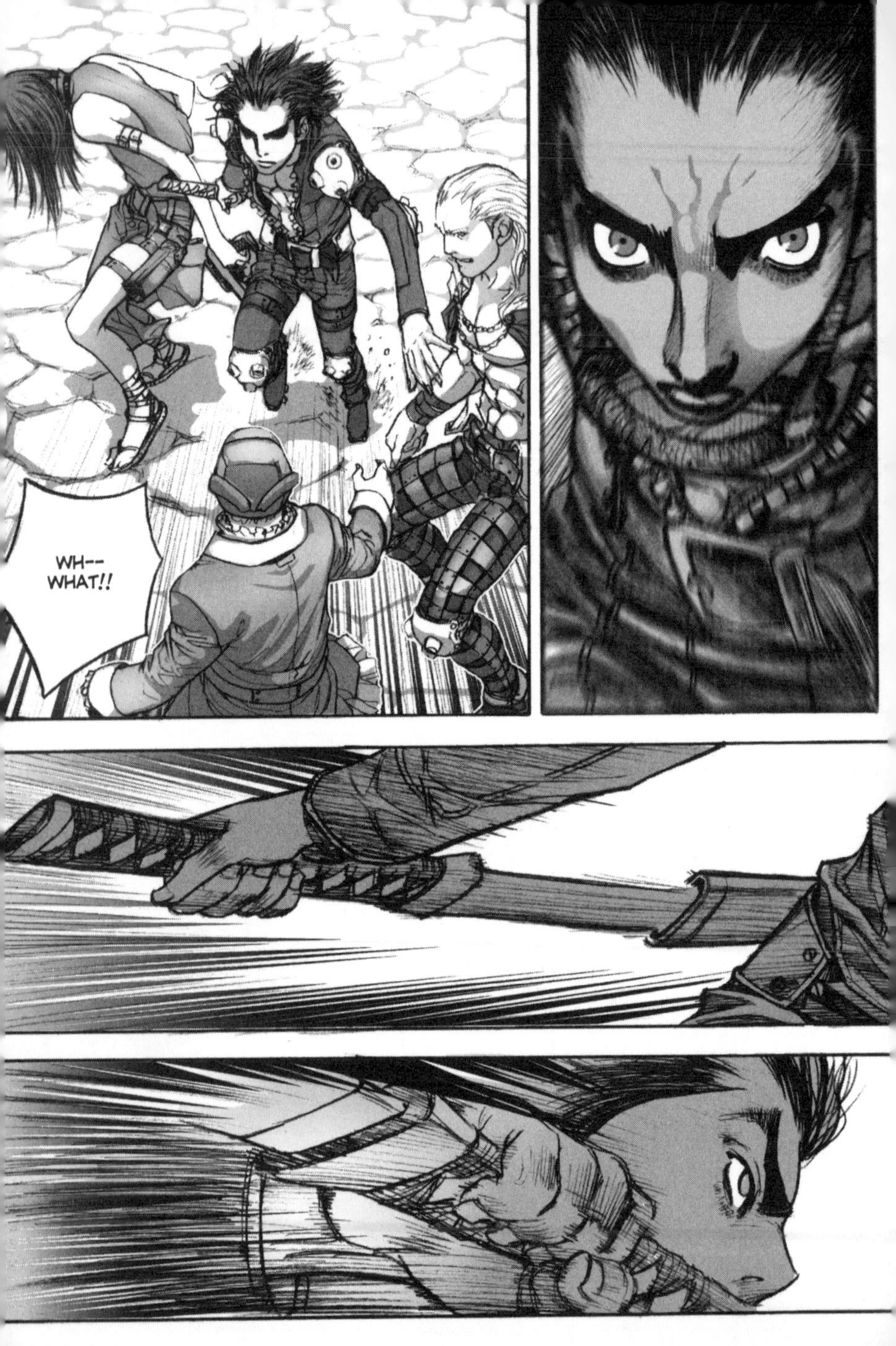
WH--
WHAT!!

WOOAAK!!

PLEASE STOP THIS!! IT'S ALL MY FAULT!!

SHHHT

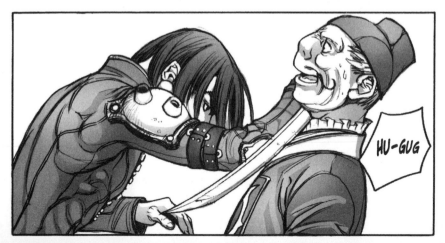

HU-GUG

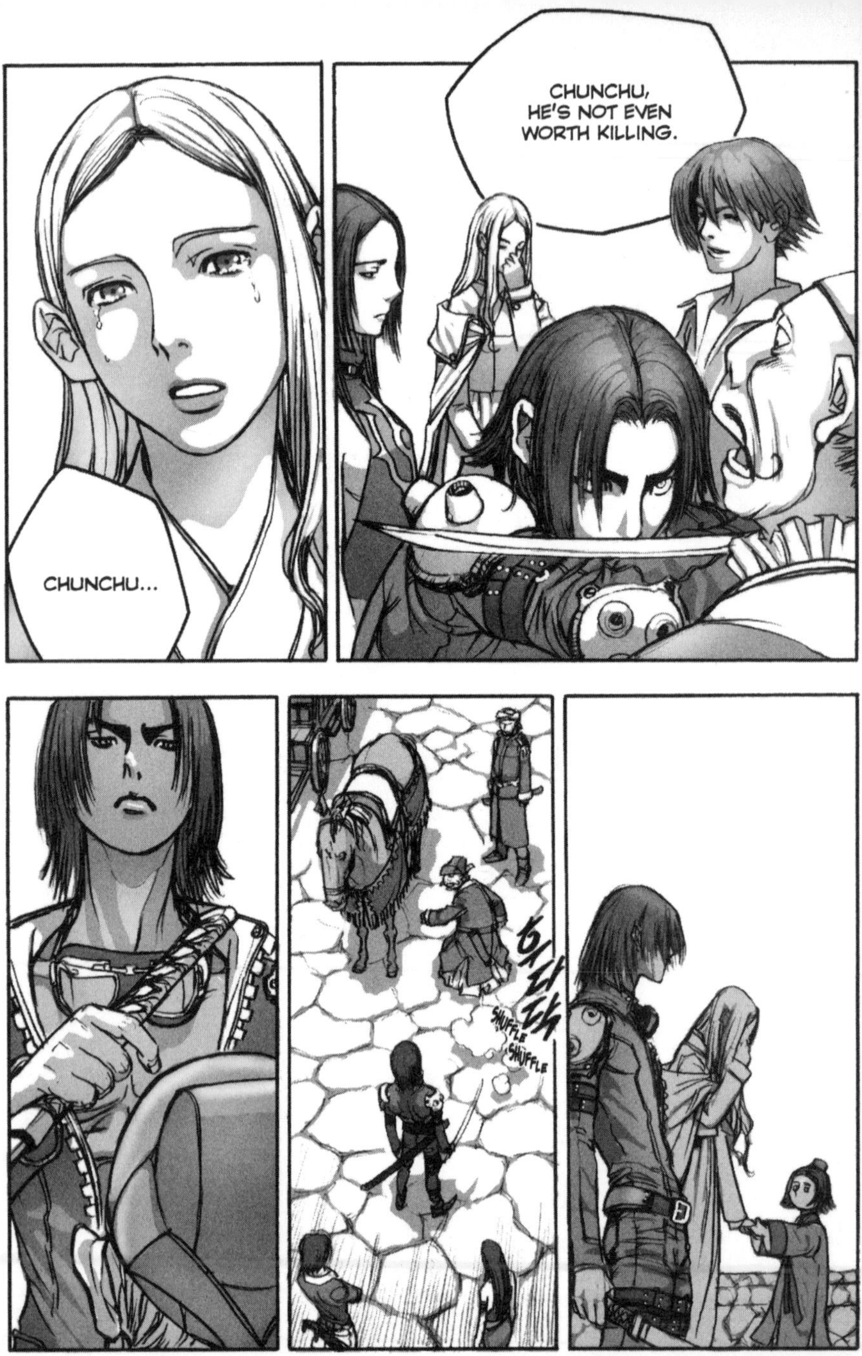
CHUNCHU...
CHUNCHU, HE'S NOT EVEN WORTH KILLING.
SHUFFLE SHUFFLE

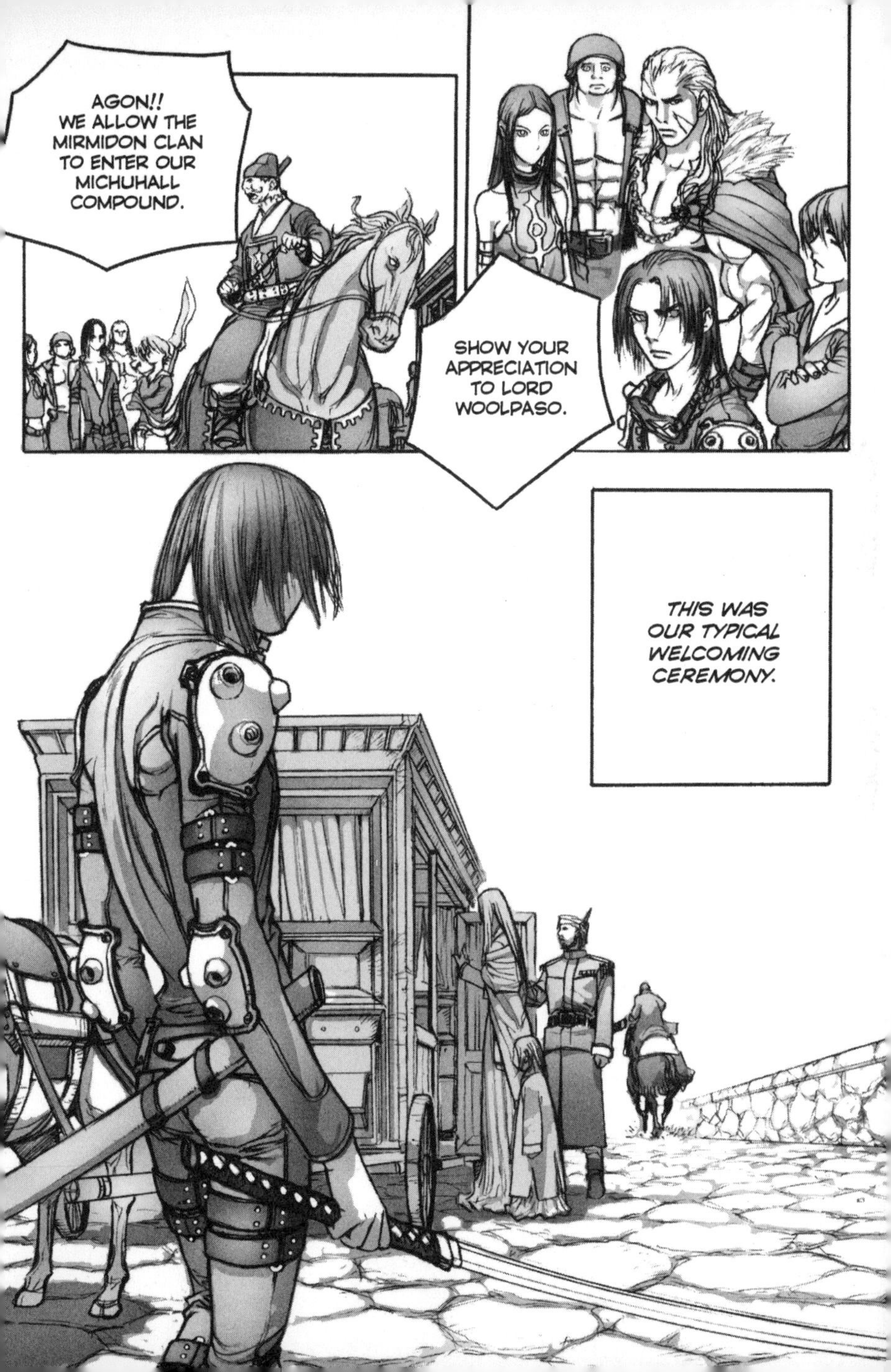
AGON!! WE ALLOW THE MIRMIDON CLAN TO ENTER OUR MICHUHALL COMPOUND.
SHOW YOUR APPRECIATION TO LORD WOOLPASO.
THIS WAS OUR TYPICAL WELCOMING CEREMONY.

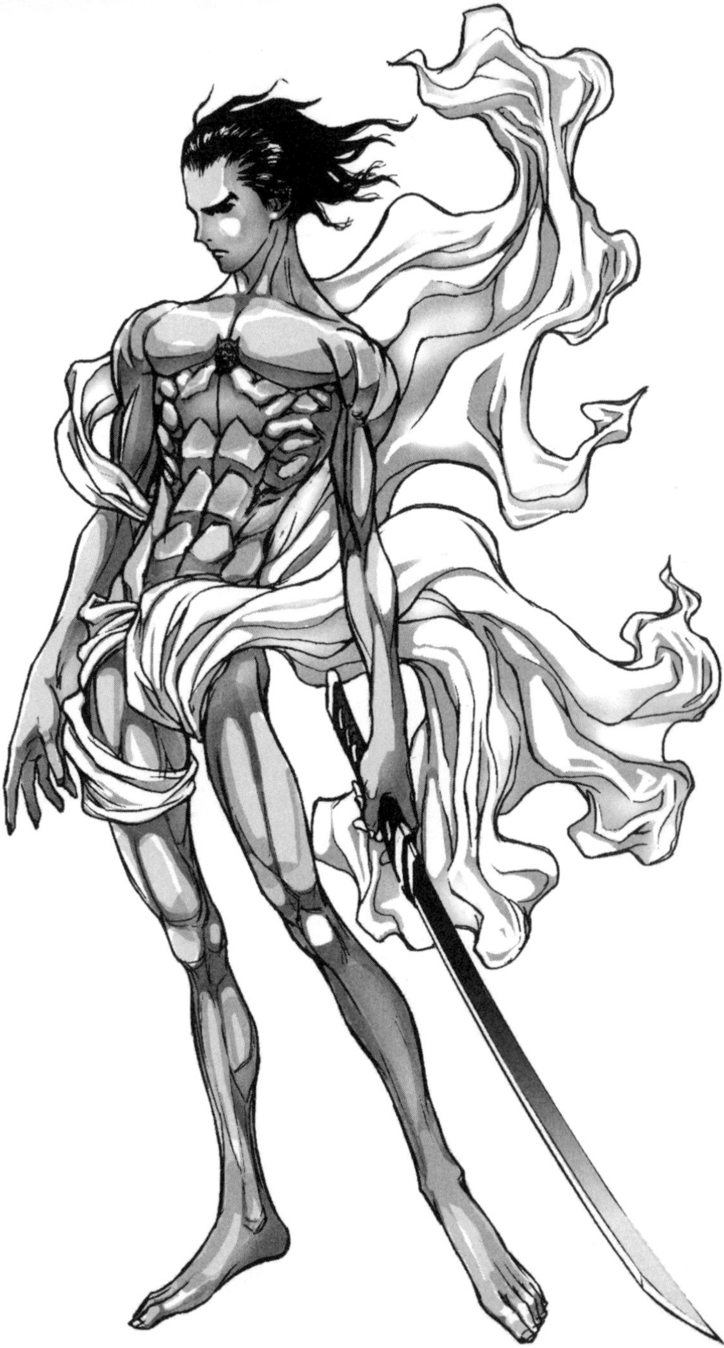

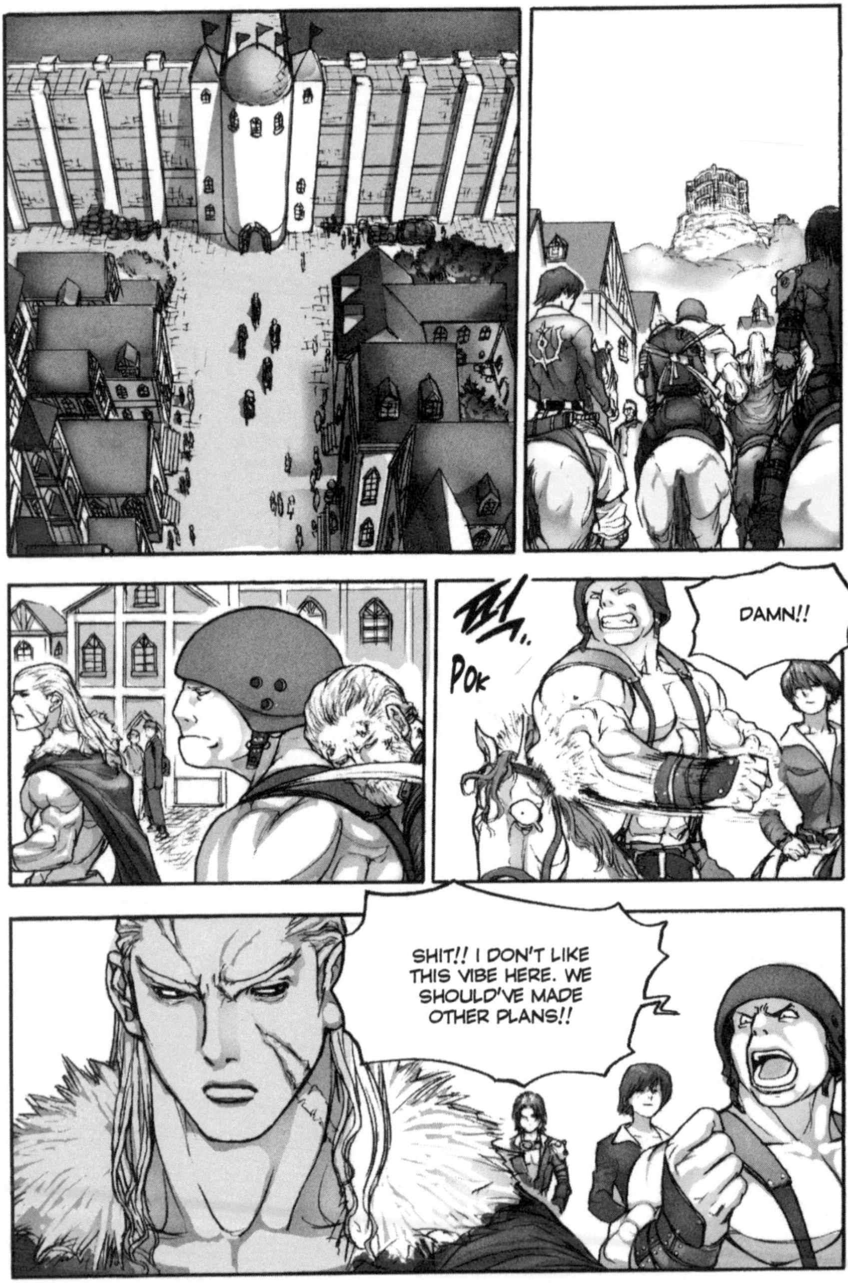
POK
DAMN!!
SHIT!! I DON'T LIKE THIS VIBE HERE. WE SHOULD'VE MADE OTHER PLANS!!

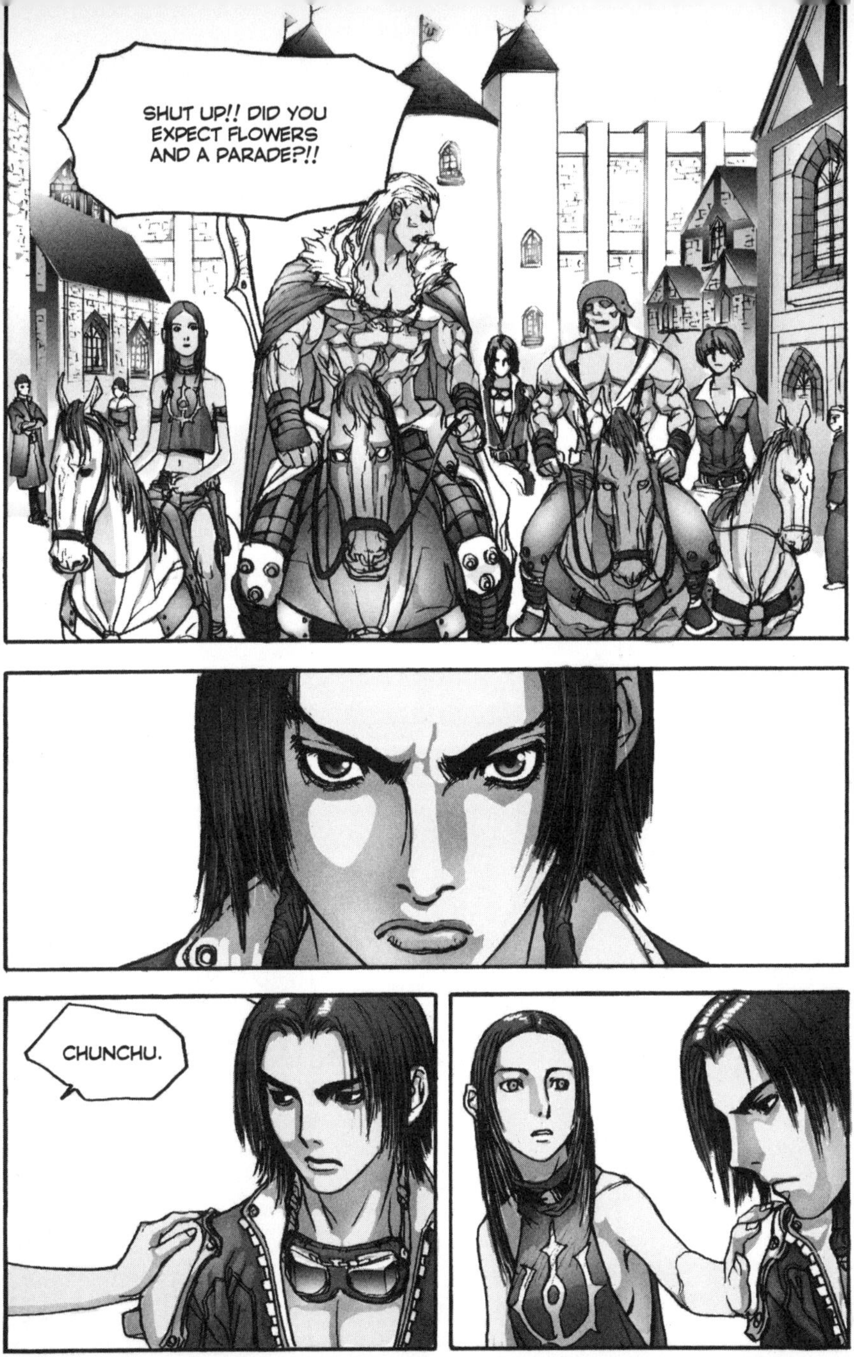
SHUT UP!! DID YOU EXPECT FLOWERS AND A PARADE?!!
CHUNCHU.

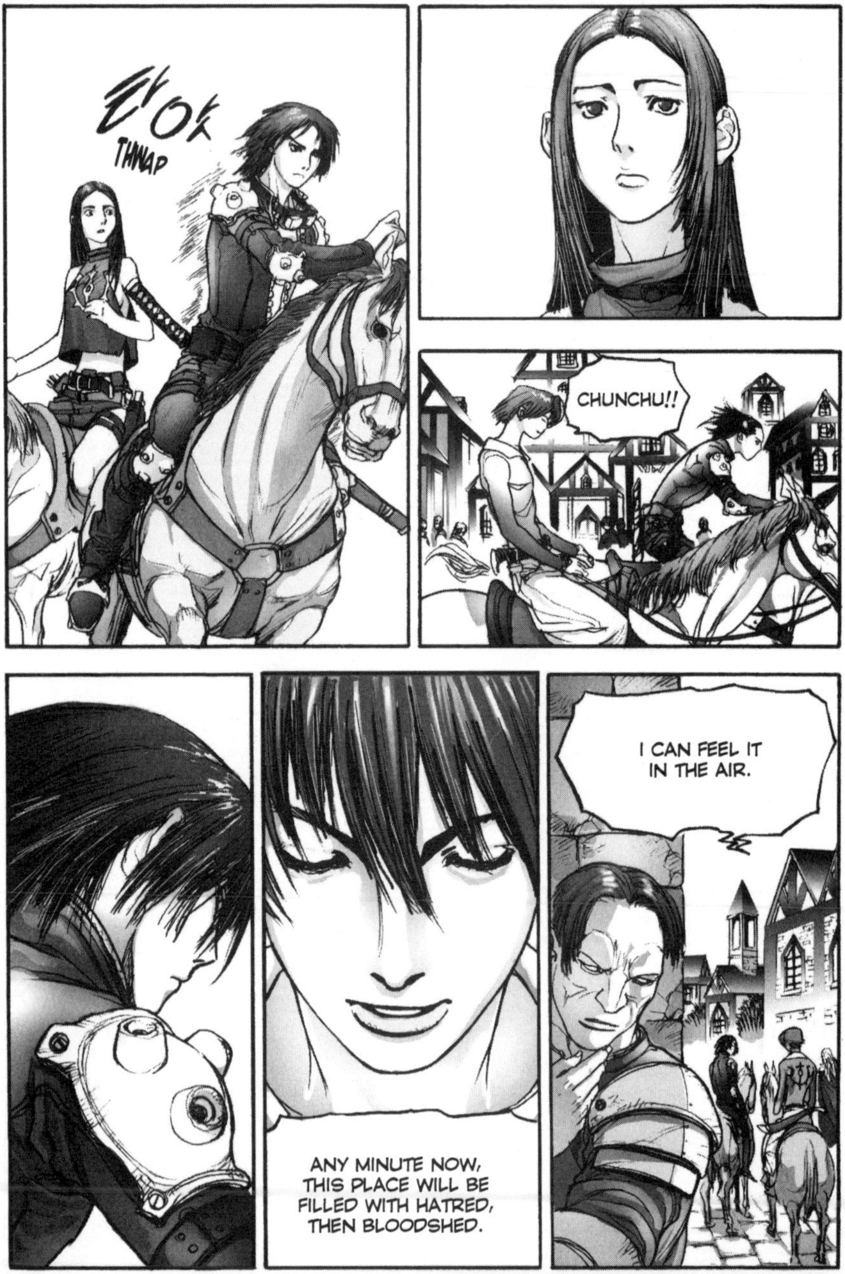

잡
THWAP
CHUNCHU!!
I CAN FEEL IT
IN THE AIR.
ANY MINUTE NOW,
THIS PLACE WILL BE
FILLED WITH HATRED,
THEN BLOODSHED.

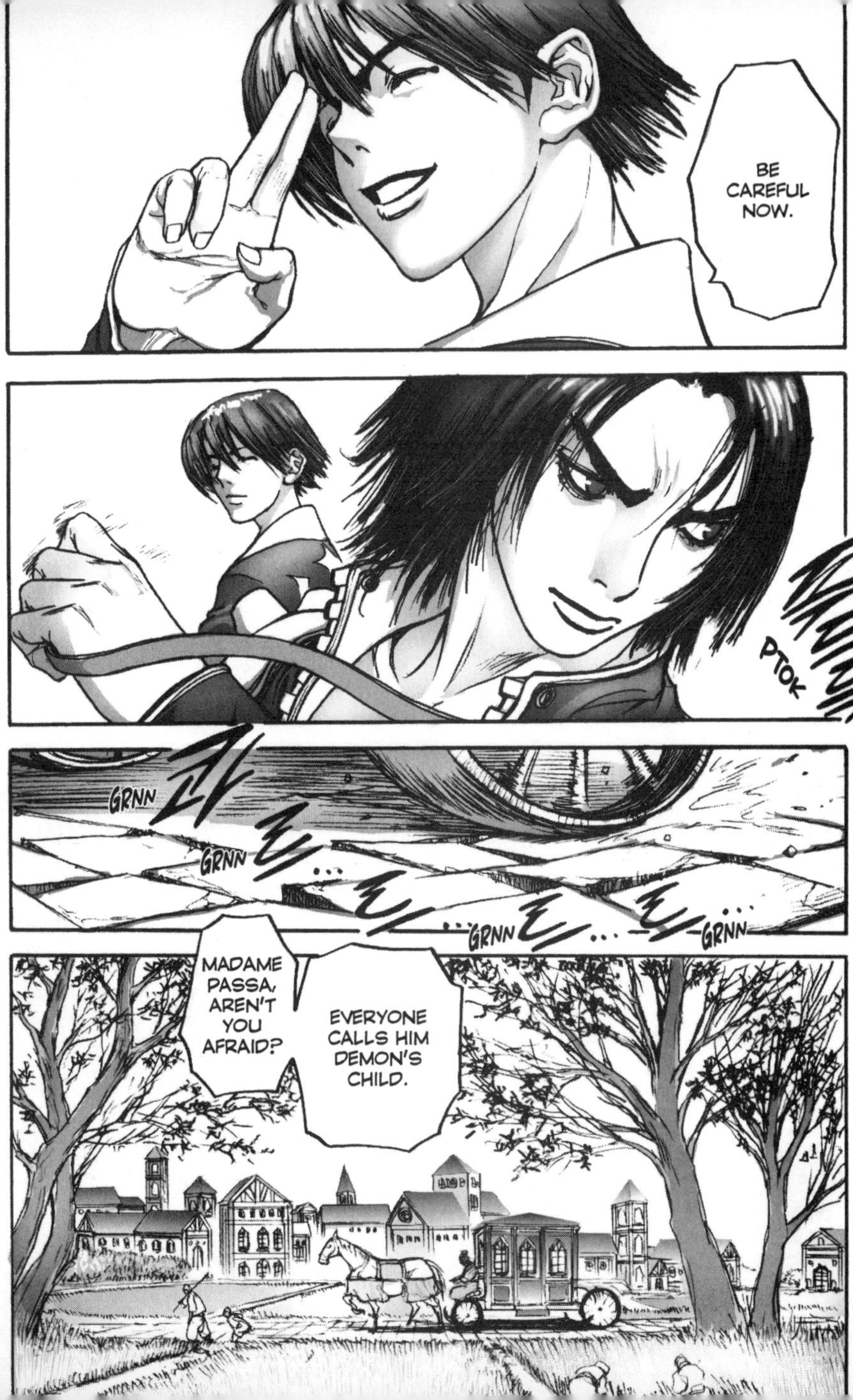
BE CAREFUL NOW.
PTOK
GRNN
GRNN
GRNN
GRNN
MADAME PASSA, AREN'T YOU AFRAID?
EVERYONE CALLS HIM DEMON'S CHILD.

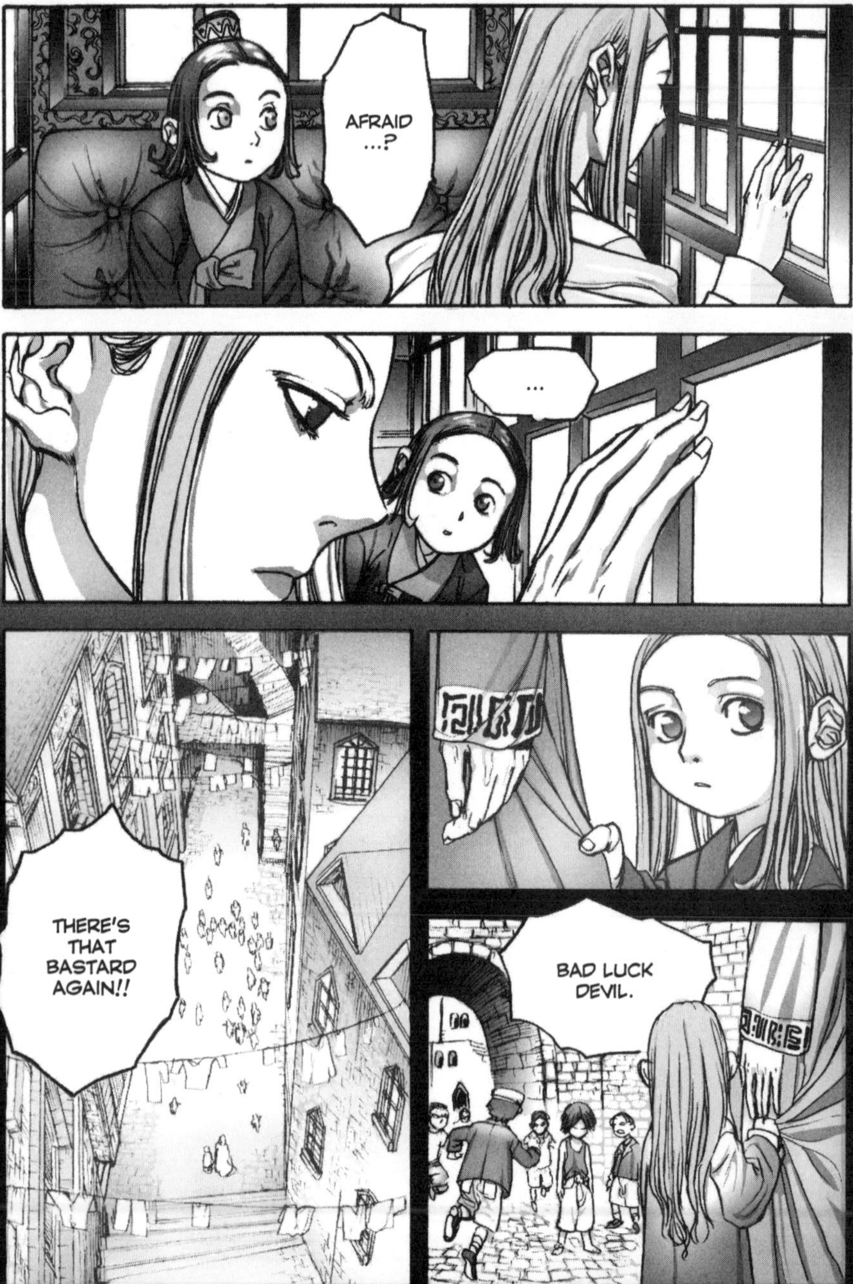
AFRAID ...?
...
THERE'S THAT BASTARD AGAIN!!
BAD LUCK DEVIL.

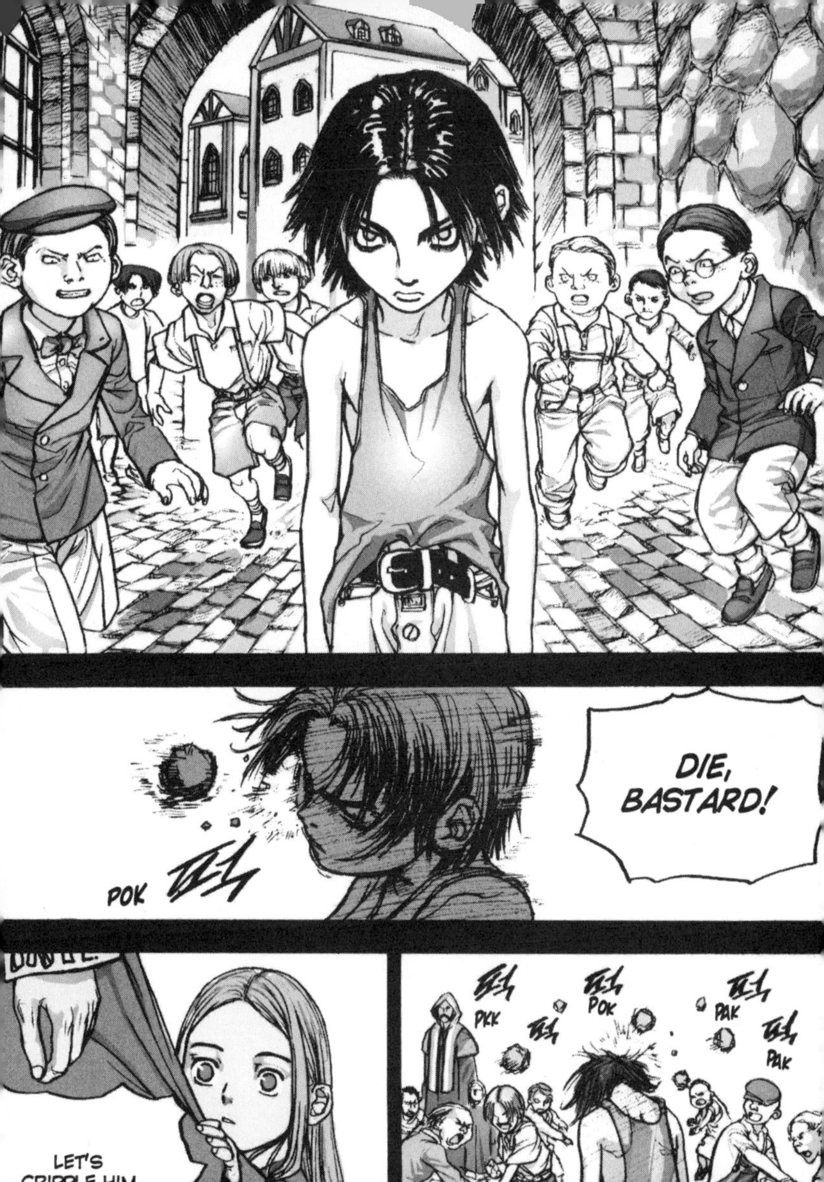
DIE, BASTARD!
POK
LET'S CRIPPLE HIM THIS TIME.
PKK
POK
PAK
PAK

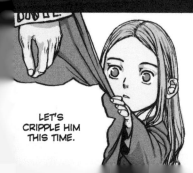

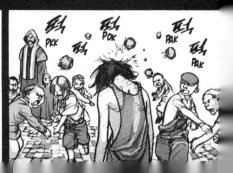

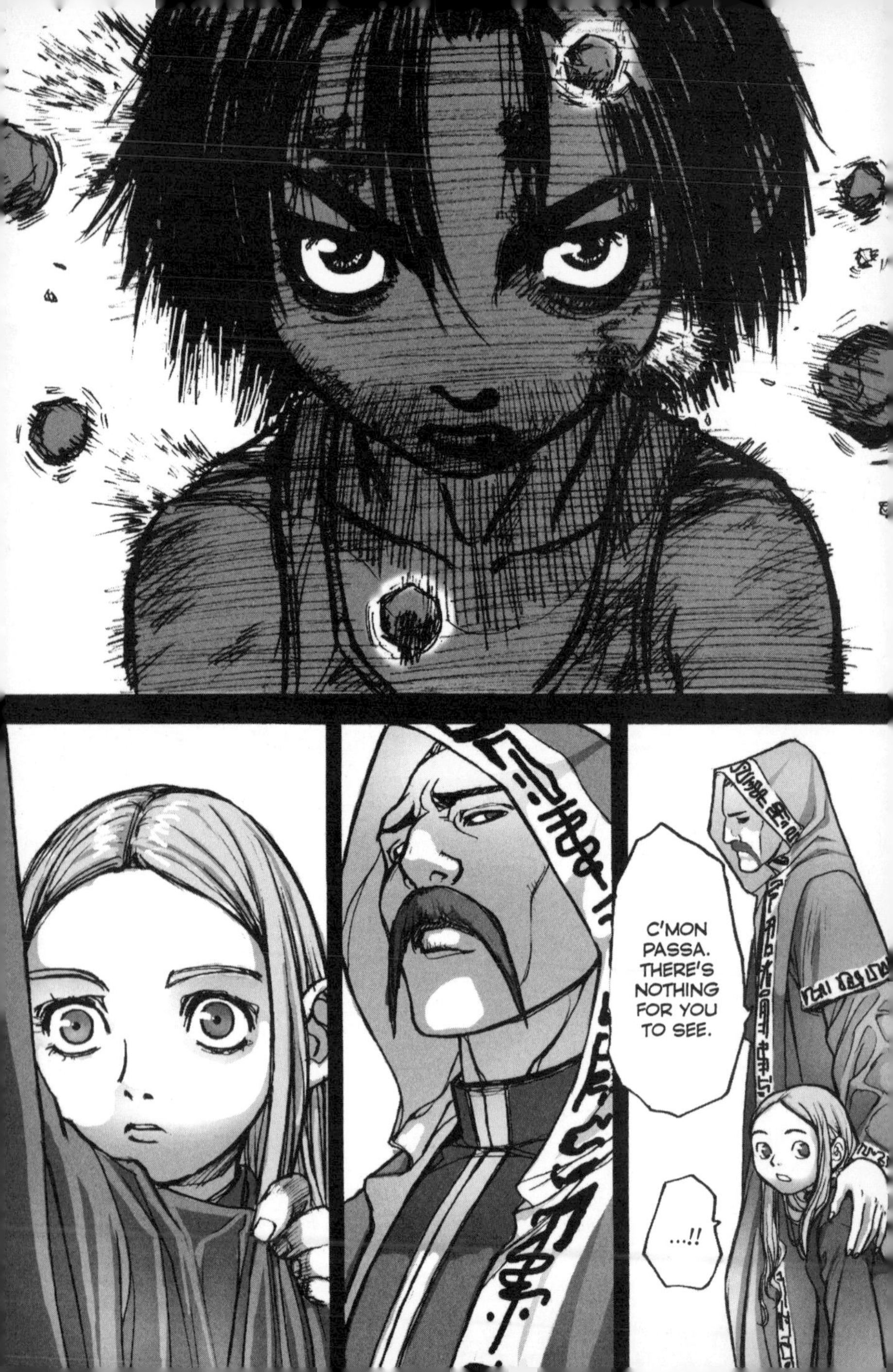
C'MON PASSA. THERE'S NOTHING FOR YOU TO SEE.
...!!

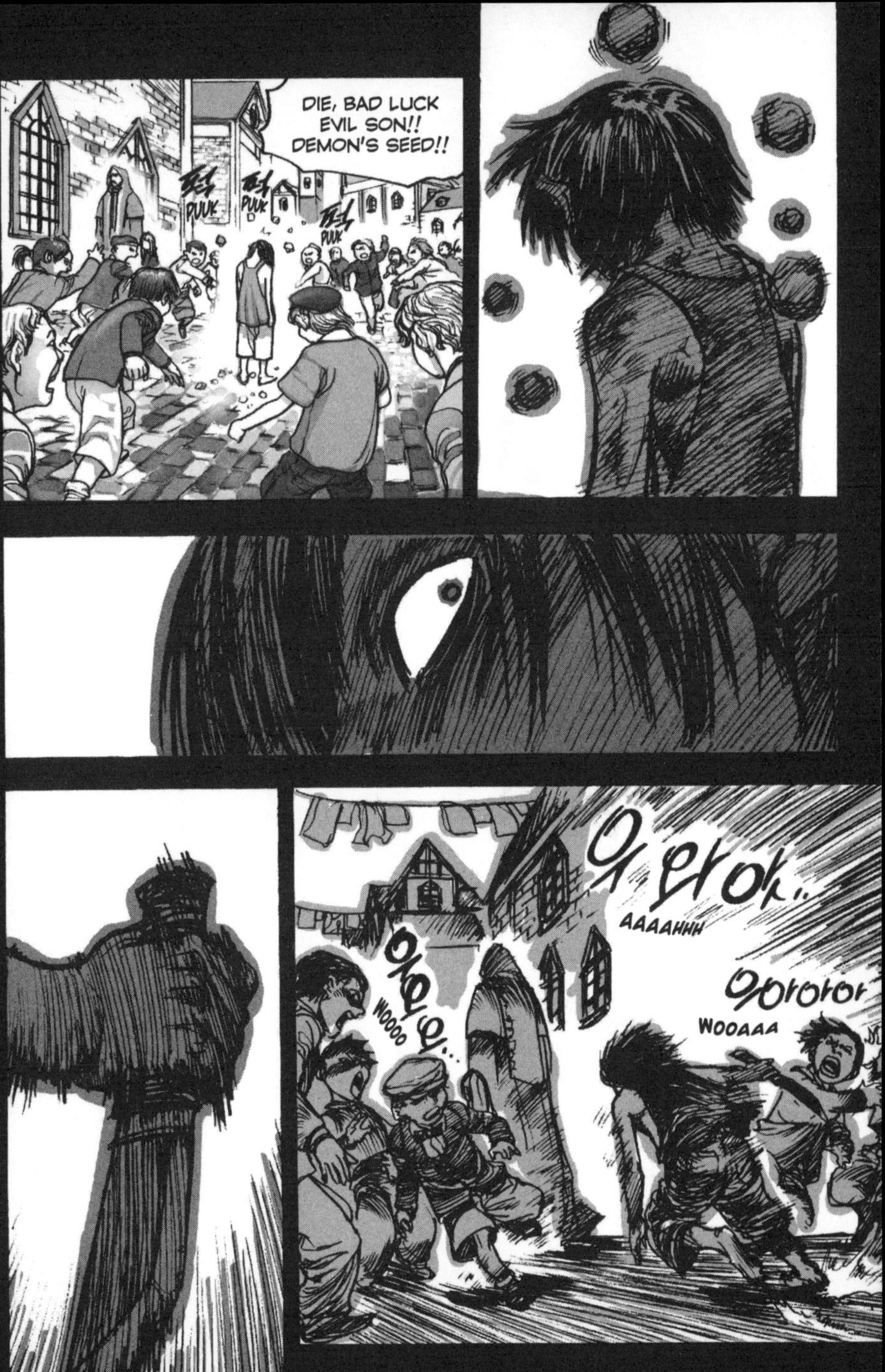
DIE, BAD LUCK EVIL SON!! DEMON'S SEED!!
PUUK
PUUK
PUUK
AAAAHHH
WOOOO
WOOAAA

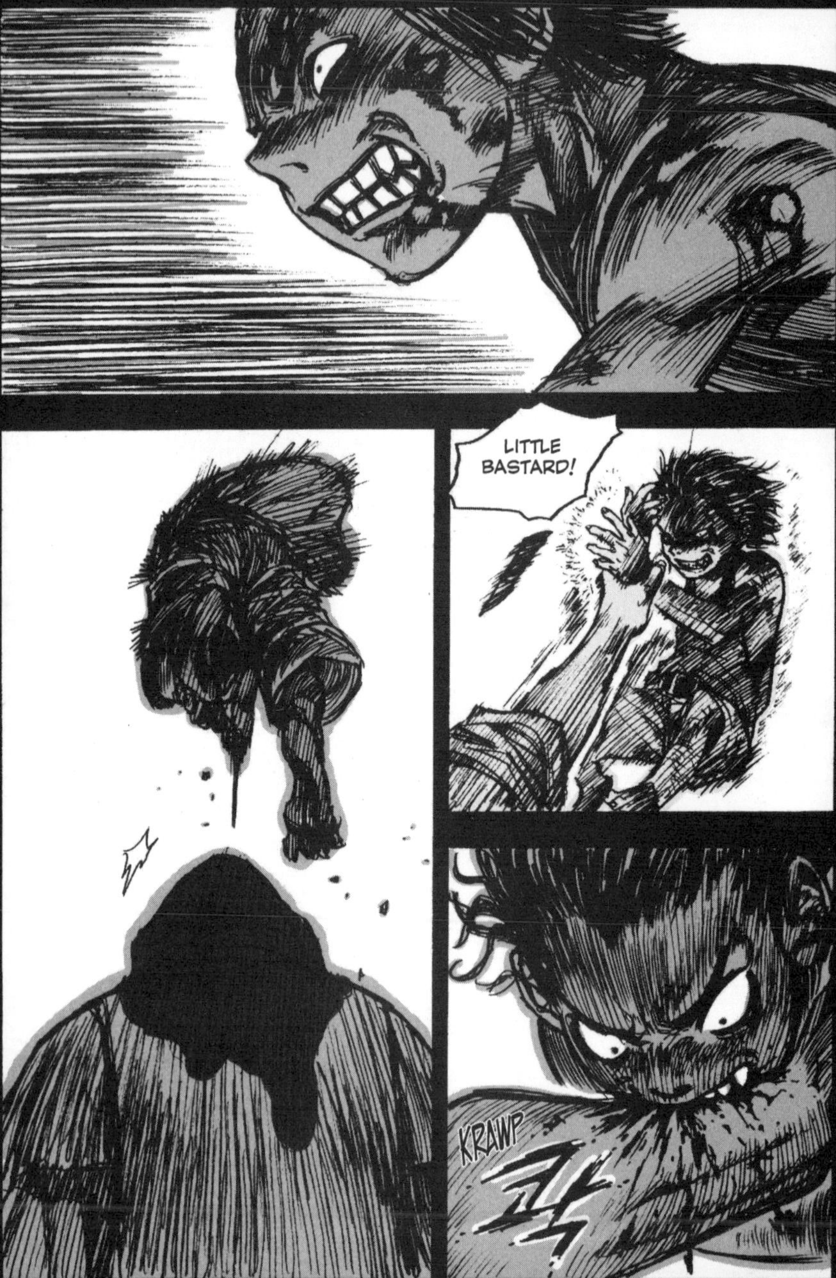
LITTLE BASTARD!
KRAWP

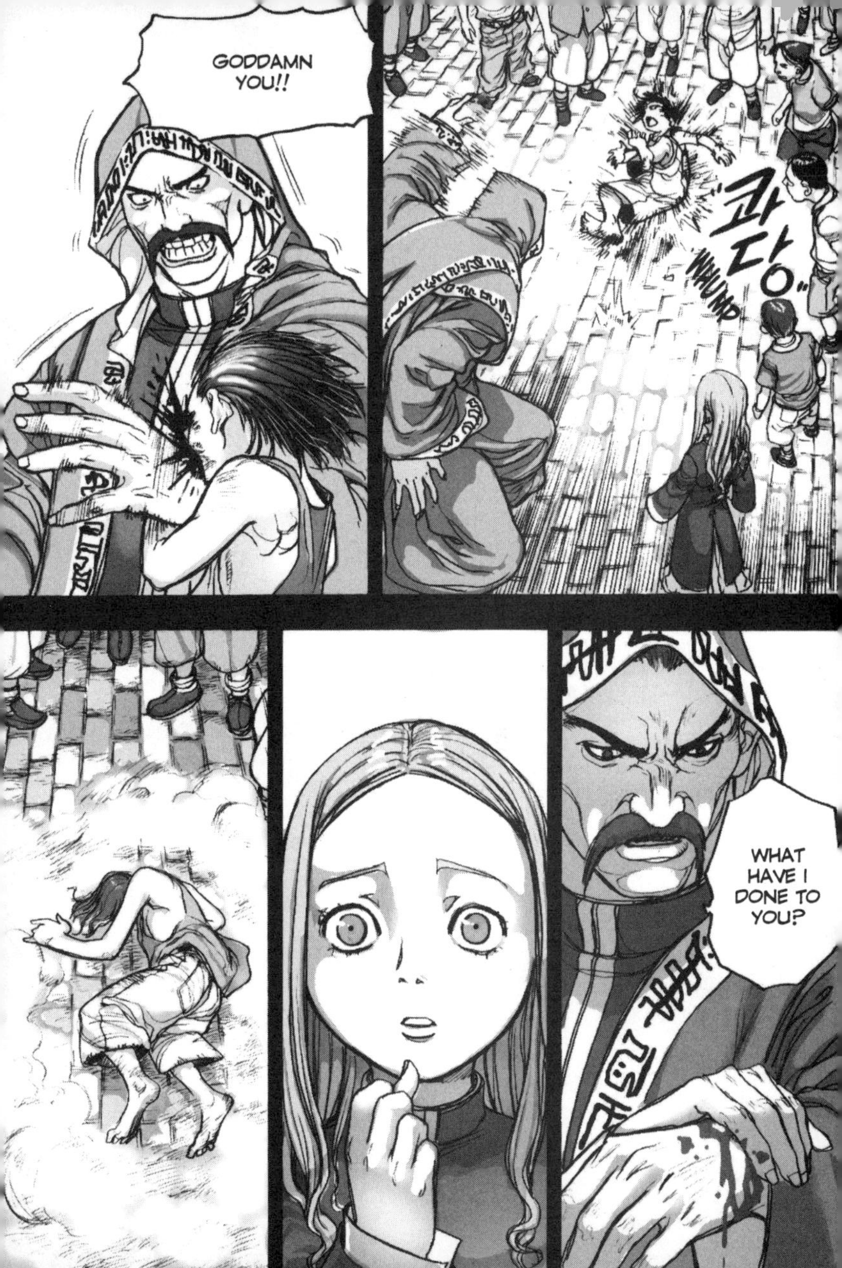
GODDAMN YOU!!
콰당
WHUMP
WHAT HAVE I DONE TO YOU?

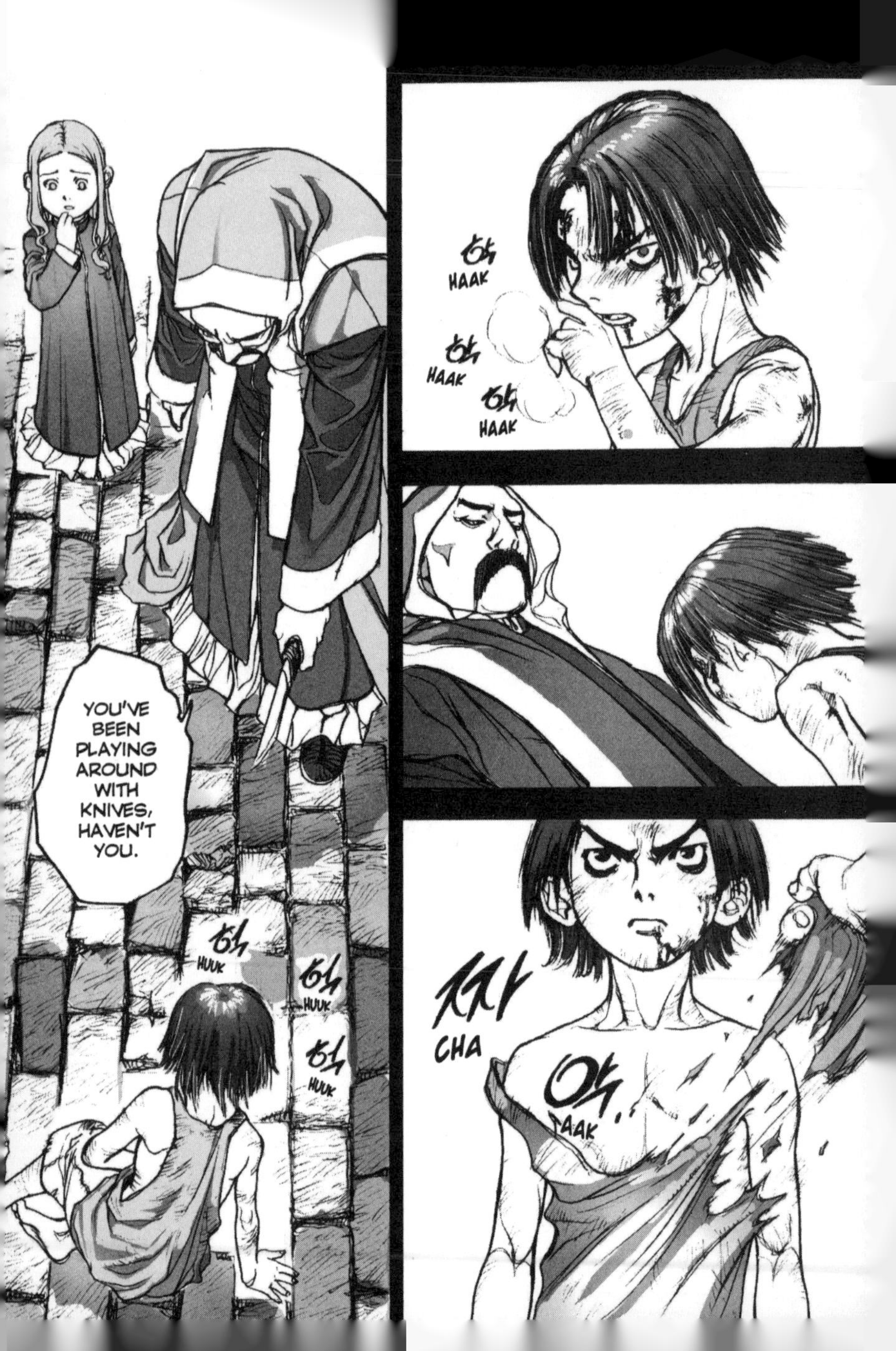
YOU'VE BEEN PLAYING AROUND WITH KNIVES, HAVEN'T YOU.
HUUK
HUUK
HUUK
HAAK
HAAK
HAAK
CHA
TAAK

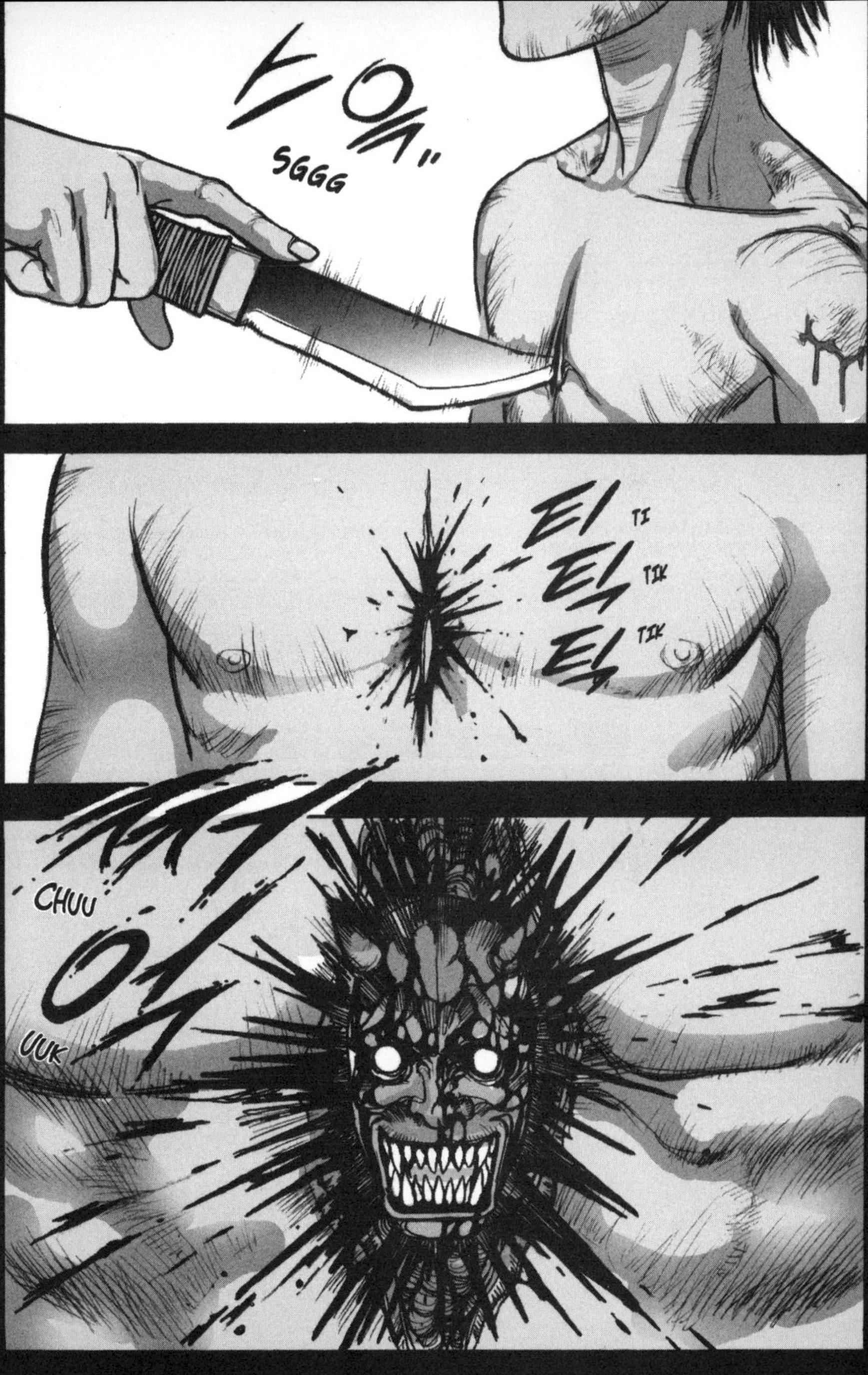
SGGG
TI
TIK
TIK
CHUU
UUK

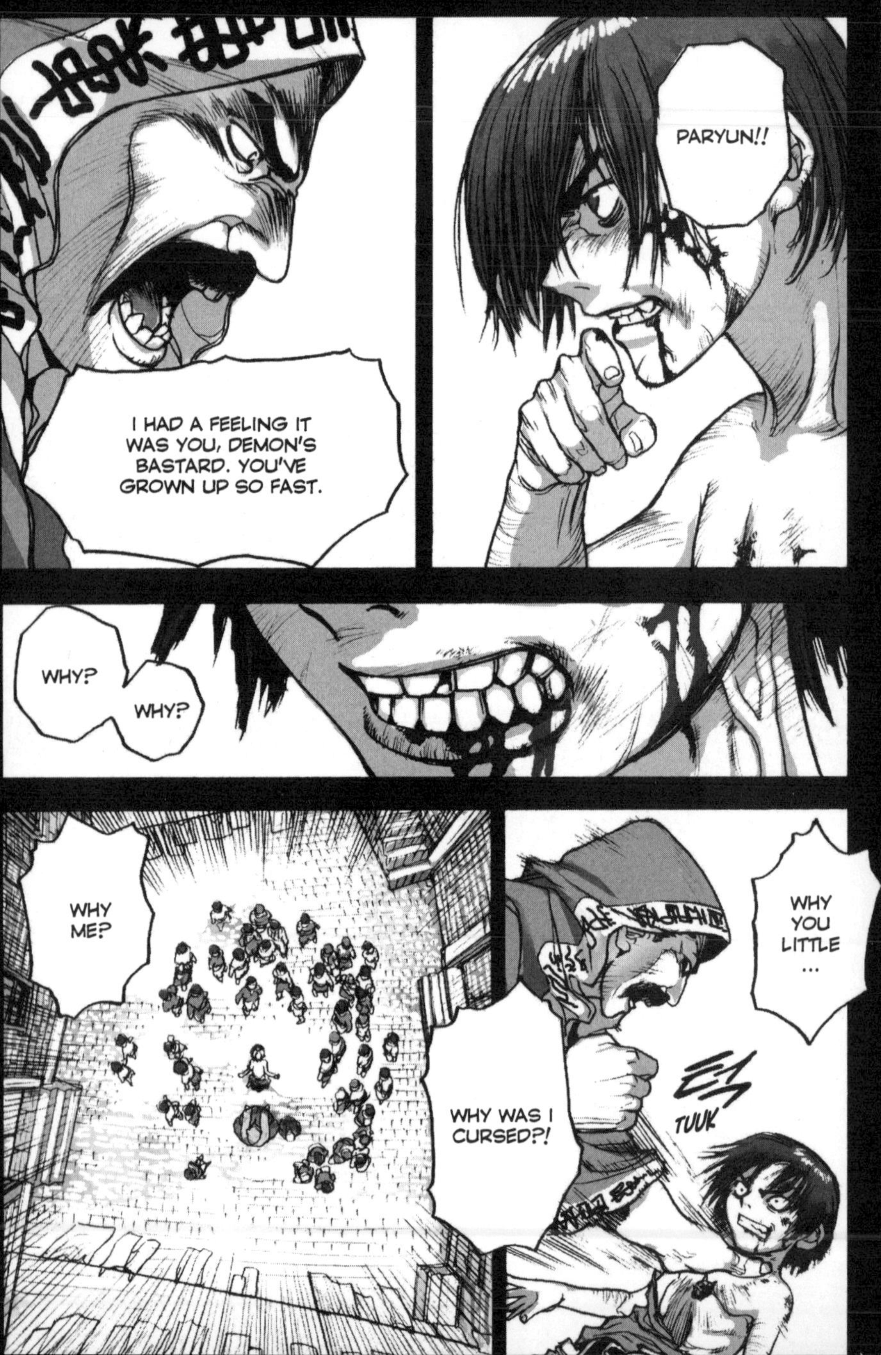
I HAD A FEELING IT WAS YOU, DEMON'S BASTARD. YOU'VE GROWN UP SO FAST.
PARYUN!!
WHY?
WHY?
WHY ME?
WHY WAS I CURSED?!
WHY YOU LITTLE ...
TUUK

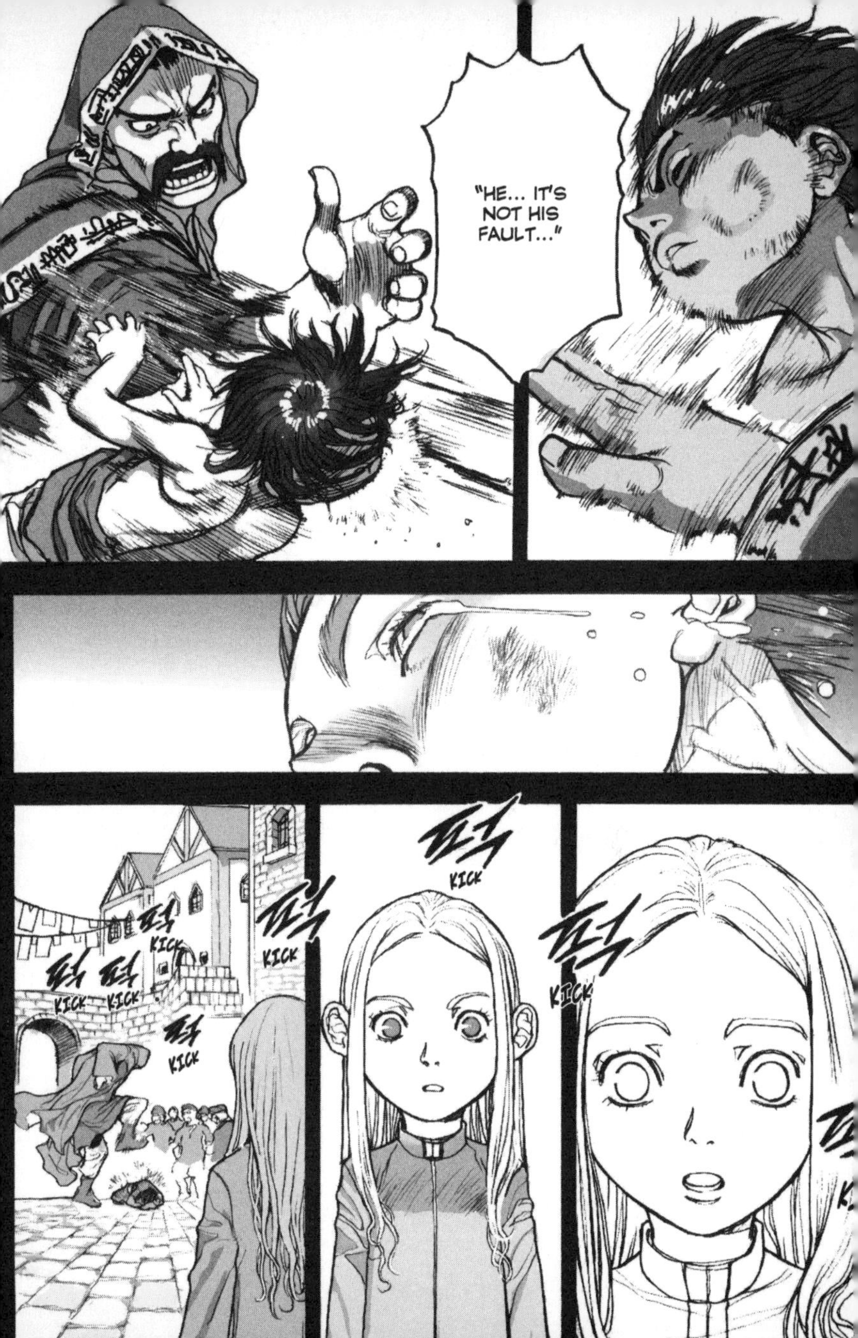
"HE... IT'S NOT HIS FAULT..."
KICK
KICK
KICK
KICK
KICK
KICK
KICK

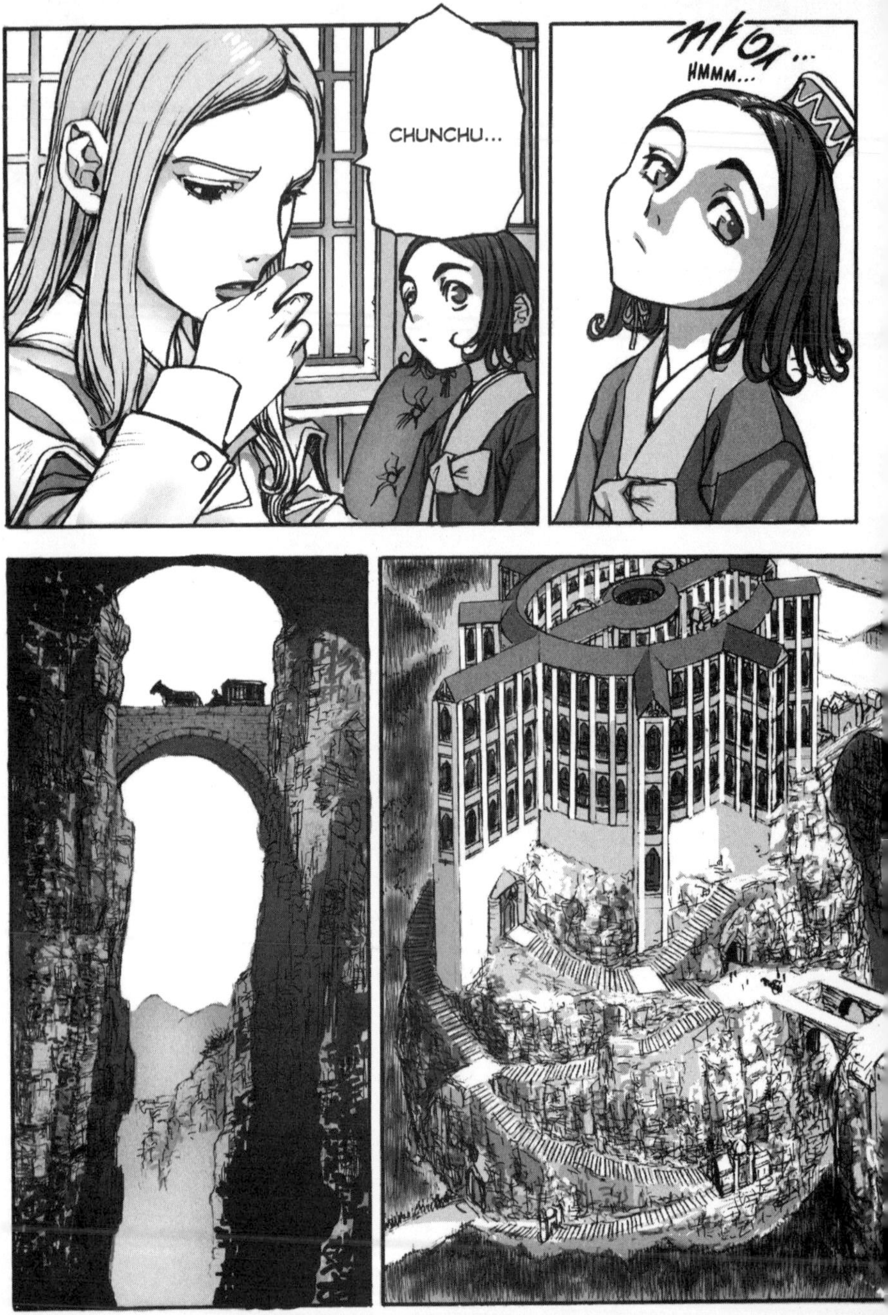

CHUNCHU...
끄덕이...
HMMM...

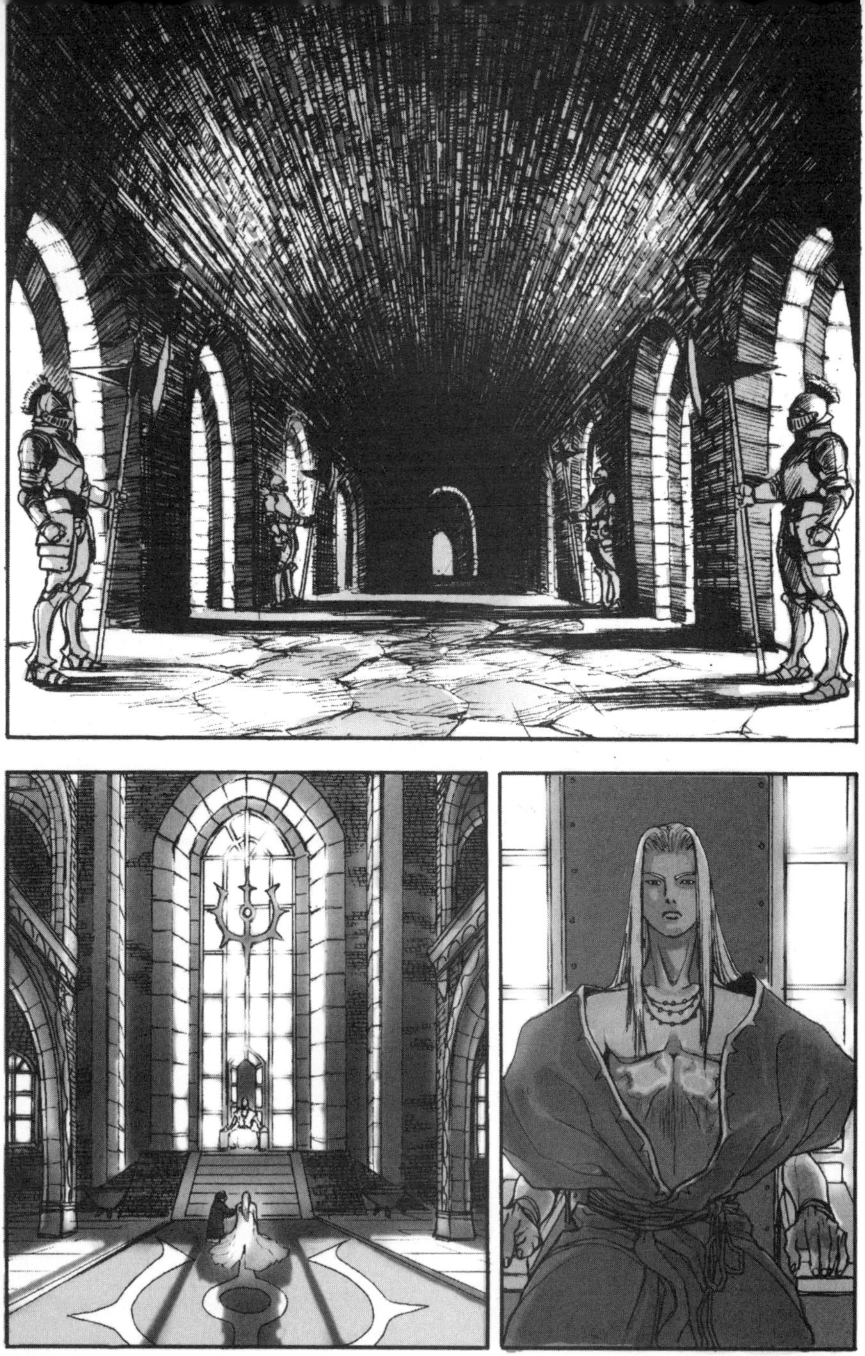

GREETINGS TO MASTER LORD WOOLPASO OF THE GREAT YEMAN EMPIRE.

I'M PASSA FROM THE HUMBLE GOMAH CLAN, NICE TO MAKE YOUR ACQUAINTANCE.

HAHAHA, IT'S ALMOST EMBARRASSING WITH THAT KIND OF FORMALITY FROM A WOMAN SOON TO BE MY WIFE.

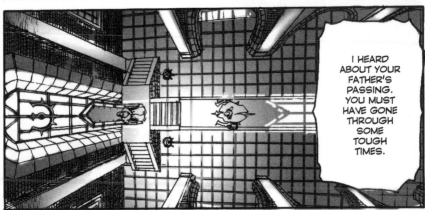

I HEARD ABOUT YOUR FATHER'S PASSING. YOU MUST HAVE GONE THROUGH SOME TOUGH TIMES.

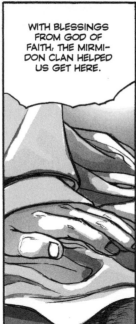

WITH BLESSINGS FROM GOD OF FAITH, THE MIRMIDON CLAN HELPED US GET HERE.

LET'S TALK ABOUT OTHER DETAILS LATER. YOU SHOULD GET SOME REST.

NO, MY LORD. WE OWE OUR LIFE TO THE MIRMIDON CLAN.

AND I WANT TO SOMEHOW PAY THEM BACK.

SK.

RRK

THE MIRMIDON CLAN IS A BUNCH OF LOW-LIFE THUGS AND THEY DON'T DESERVE ANYTHING.

B... BUT...

I THINK YOU'RE VERY TIRED.

WHY DON'T YOU GO BACK TO YOUR QUARTERS.

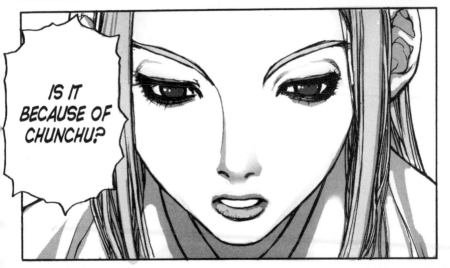

IS IT BECAUSE OF CHUNCHU?

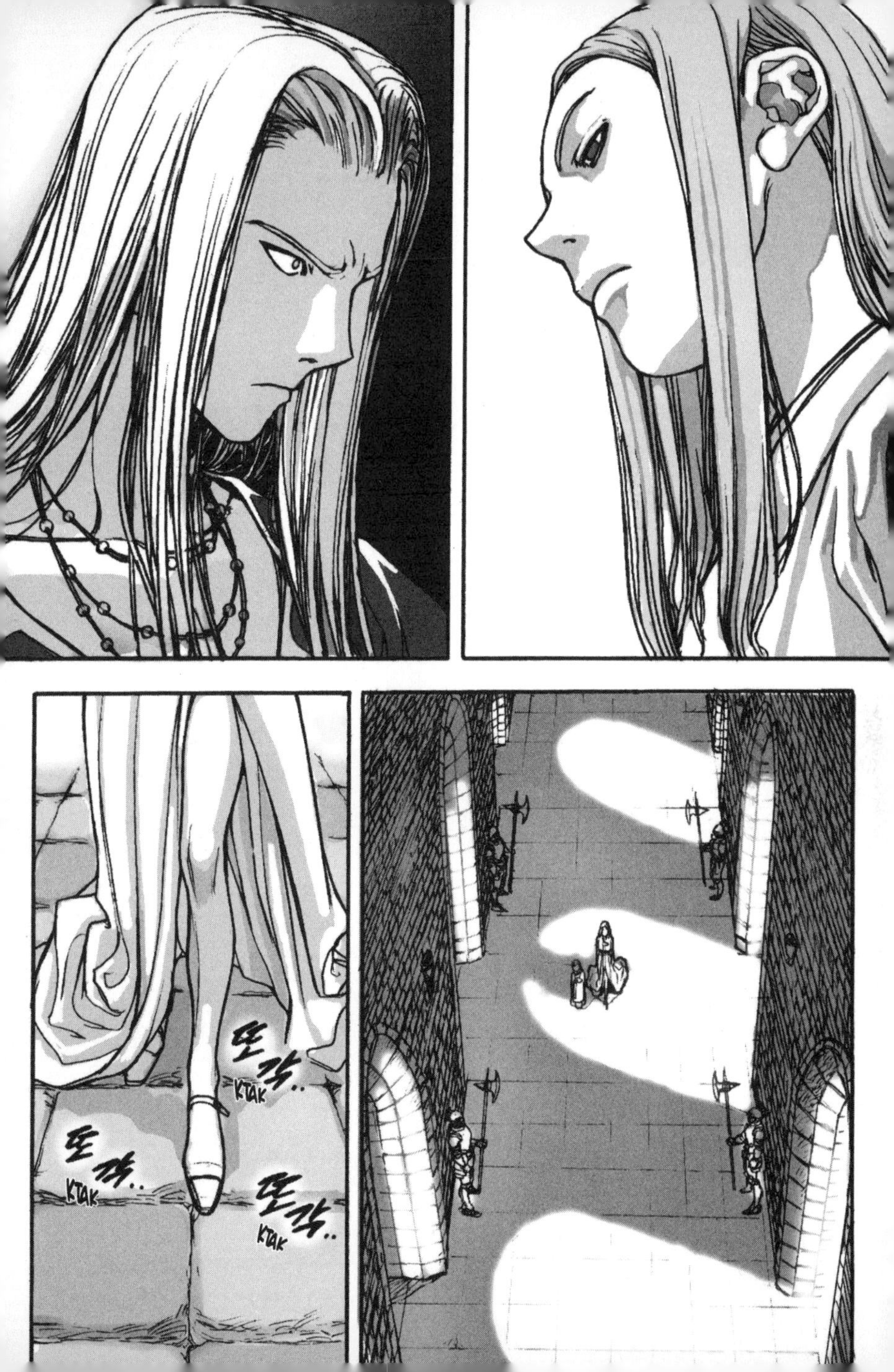
또각..
KTAK
또각..
KTAK
또각..
KTAK

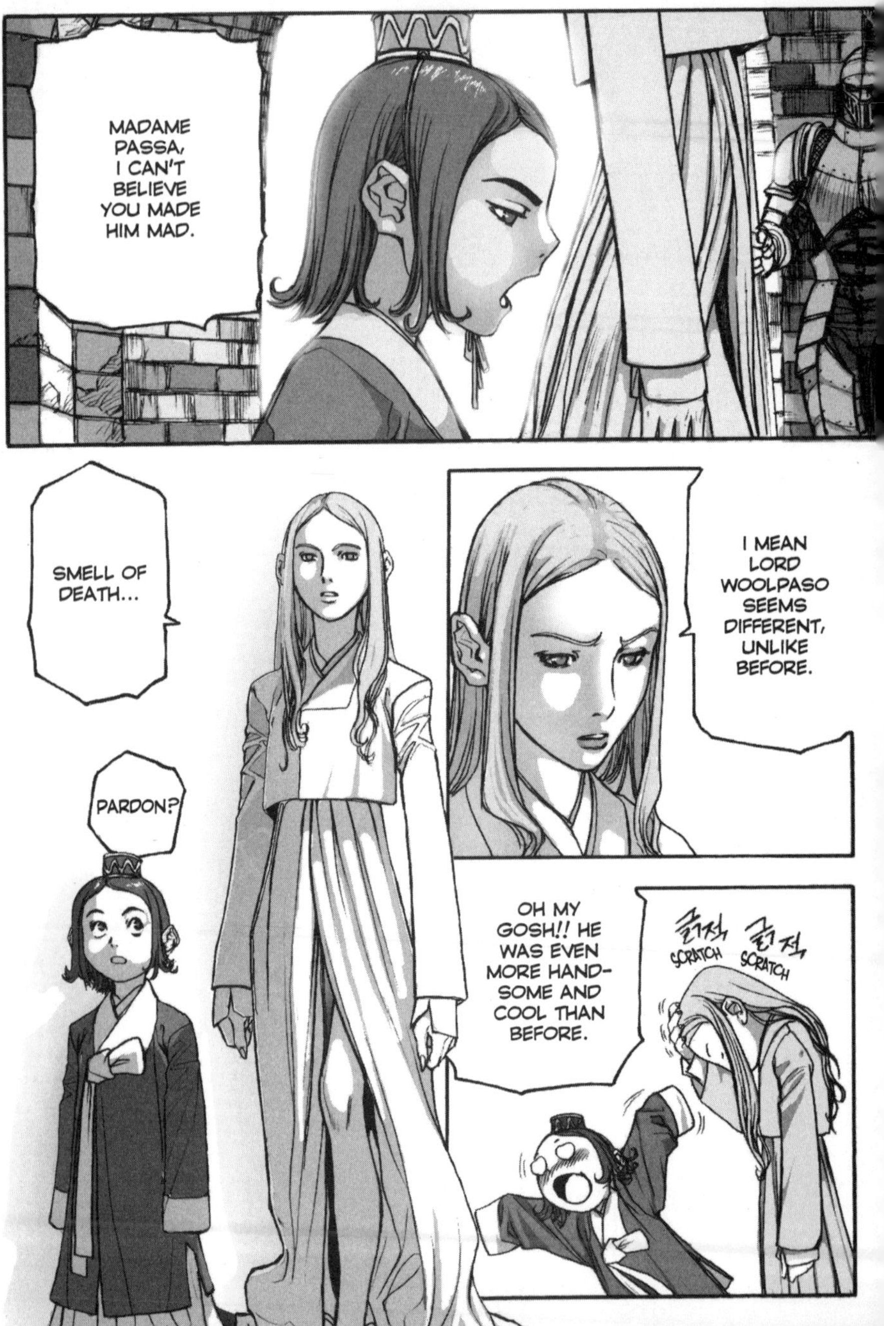
MADAME PASSA, I CAN'T BELIEVE YOU MADE HIM MAD.
I MEAN LORD WOOLPASO SEEMS DIFFERENT, UNLIKE BEFORE.
SMELL OF DEATH...
PARDON?
OH MY GOSH!! HE WAS EVEN MORE HAND-SOME AND COOL THAN BEFORE.
긁적 SCRATCH
긁적 SCRATCH

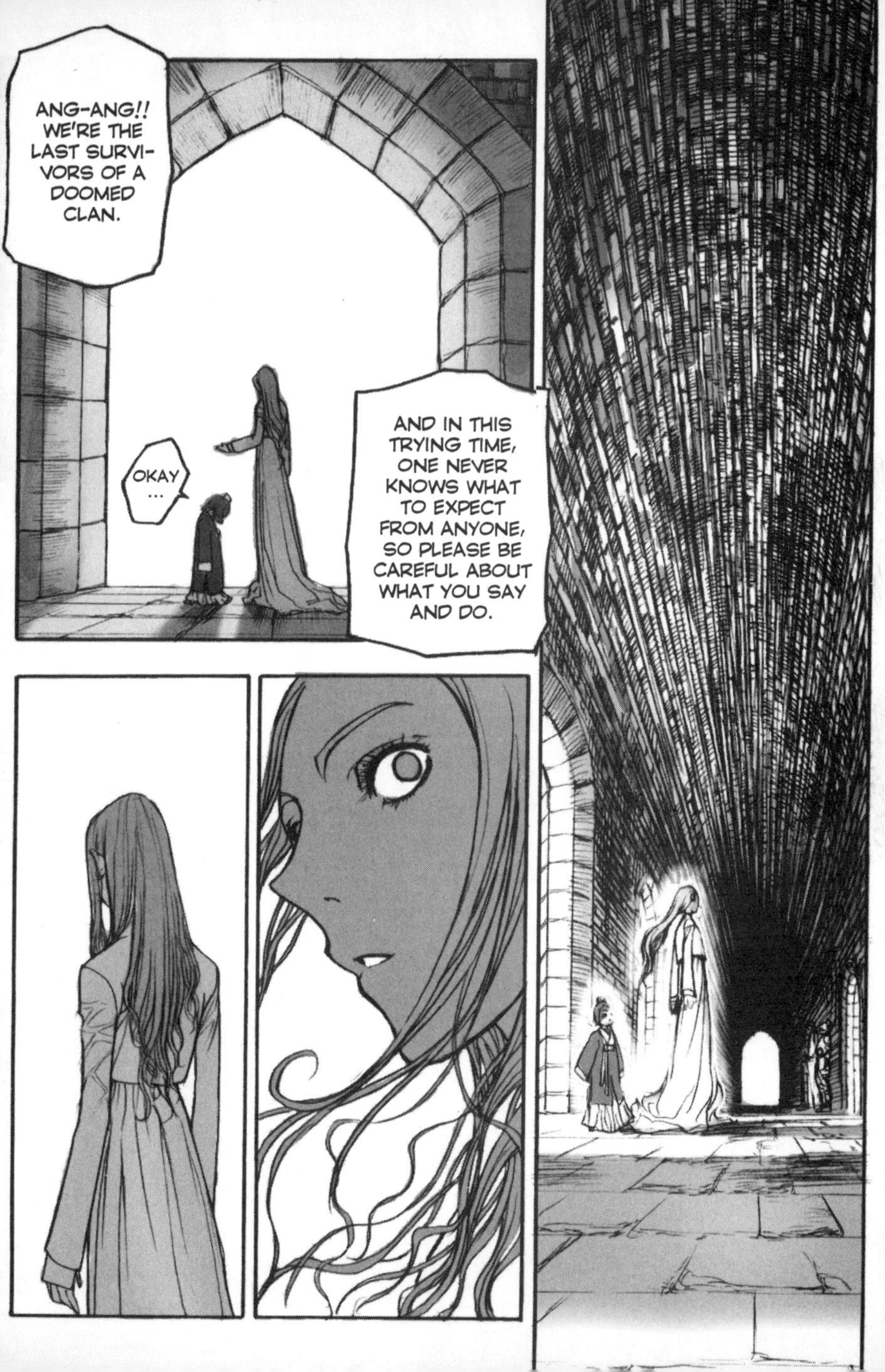

ANG-ANG!! WE'RE THE LAST SURVIVORS OF A DOOMED CLAN.
OKAY ...
AND IN THIS TRYING TIME, ONE NEVER KNOWS WHAT TO EXPECT FROM ANYONE, SO PLEASE BE CAREFUL ABOUT WHAT YOU SAY AND DO.

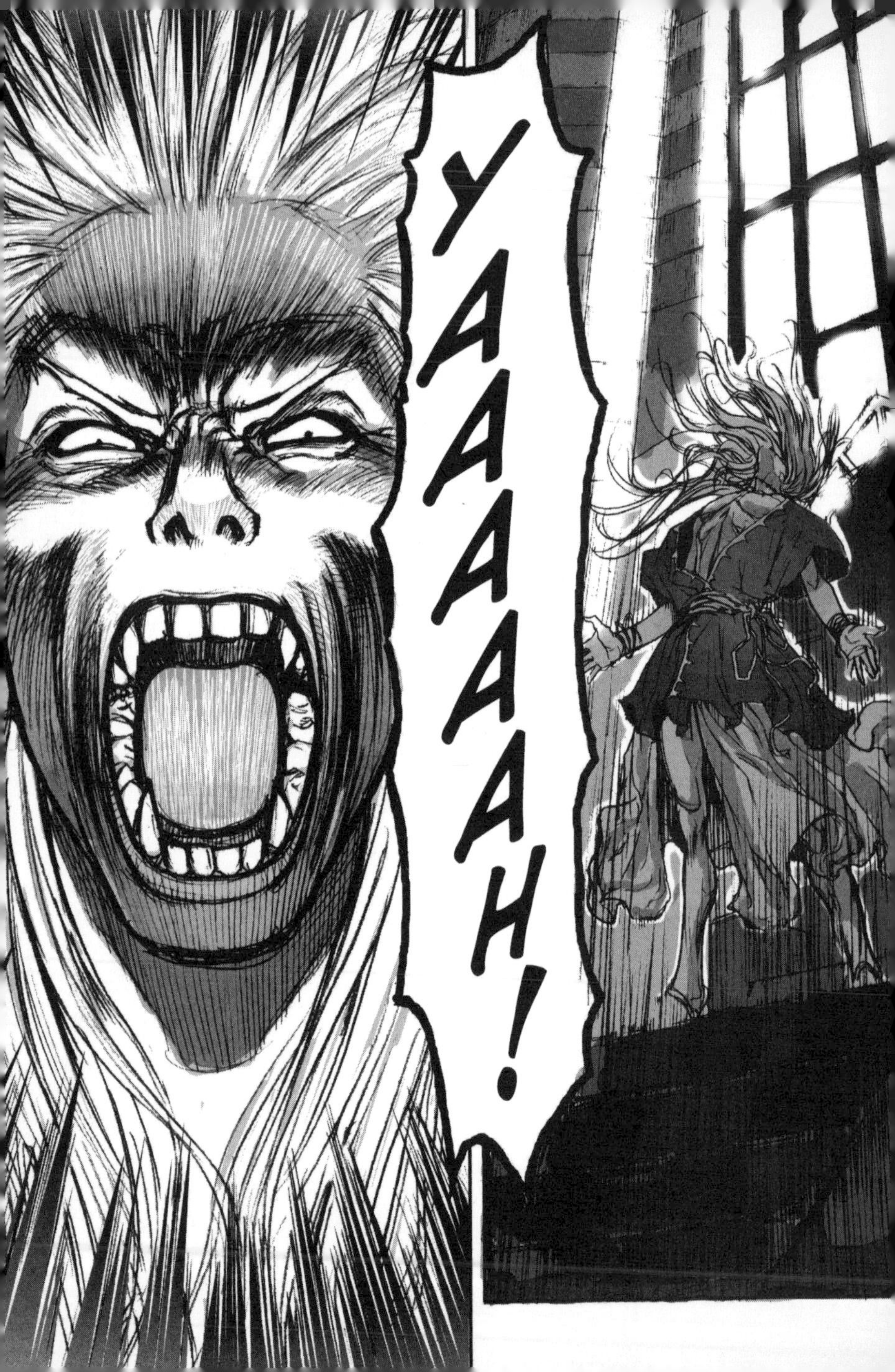
YAAAAAH!

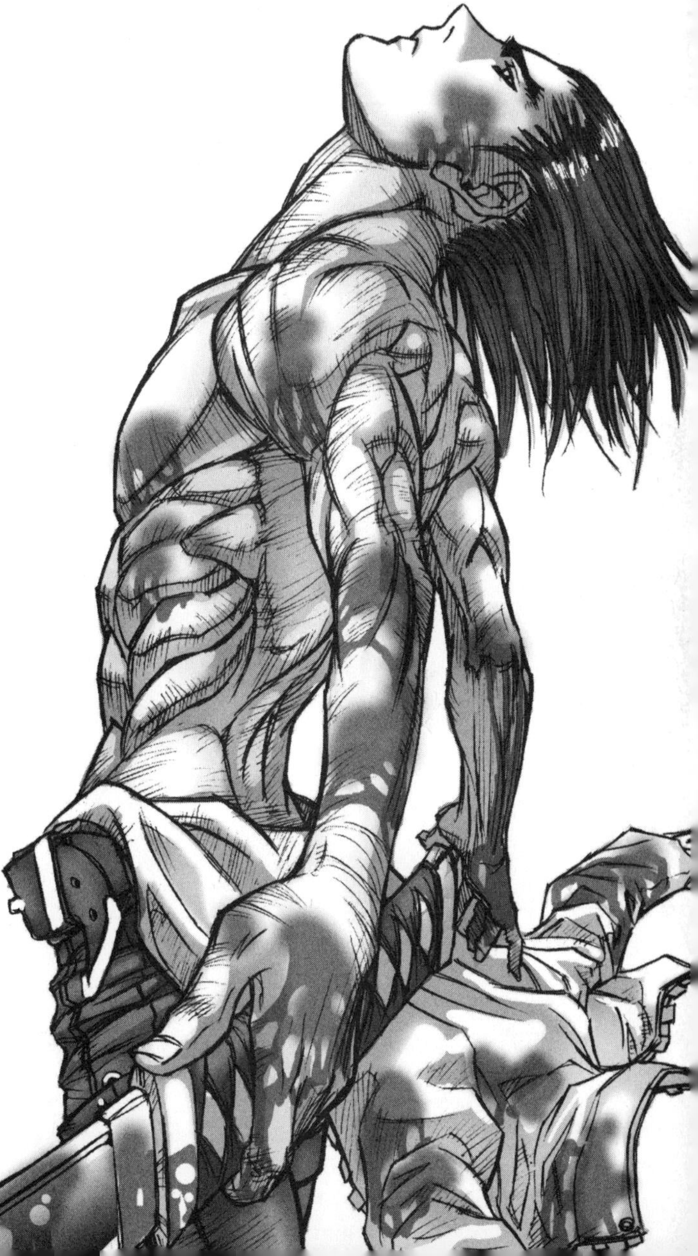

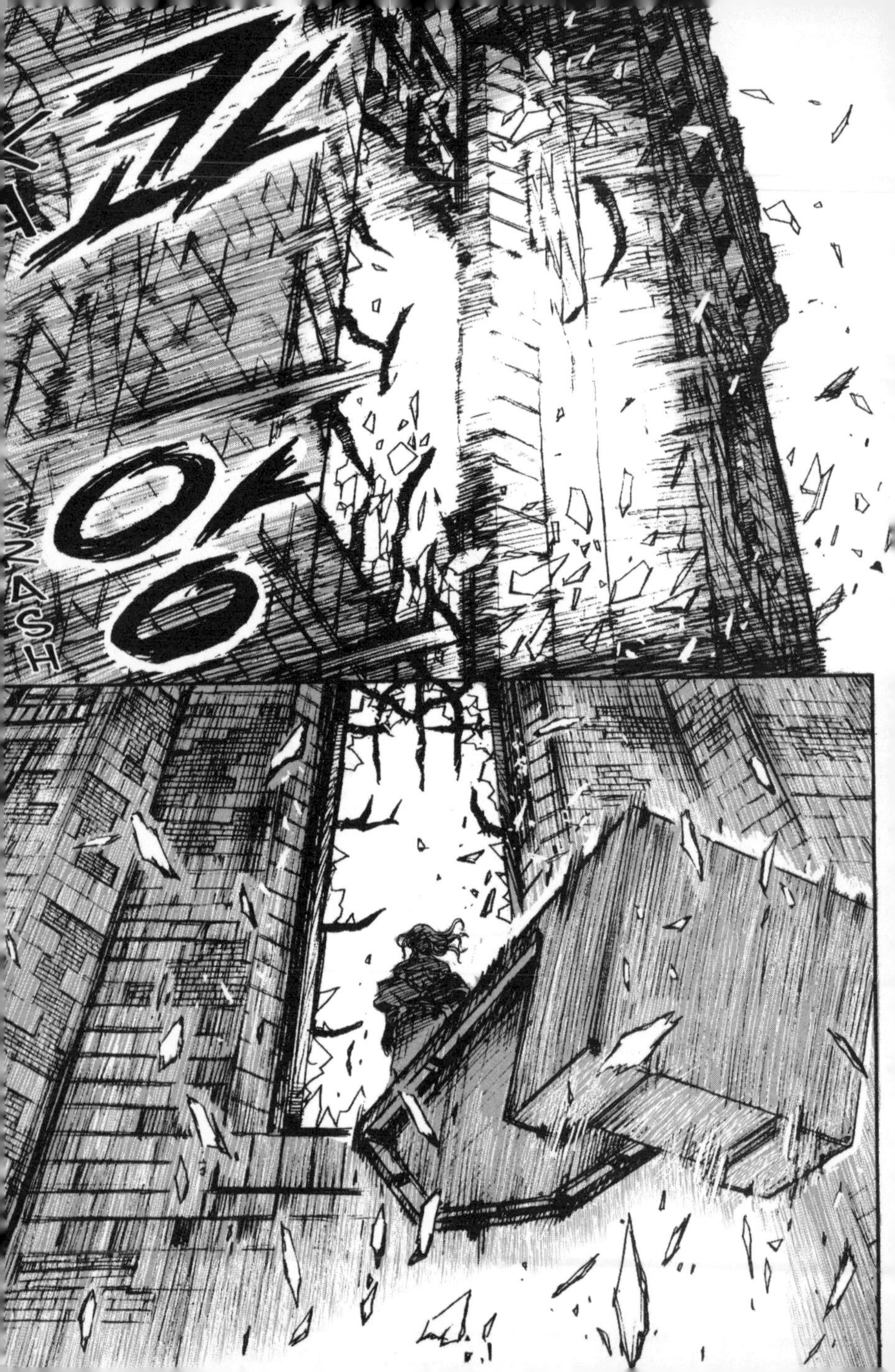
KRASH

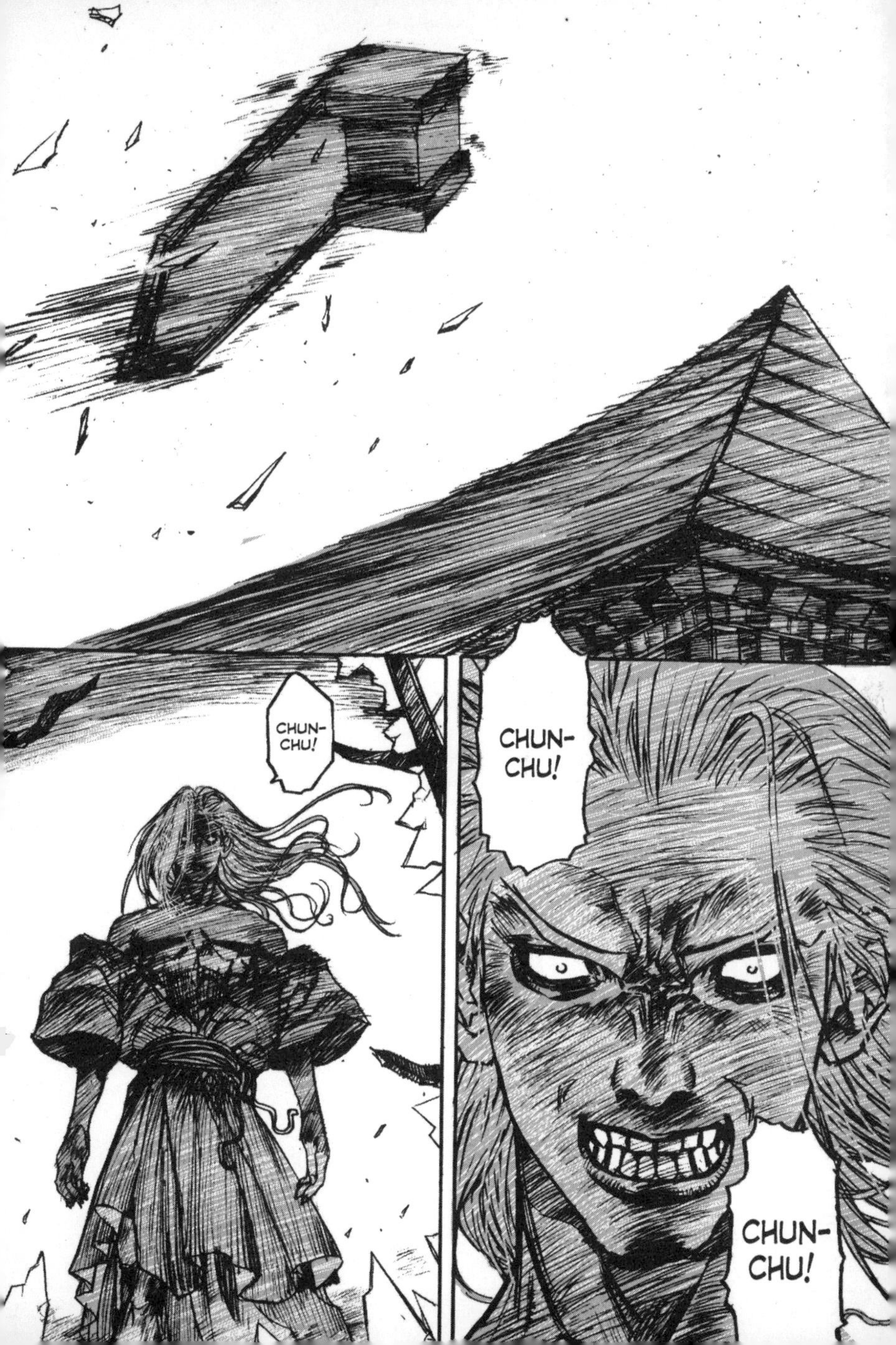
CHUN-
CHU!
CHUN-
CHU!
CHUN-
CHU!

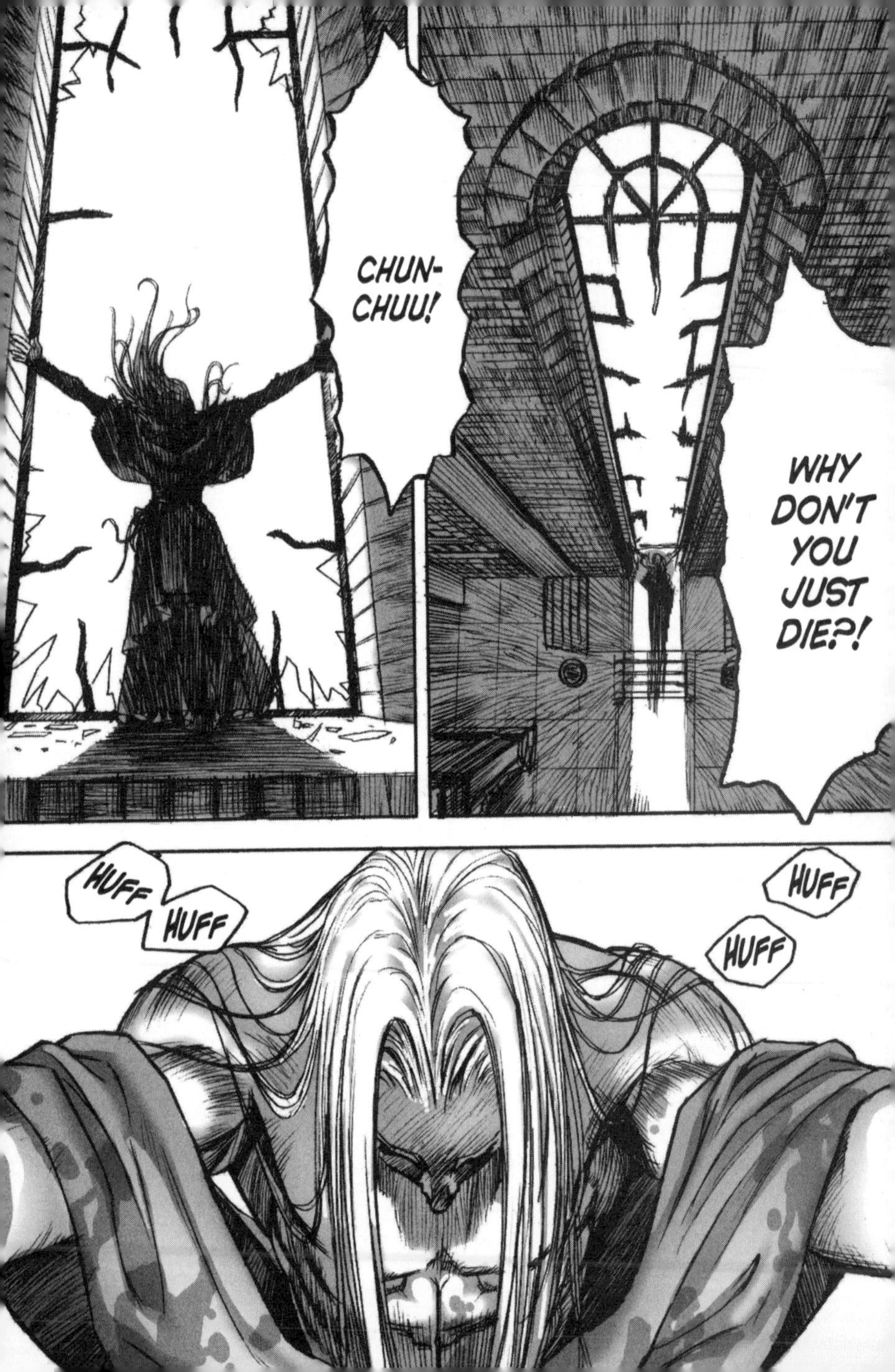
WHY DON'T YOU JUST DIE?!
CHUN-CHUU!
HUFF
HUFF
HUFF
HUFF

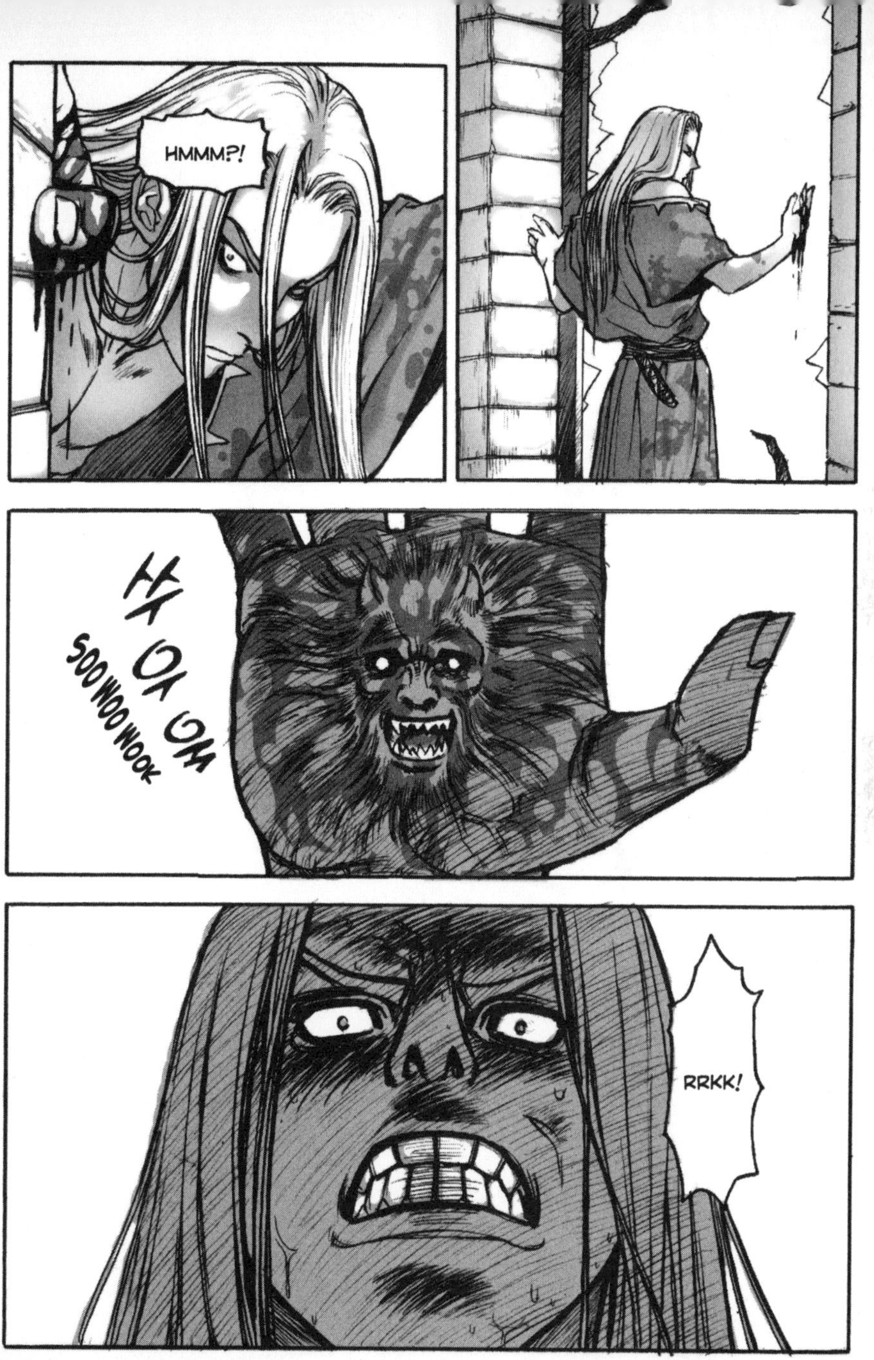
HMMM?!
SOO WOO WOOK
RRKK!

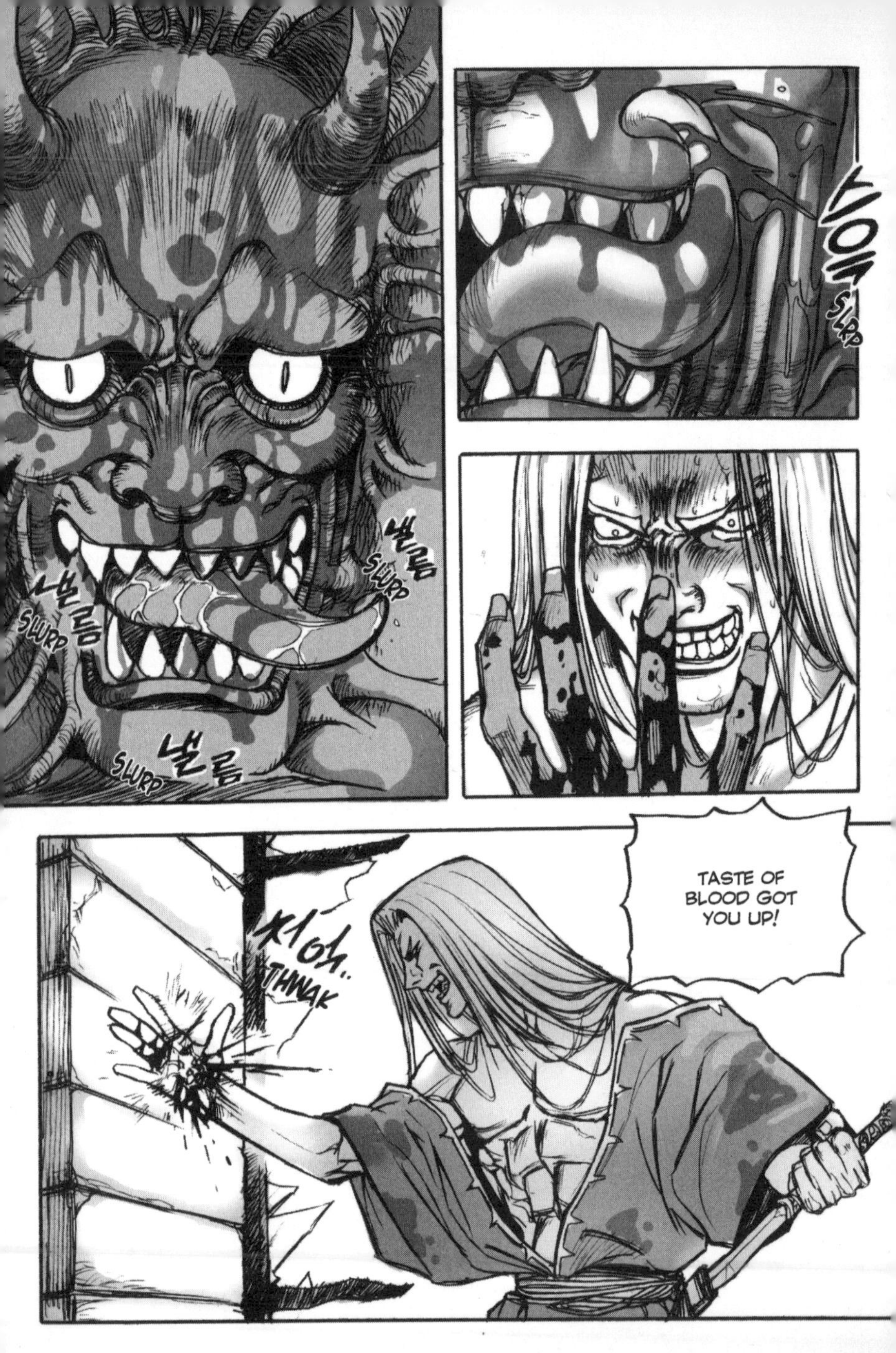

SLRP
낼름
SLURP
낼름
SLURP
낼름
SLURP
TASTE OF BLOOD GOT YOU UP!
THWAK

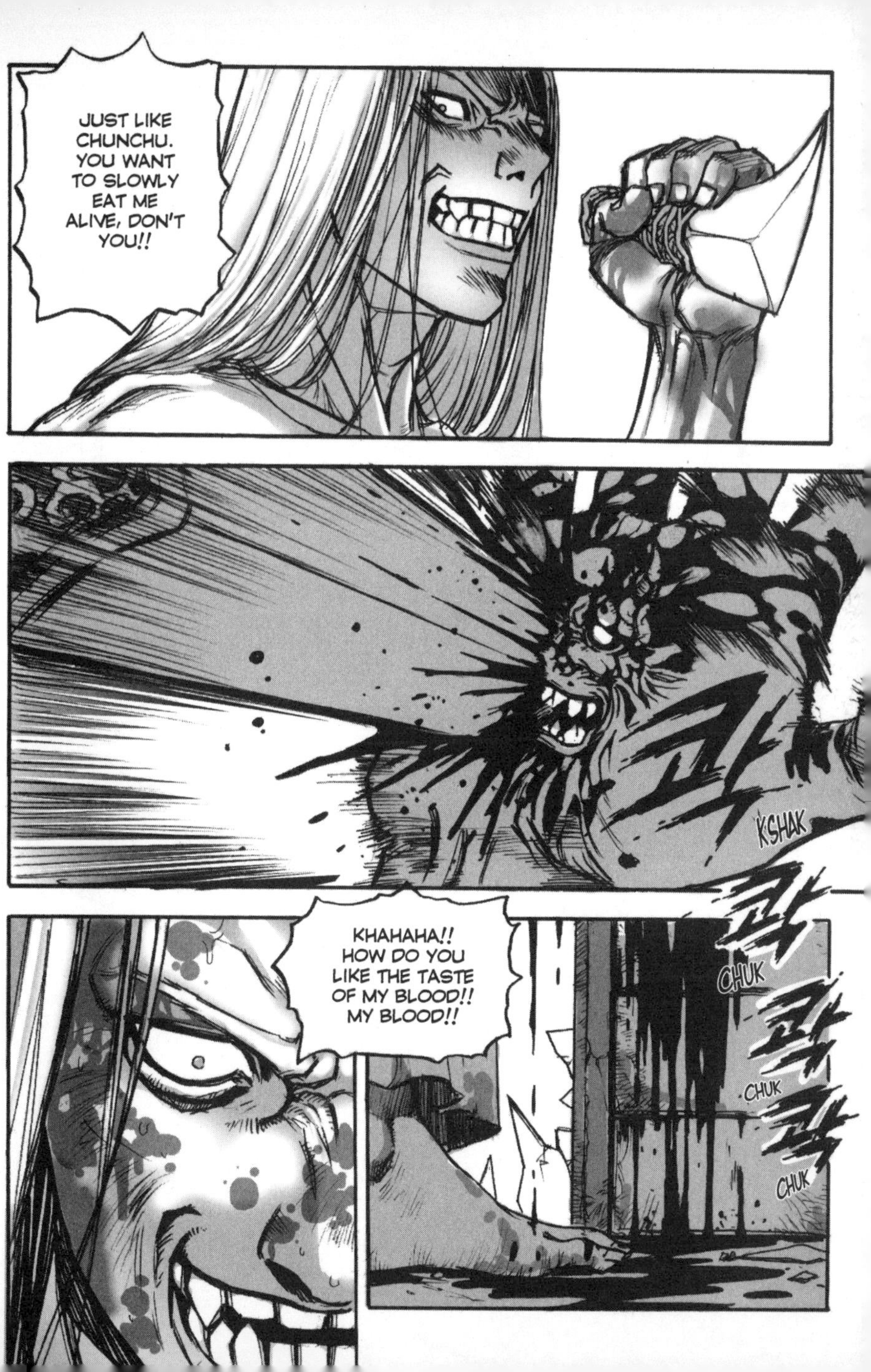
JUST LIKE CHUNCHU. YOU WANT TO SLOWLY EAT ME ALIVE, DON'T YOU!!
K'SHAK
KHAHAHA!! HOW DO YOU LIKE THE TASTE OF MY BLOOD!! MY BLOOD!!
CHUK
CHUK
CHUK

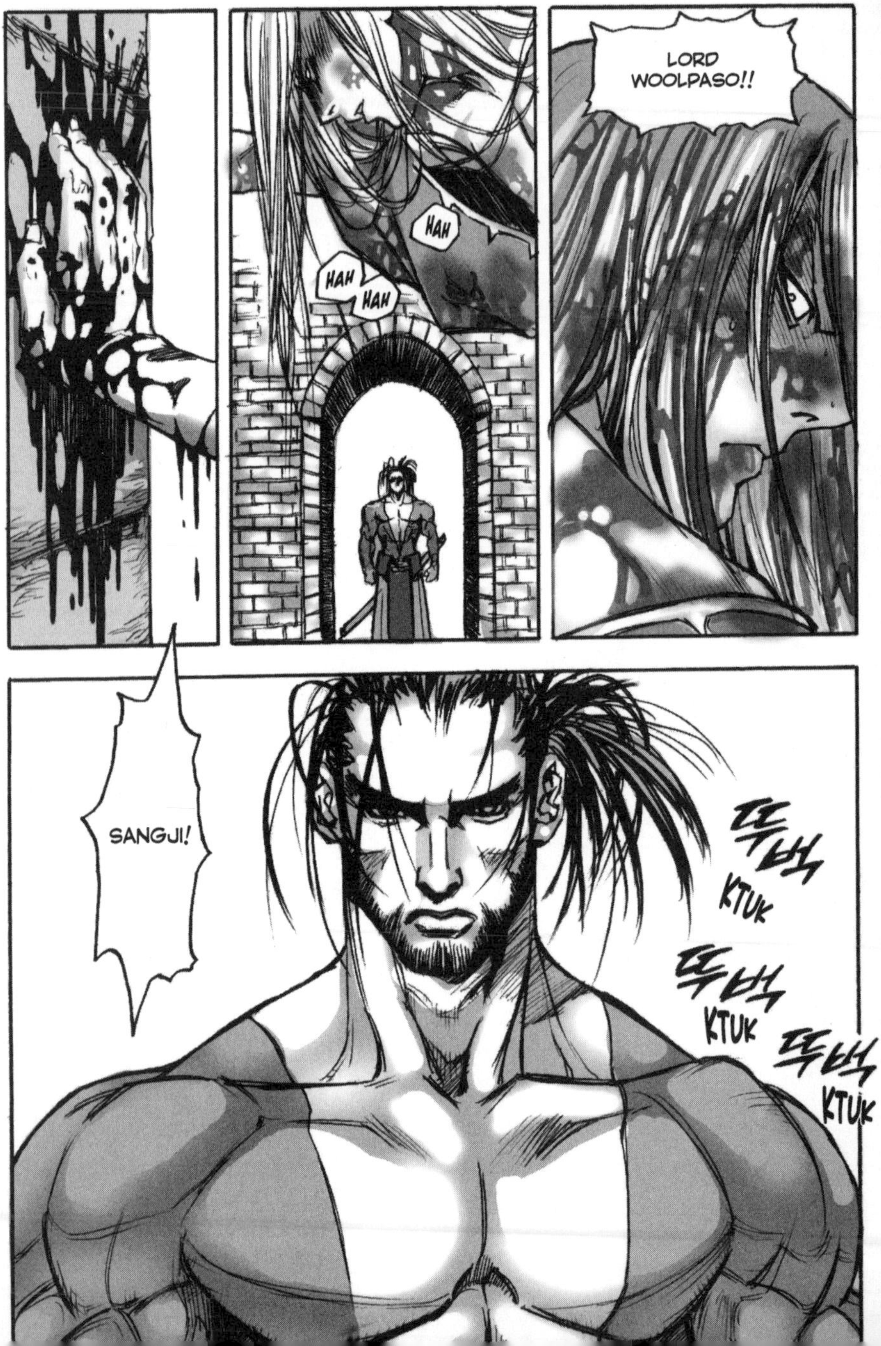
HAH
HAH
HAH
LORD WOOLPASO!!
SANGJI!
뚜벅
KTUK
뚜벅
KTUK
뚜벅
KTUK

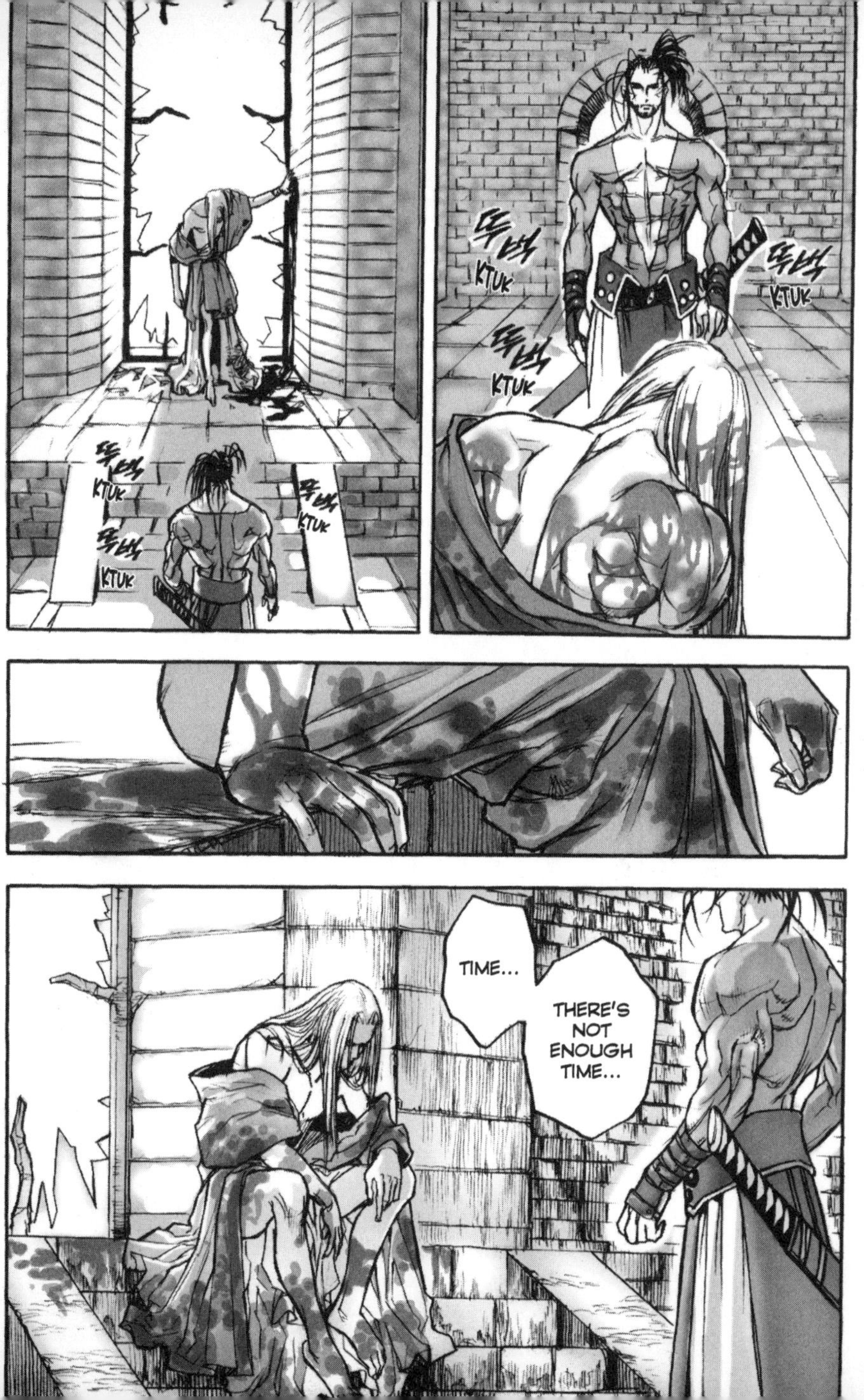

뚝벅
KTUK
뚝벅
KTUK
뚝벅
KTUK
뚝벅
KTUK
뚝벅
KTUK
뚝벅
KTUK
TIME...
THERE'S NOT ENOUGH TIME...

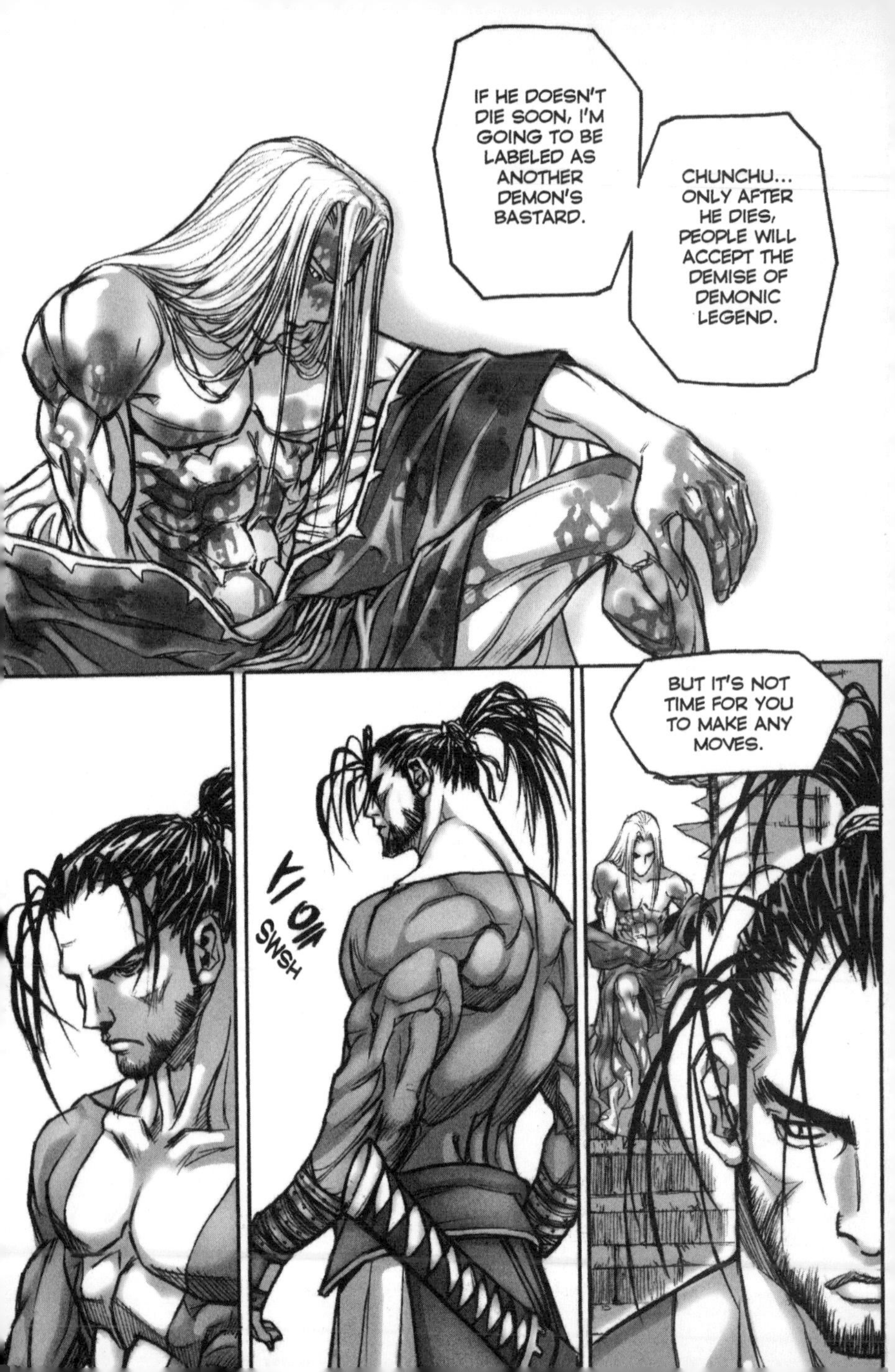
IF HE DOESN'T DIE SOON, I'M GOING TO BE LABELED AS ANOTHER DEMON'S BASTARD.
CHUNCHU... ONLY AFTER HE DIES, PEOPLE WILL ACCEPT THE DEMISE OF DEMONIC LEGEND.
SWSH
BUT IT'S NOT TIME FOR YOU TO MAKE ANY MOVES.

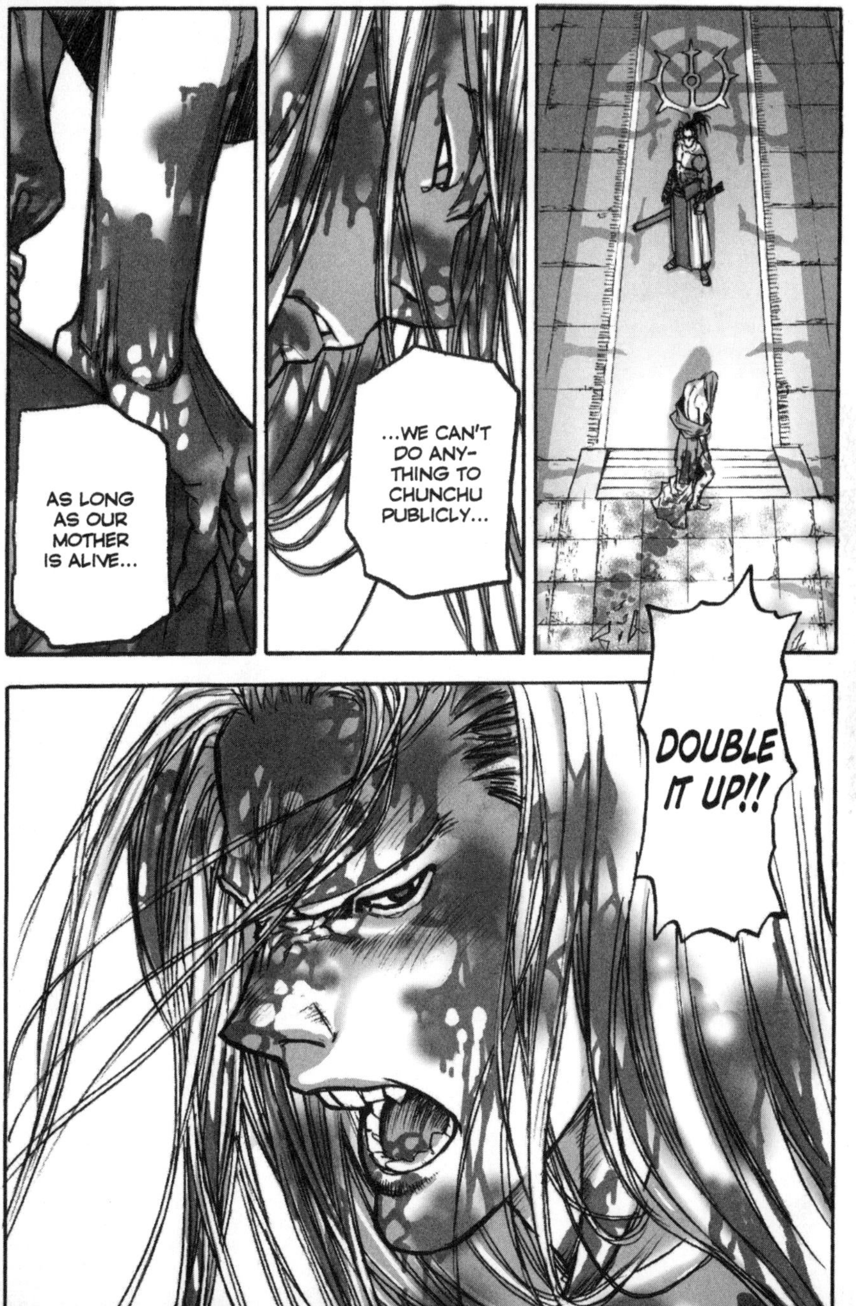

AS LONG AS OUR MOTHER IS ALIVE...
...WE CAN'T DO ANY-THING TO CHUNCHU PUBLICLY...
DOUBLE IT UP!!

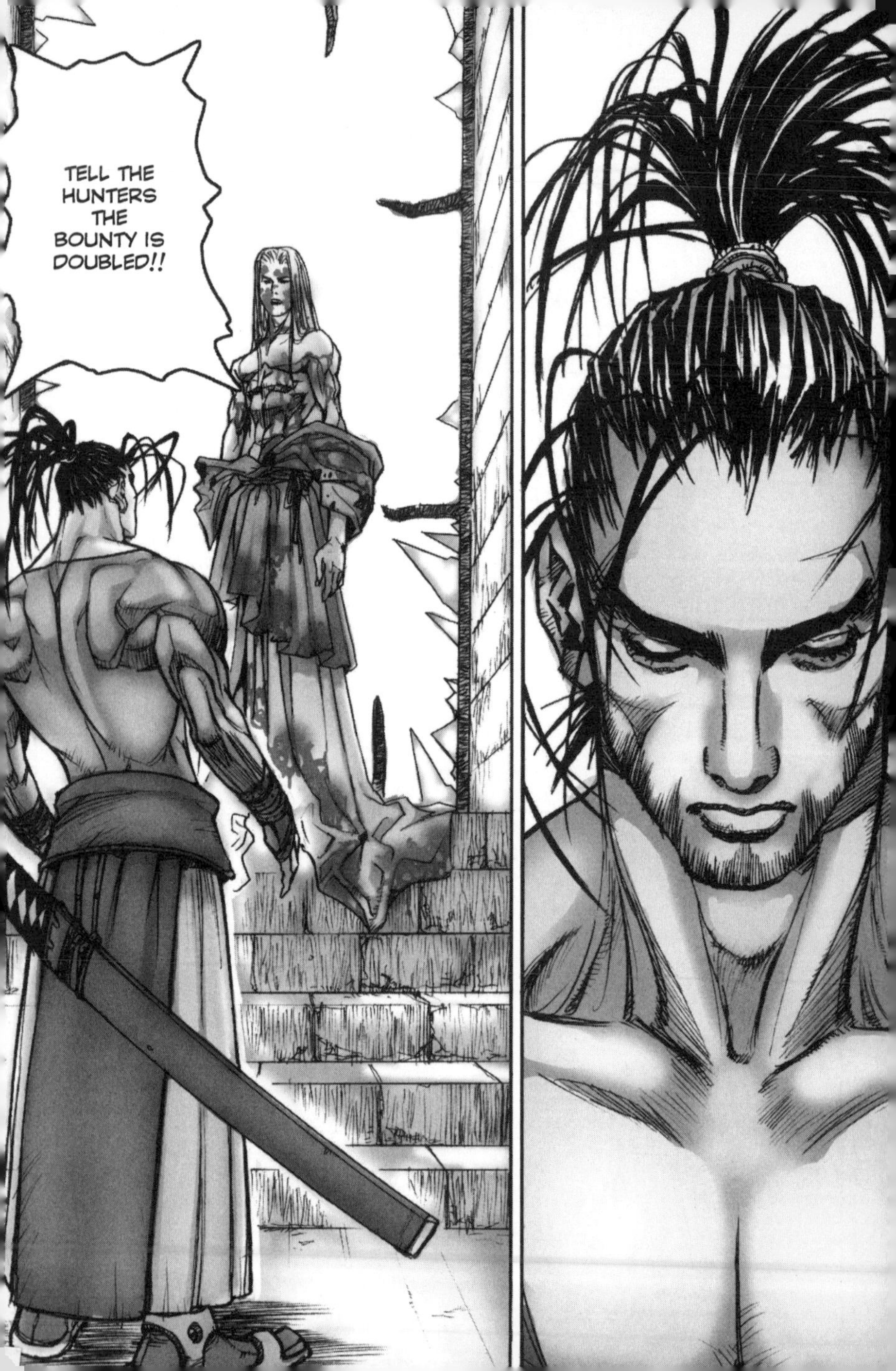
TELL THE HUNTERS THE BOUNTY IS DOUBLED!!

CHAK .. CHAK .. CHAK ..

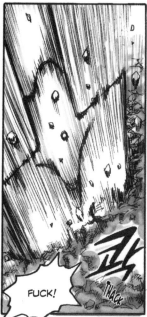

FUCK!

THACK

FUCK! FUCK! FUCK! SHIT!

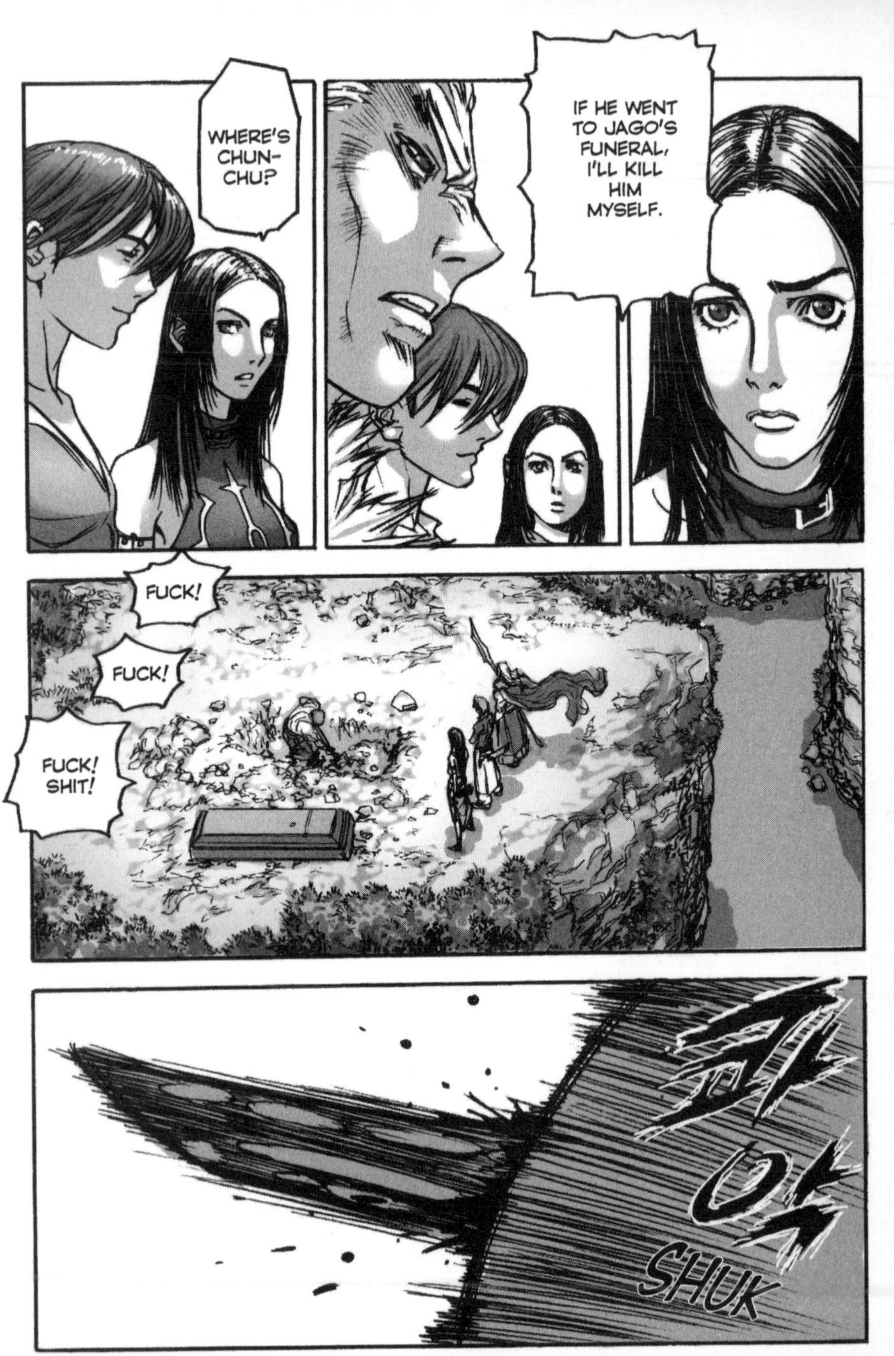
WHERE'S CHUN-CHU?
IF HE WENT TO JAGO'S FUNERAL, I'LL KILL HIM MYSELF.
FUCK!
FUCK!
FUCK! SHIT!
SHUK

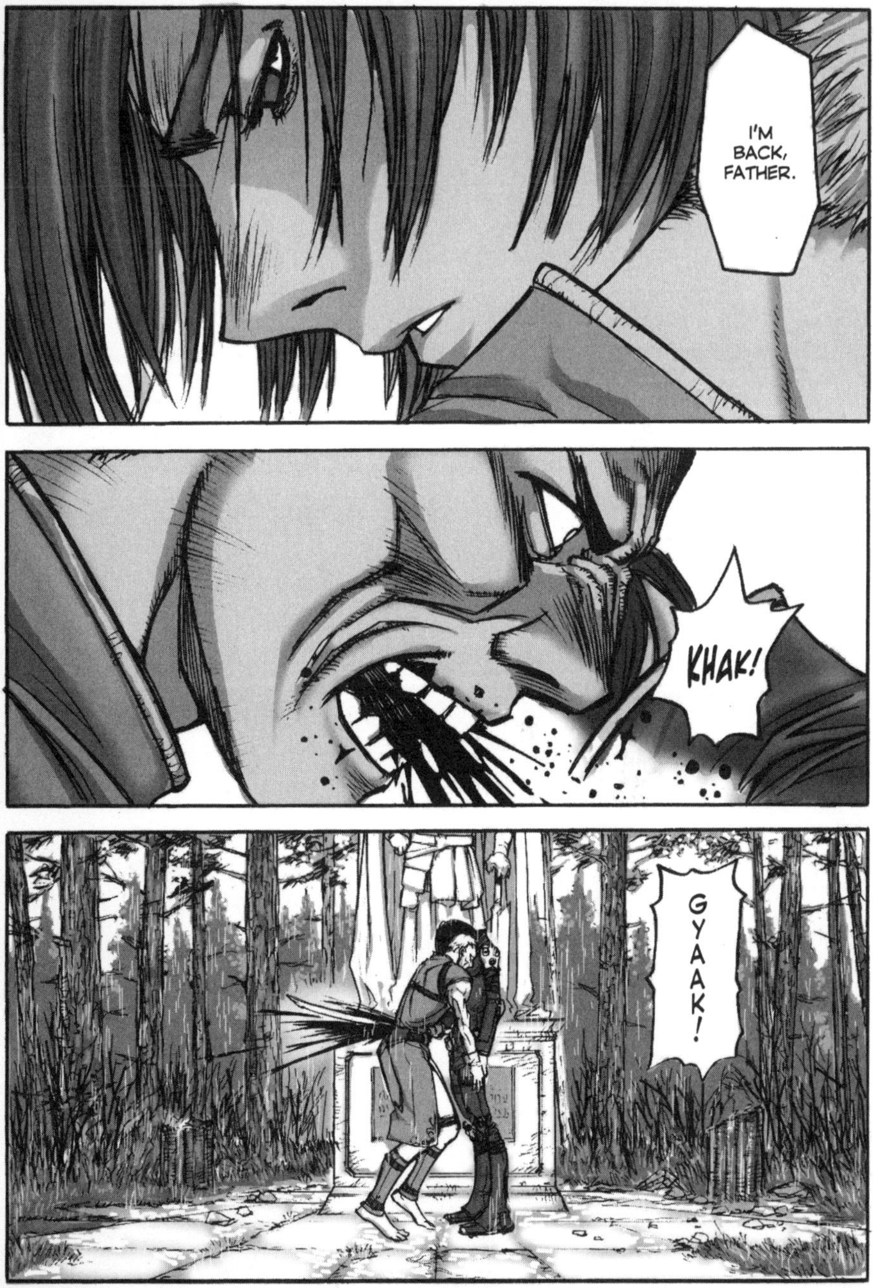
I'M BACK, FATHER.
KHAK!
GYAAK!

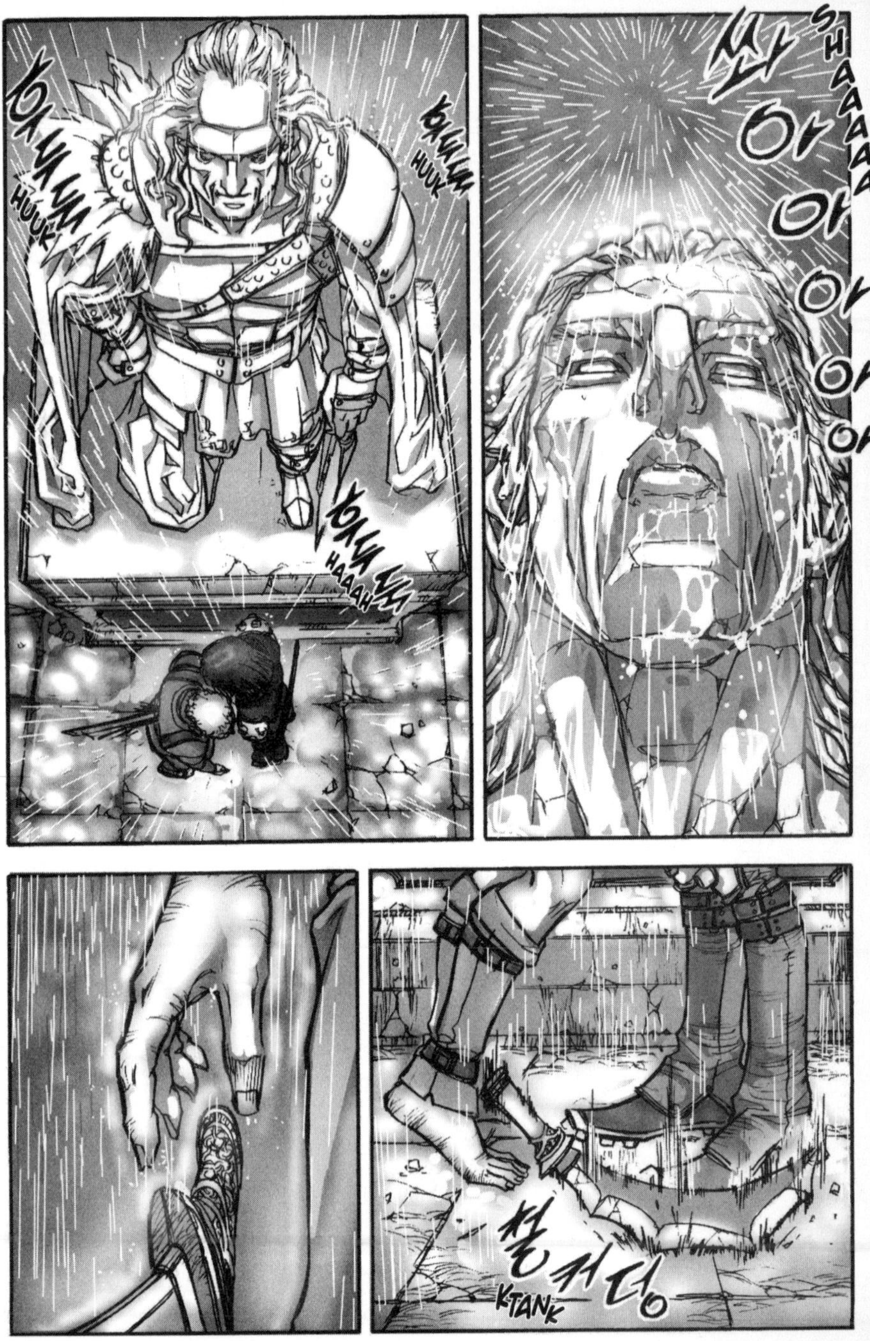
HUUK
HUUK
HAAAAH
SHAAAAAAA
K-TANK

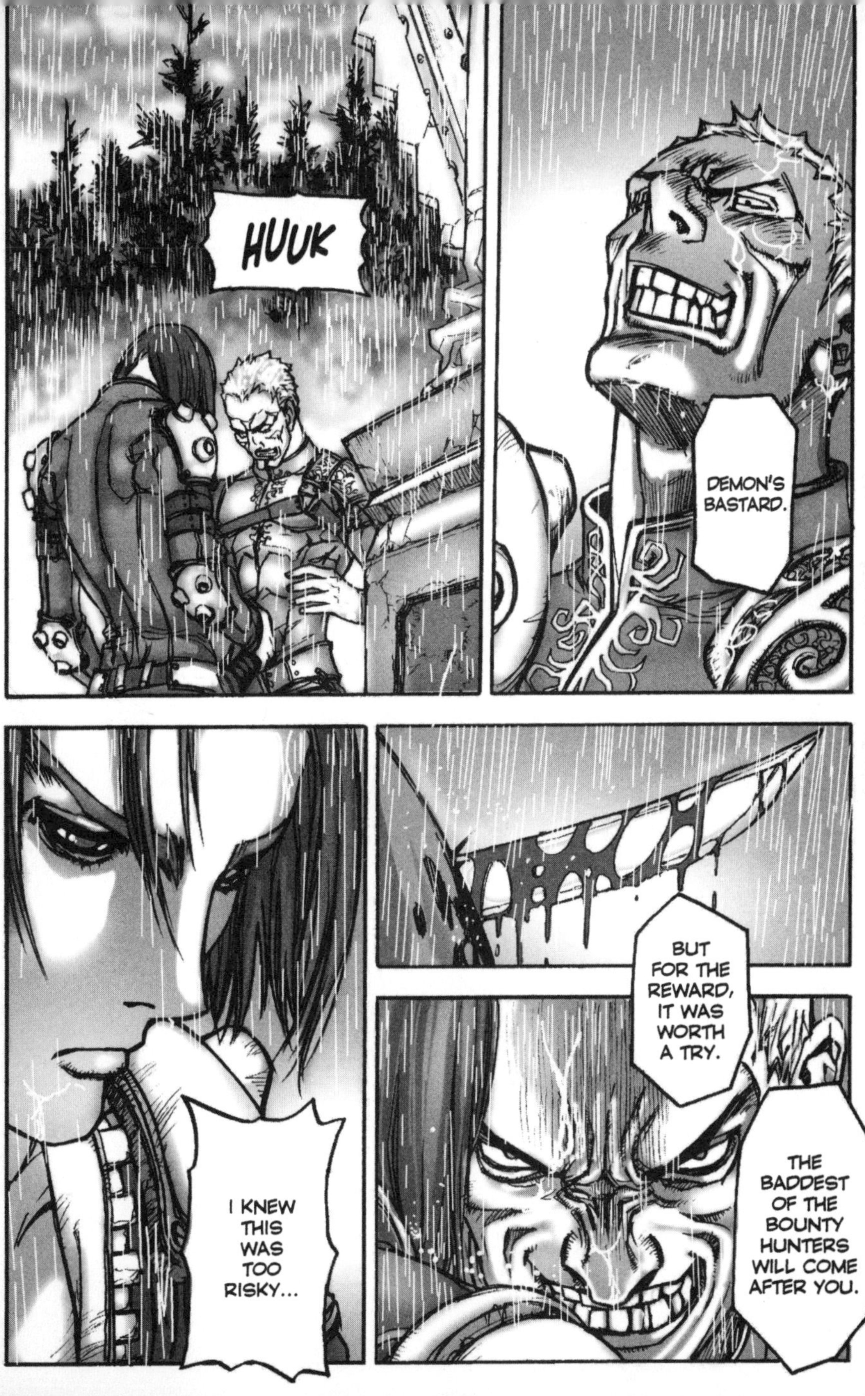
HUUK
DEMON'S BASTARD.
BUT FOR THE REWARD, IT WAS WORTH A TRY.
I KNEW THIS WAS TOO RISKY...
THE BADDEST OF THE BOUNTY HUNTERS WILL COME AFTER YOU.

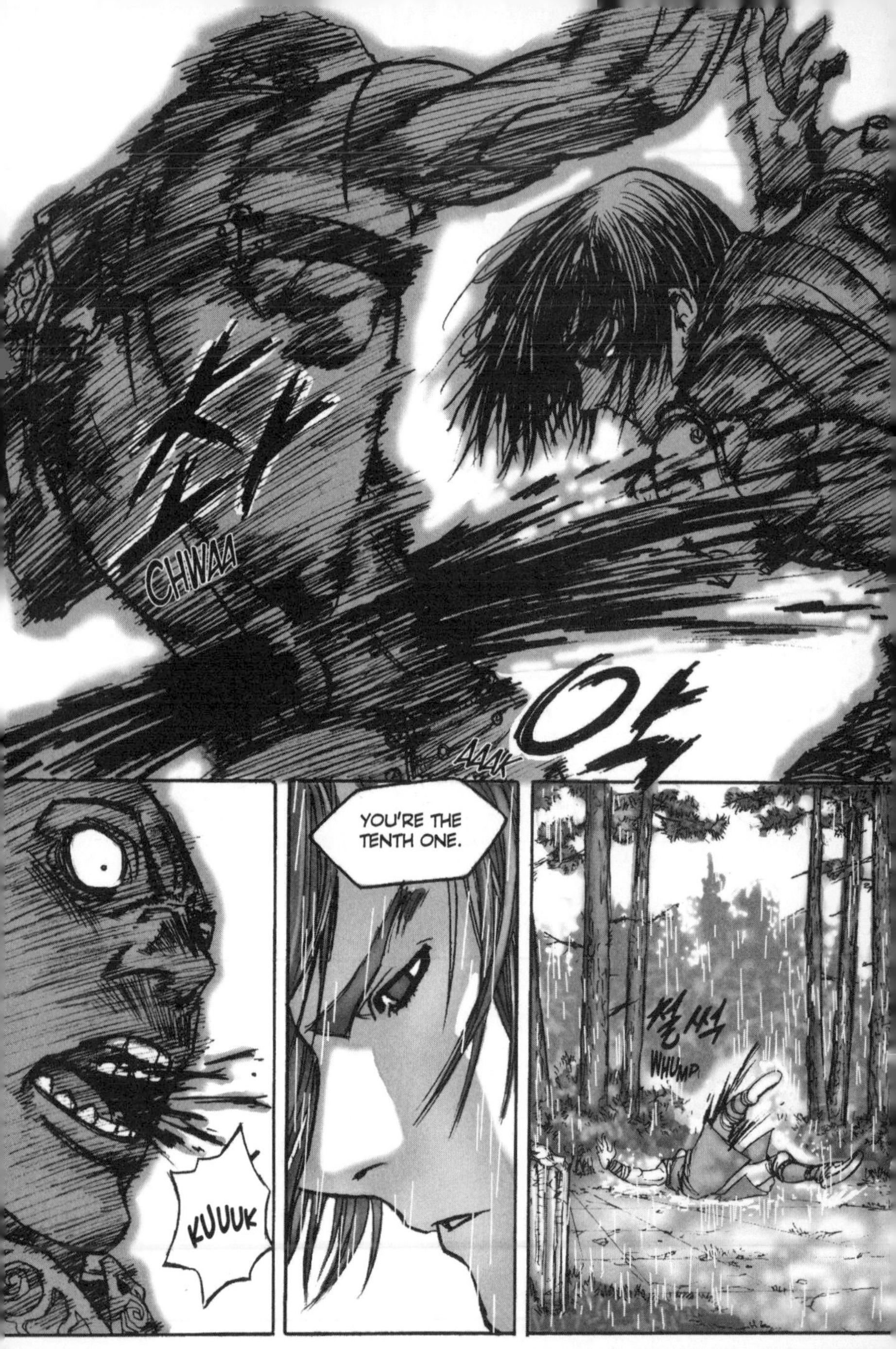

CHWAA
AAAK
YOU'RE THE TENTH ONE.
KUUUK
WHUMP

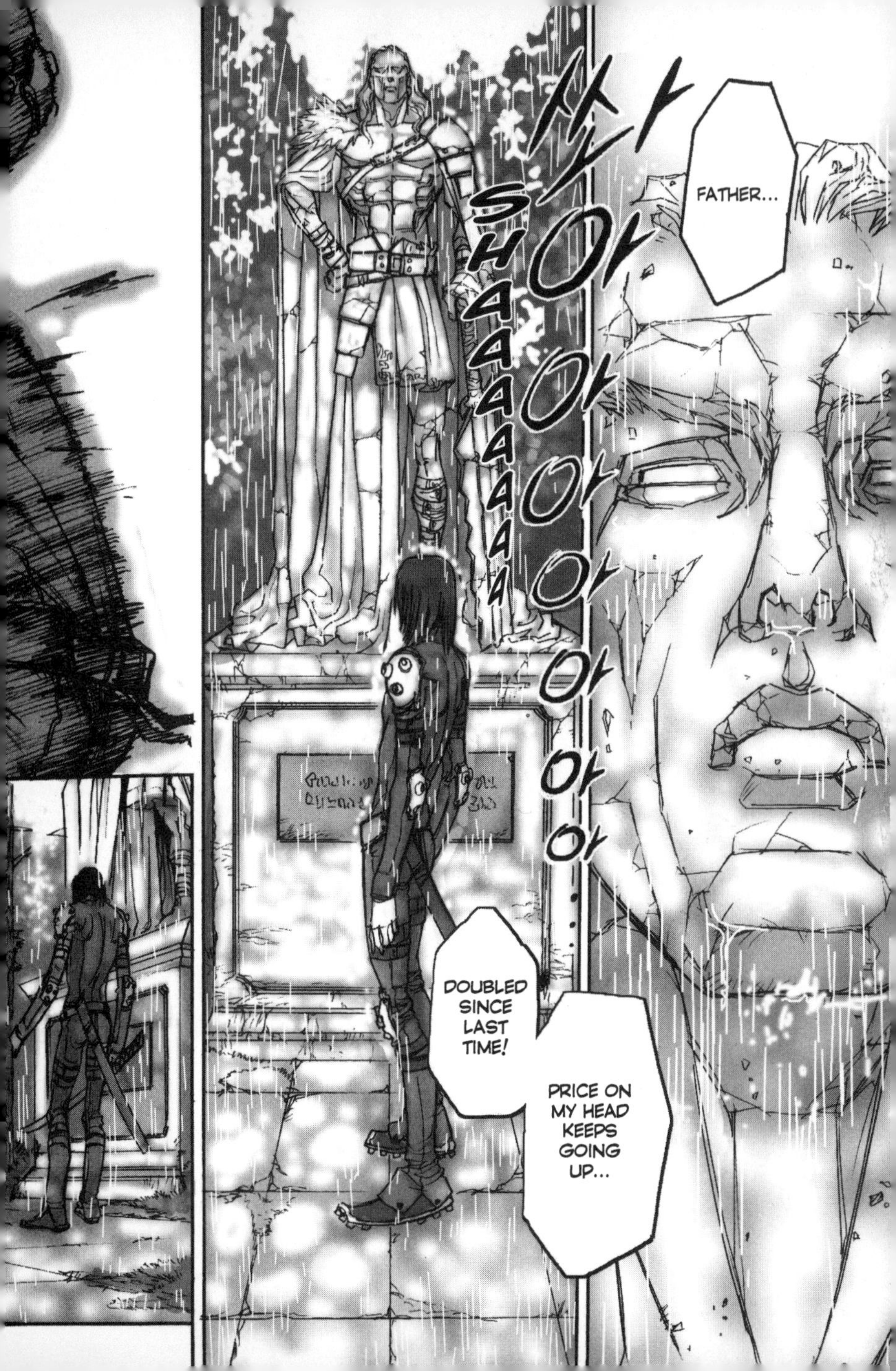
FATHER...
SHAAAAAAAAAA
KYYOOOOOOOOOO
DOUBLED SINCE LAST TIME!
PRICE ON MY HEAD KEEPS GOING UP...

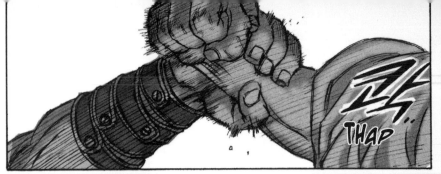

THAP

SO, THIS IS THE WAY YOU TREAT THE FUTURE OF OUR WORLD.

CHIEF PARYUN OF THE GOMAH CLAN.

YOU'RE CHIEF ABULCHAN OF MIRMIDON, WHAT ARE YOU DOING HERE?

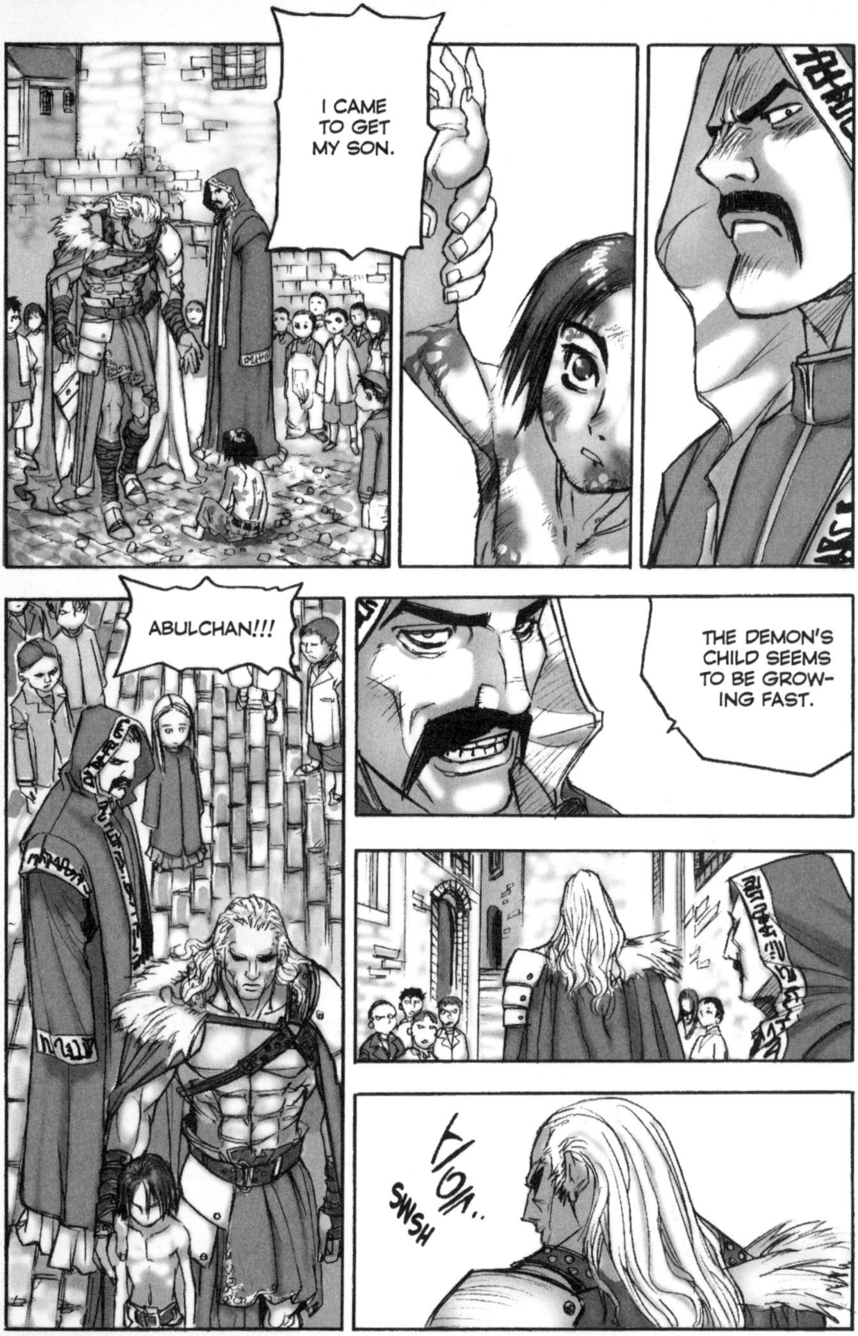
I CAME TO GET MY SON.
ABULCHAN!!!
THE DEMON'S CHILD SEEMS TO BE GROWING FAST.
SWSH

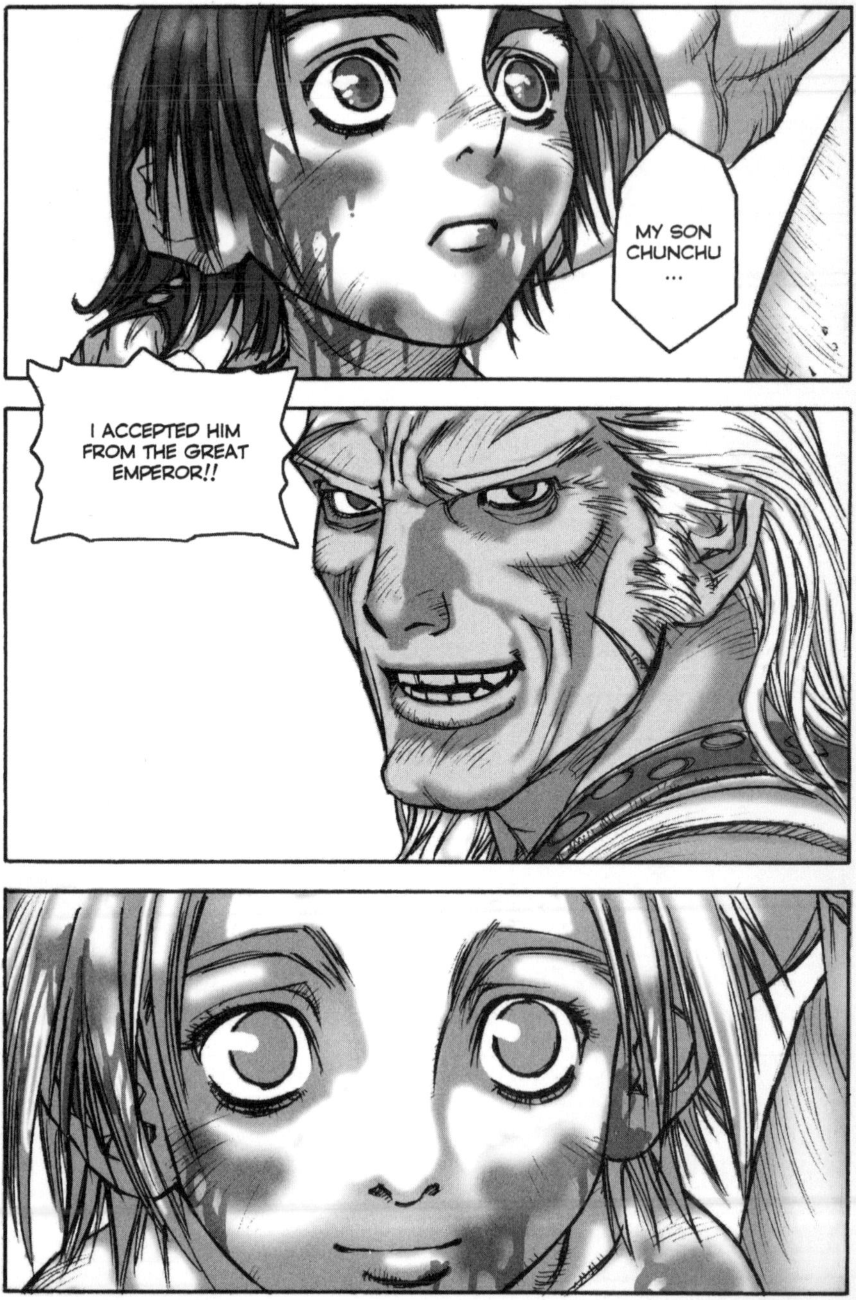
MY SON CHUNCHU ...
I ACCEPTED HIM FROM THE GREAT EMPEROR!!

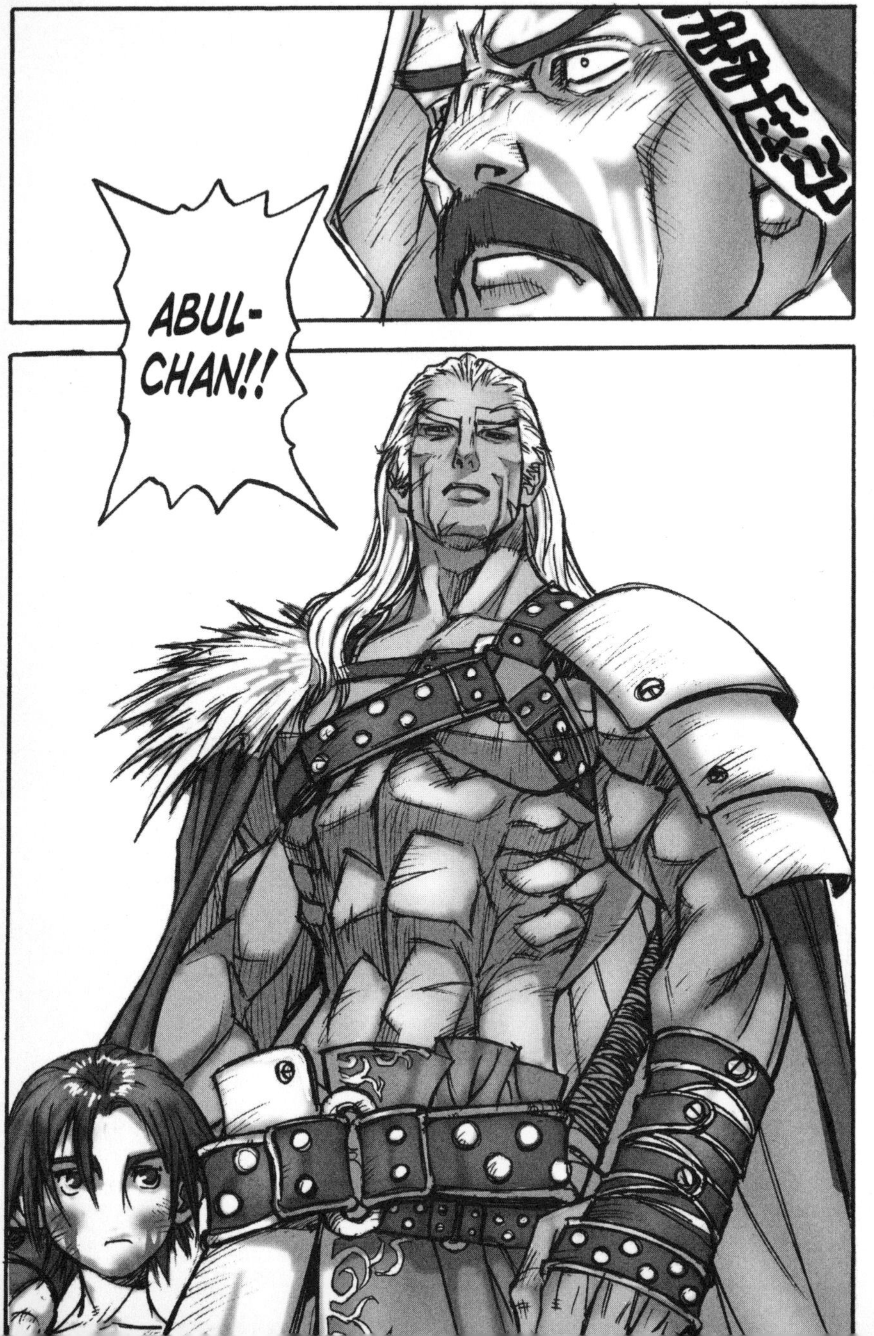
ABUL-
CHAN!!

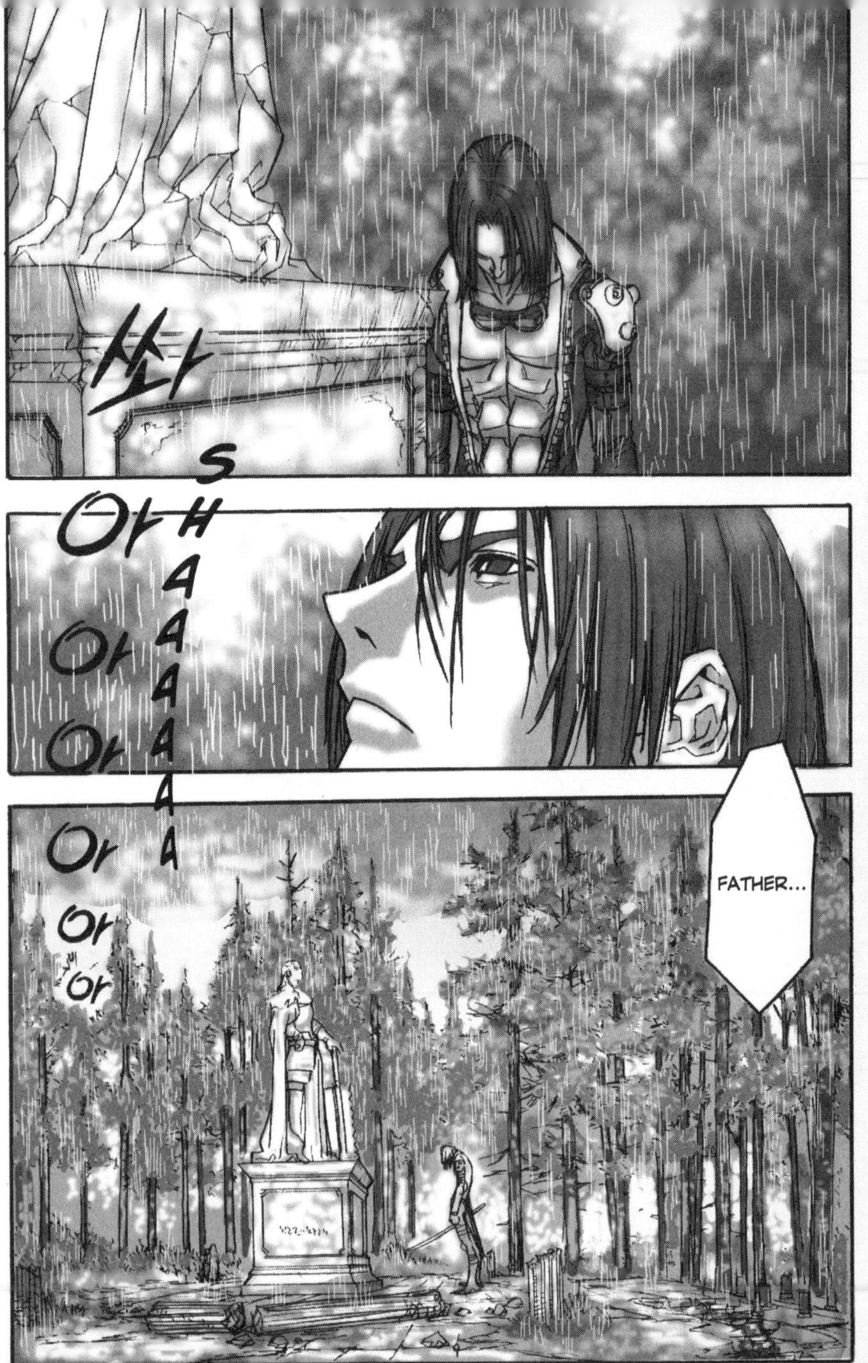
SHAAAAAA
FATHER...

CHUNCHU TO CONTINUE IN VOLUME 2

PARK JOONG-KI'S

S·H·A·M·A·N
WARRIOR

One of Korea's top five best-selling manhwa titles! From the desert wastelands emerge two mysterious warriors, master wizard Yarong and his faithful servant Batu. On a grave mission from their king, they have yet to realize the whirlwind of political movements and secret plots which will soon engulf them and change their lives forever. When Yarong is injured in battle, Batu must fulfill a secret promise to leave Yarong's side and protect his master's child. As Batu seeks to find and hide the infant, Yarong reveals another secret to those who have tracked him down to finish him off—the deadly, hidden power of a Shaman Warrior!

Volume 1
ISBN-10: 1-59307-638-X
ISBN-13: 978-1-59307-638-2

Volume 2
ISBN-10: 1-59307-749-1
ISBN-13: 978-1-59307-749-5

Volume 3
ISBN-10: 1-59307-769-6
ISBN-13: 978-1-59307-769-3

$12.95 EACH!

Previews for *SHAMAN WARRIOR* and other DARK HORSE MANHWA titles can be found at darkhorse.com!

DARK HORSE MANHWA